TURKEY'S NEO-OTTOMANIST MOMENT
A EURASIANIST ODYSSEY

Cengiz Çandar has written a thought provoking and tremendously insightful book on contemporary Turkish foreign policy rooted in a deep understanding of Turkish history and politics. Çandar's insights are grounded in experiences as a journalist and foreign policy advisor.

As one who brought the term Neo-Ottomanism to Turkey he is able to explain it in all its many positive and negative facets and place it in today's foreign policy discourse. He knows the international arena and Turkey's place in it. He knows the West, he knows the Balkans, the Caucasus, and the Middle East. He takes his readers from the Mediterranean to Russia and to China. He has worked with Turkey's leaders and understands their motivations.

This book goes a long way to explain Turkey's strident foreign policy today. It is a wonderfully informative and enjoyable read!

-   *Lenore G. **Martin**, Professor, Co-Chair of the Study Group on Modern Turkey, Center for Middle Eastern Studies, Harvard University*

No one better understands and explains "Neo-Ottomanism" than Cengiz Çandar, who coined the term almost 30 years ago, long before it became a fashionable concept capturing the evolution of Turkish foreign policy. And very few writers can so beautifully weave professional insights, objective analysis and anecdotal flair. By transcending easy clichés and lazy analogies, Çandar has produced a definitive account. If you could only read one book on Turkish foreign policy, this is it.

-   *Ömer **Taşpınar**, Professor, National War College, and The Johns Hopkins University (SAIS). Specialist on Turkey, Turkish foreign policy, Turkish-U.S. relations, and the European Union. Former Director of the Turkey Program at the Brookings Institution.*

What makes Erdogan's Turkey so thick? Is Ankara's international conduct driven by (neo)imperial outlook or is it guided by Realpolitik considerations? Is Turkey's policies neo-Ottomanist or is it primarily a Eurasianist power? In his new book, Turkey's Neo-Ottomanist Moment: A Eurasianist Odyssey, Cengiz Çandar, a veteran foreign policy analyst, advances a lucid explanation of his country's increasingly assertive behavior. His seemingly paradoxical conclusion is aptly encapsulated in the book's title. In contemporary Turkey's context, neo-Ottomanism and Eurasianism are the two facets of a specific political mindset characterized by authoritarian tendencies, illiberal instincts, nationalist sentiments, imperial nostalgia, and strong animus towards the West. It is this mindset, Çandar persuasively argues, that it is beyond Ankara's muscular policies in the Middle East, makes Turkey such an awkward partner for the US and the EU, and explains its contradictory relationship with Putin's Russia: "Eurasianism" provides the platform for cooperation with Moscow, while "neo-Ottomanism" makes more than enough room for competition.

Çandar's book is an intellectual tour de force and a must-read for anyone interested in the intertwined problem of contemporary Turkey's identity and foreign policy.

- *Igor **Torbakov**, Historian, Specialist on Russian and Eurasian history and politics, former research scholar at the Russian Academy of Sciences. Analyst for Russia's and Turkey's geopolitical discourses.*

To my girls; Elâ Tara (the youngest), Defne, Tuba, and my boy Christoph,

POLICY SERIES: 10

Turkey's Neo-Ottomanist Moment

A Eurasianist Odyssey

Cengiz Çandar

First published in 2021 by Transnational Press London in the United Kingdom, 13 Stamford Place, Sale, M33 3BT, UK.
www.tplondon.com

Transnational Press London® and the logo and its affiliated brands are registered trademarks.

Requests for permission to reproduce material from this work should be sent to:
sales@tplondon.com

Paperback
ISBN: 978-1-80135-044-0
Digital
ISBN: 978-1-80135-049-5

Cover Design: Nihal Yazgan

Transnational Press London Ltd. is a company registered in England and Wales No. 8771684

TURKEY'S NEO-OTTOMANIST MOMENT
A EURASIANIST ODYSSEY

Cengiz Çandar

TRANSNATIONAL PRESS LONDON

2021

CONTENTS

ACKNOWLEDGMENTS

The Swedish Institute for International Affairs (Utrikespolitiska Institutet in Swedish, better known by its acronym UI), and the director of its Middle East and North Africa (MENA) Program Rouzbeh Farsi, have to take precedence in my list of acknowledgments regarding this book. I am a Senior Fellow at the UI and affiliated with its MENA Programme. *Turkey's Neo-Ottomanist Moment, A Eurasian Odyssey* was initially intended to become a publication of the UI. I had committed myself to write a paper for the UI on Turkey's Syria policy within the context of Turkish-Russian relations. My plan was to submit the document in 2020 to Rouzbeh, who was patiently waiting for my delivery. With Turkey's activism in foreign policy – from North Africa to the South Caucasus, and from the Eastern Mediterranean to the Black Sea and the Caspian geopolitics – the scope of my project continuously widened. Delivery was delayed indefinitely, and when I finally considered the project to be complete, my manuscript's limits were well beyond what was reasonable for the UI to publish as a paper. Rouzbeh was always gentle with me and always forthcoming even though ultimately I did not present my work to the Utrikespolitiska Institutet for publication. Therefore, my gratitude goes out to the UI and Rouzbeh Parsi. They have an unmistakable share in the coming to fruition of *Turkey's* Neo-Ottomanist Moment, A Eurasian Odyssey.

Perhaps I must also acknowledge that the long dark days of autumn and winter in Sweden, where I had to confine myself to self-isolation due to the year of the COVID-19 pandemic which hit my host country severely, played a significant role in the writing of Turkey's Neo-Ottomanist Moment, A Eurasianist Odyssey. The imposed immobility provided me the focus and ample time necessary to write a book.

As I have already acknowledged in the preface, my wife Tuba played an unrivaled part in this oeuvre. Her role was two-fold: not only did she hold up under the long, dark, cold days of the Swedish winter that is so foreign to her Mediterranean temperament, she endured my unbearable presence indoors, where I made life even more boring for her by not raising my head from my computer and barely speaking a word day or night. She is the person who encouraged me to expand my work into a book after looking at the original draft, even though it would mean further boredom and sacrifices on her part. She nevertheless graciously compromised.

As in my previous book, I was fortunate having Carol Ross as my native

English editor. Without her contribution, I am not sure what this book would have looked like. I express my gratitude to her.

I feel like an exceptionally lucky person to have Dr. Erdi Öztürk, a rising star among young Turkish scholars, as my dear friend. He was always ready to offer his selfless assistance to me, and as always, he guided me into unchartered territory. Without him, I wonder how this book could have materialized.

My special gratitude goes to Prof. Ibrahim Sirkeci, my eminent publisher. From day one, he was so generous in offering the services of Transnational Press London. He believed in me and what I might present, and with the ease of mind he provided, I was able to bring *Turkey's Neo-Ottomanist Moment, A Eurasian Odyssey* to completion with self-confidence. It is to him, and the editors of Transnational Press London, that the last but not the least of my acknowledgments are given.

ABOUT THE AUTHOR

Cengiz Çandar, scholar and journalist, is the leading expert on Turkish foreign policy, the main architect of the Turkish-Kurdish rapprochement as President Turgut Özal's advisor in the 1990s. Author and contributor of several publications in Turkish and English on Turkey, the Middle East and international relations, a co-author *Turkey's Transformation and American Policy*, New York, 2000 and *The United States and Turkey – Allies in Need*, New York, 2003, both are Century Foundation publications and *The Future of Turkish Foreign Policy*, MIT Press, 2004. His *Turkey's Mission Impossible, War and Peace with the Kurds* published in the U.S. in 2020. Çandar is Distinguished Visiting Scholar at the Stockholm University Institute for Turkish Studies (SUITS) and Senior Associate Fellow at the Swedish Institute of International Affairs (UI).

Turkey's neo-Ottomanist Moment, A Eurasianist Odyssey, is the most comprehensive account to date of the transformation of Turkey's foreign policy related to its regime change. With first-hand knowledge, Cengiz Çandar tells the story of the emergence of Recep Tayyip Erdoğan's revisionist Turkey in global affairs. References from almost 90 different names from around 20 countries, he also reflects how the international expertise on Turkey viewed Turkey.

PREFACE

"This book was written not because I knew the answers to the questions it poses, or even because I had any particular knowledge of the many subjects and fields it touches upon, because I myself wanted to read such a book. It is a book I would have preferred someone else to have written so I could enjoy reading it without the work of authorship. But no one else took up the assignment."

These lines are the introductory statement to S. Frederick Starr's magnum opus, *Lost Enlightenment, Central Asia's Golden Age from the Arab Conquest to Tamerlane*.[1] On the front cover the President of Afghanistan Ashraf Ghani describes the work as "a fantastic book". It is a fantastic book, indeed. To me, equally fantastic is these opening lines and indeed the whole preface. I met F. Frederick Starr only once in my life for around two hours in 2002 when we both were in the jury for Ömer Taşpınar's doctoral dissertation at The Johns Hopkins University School of Advanced International Studies (SAIS). One of the four jury members, my good friend, late Prof. Fouad Ajami, was reluctant to take the train from New York City to Washington to attend. Upon his approval to substitute him, I traveled overseas from Istanbul to Washington for that purpose. Ömer, whom I had known closely and later became an internationally renowned expert on Turkish foreign policy and the U.S. national security policies, had his dissertation on a very controversial but relevant issue: *Kurdish nationalism and political Islam in Turkey: Kemalist identity in transition.* That was the occasion I acquainted with Starr. Years later I avidly read his *Lost Enlightenment*, a book that will remain forever in my top ten, a priceless scholarly jewel.

I never forgot the promise I made to myself that I would one day quote his preface if I could write a book I could enjoy reading without the work of authorship. Like him, because no one took up the assignment, it has fallen upon me to accomplish the mission. Perhaps, it was incumbent upon no one but me to take the assignment of writing *Turkey's Neo-Ottomanist Moment, A Eurasian Odyssey.*

It had to be.

Although the reputation of the foremost Middle East expert in Turkey stuck on me for years, my professional training was on diplomacy and international relations. I did not leave any inch of the Greater Middle East from Afghanistan

---

[1] S. Frederick Starr, *Lost Enlightenment, Central Asia's Golden Age from the Arab Conquest to Tamerlane*, Princeton University Press, 2013

to Morocco, from Yemen and Sudan to Mesopotamia and Levant untouched in my long professional journalistic career. Over the years, I have developed acquaintances and even close personal relations with many historical figures ranging from Israelis to Palestinians, Iranians, Arabs, Turks, and Kurds. I taught the modern history of the Middle East in various universities in Istanbul. But my affiliation with the Middle East did not prevent me from following, contemplating, and being on the spot for the momentous changes that had taken place on the other corners of the globe.

Before the fall of the Berlin Wall, my focus had moved to Eastern Europe and the Soviet Union. I was in East Berlin on that unforgettable day recorded in history as the end of the Cold War. I was in Prague during the Velvet Revolution. I was in Moscow in 1991 when Gorbachev was ousted by a coup, to return a few days later, that followed the dissolution of the Soviet Union. I was the first Turkish journalist to be in every corner of the South Caucasus and Central Asia when the former Soviet republics transformed into independent states. I was in Hungary and Poland during the last days of the communist rule and the first days of its aftermath. I was often in the Balkans, from Albania to Bulgaria, and during Yugoslavia's break-up, from Macedonia and Croatia to Bosnia-Herzegovina. During the 1980s, my focus was Greek-Turkish relations and the Cyprus question. I have been all over Greece and on both sides of Cyprus island. I knew and met practically all the Greek and Turkish decision-makers and political personalities. I attended almost all conferences under the aegis of the United Nations from New York to Geneva, from Brussels to Davos, to settle the Cyprus question and the Turco-Greek conflict.

In retrospect, it should not be surprising President Turgut Özal asked me to work for him as his aide on international politics, which I did enthusiastically from 1991 until he passed away in 1993.

In 1992, I coined the concept of "neo-Ottomanism" as a proposition for the Turkish foreign policy in the new post-Cold war era, therefore for the attribute "Özalian neo-Ottomanism", I have some share.

At the turn of the century, I lived in Washington for two years, spent time in two prestigious think-tanks working on Turkish-American relations and the future of political Islam in Turkey. Following a short period of my return, Turkey had a new political reality: the rule of a party having roots in political Islam. Its leaders, above all, Abdullah Gül and Recep Tayyip Erdoğan knew me well. They had an ear to my views and analysis on foreign policy matters. From day one of their government, I traveled with them mainly in Europe; almost every official visit carried them to the United States. I was among the pioneers of Turkey's accession struggle to the European Union. I had the opportunity of frequently exchanging opinions with Turkey's new decision-makers, including Ahmet Davutoğlu, the ideologue and strategist of foreign policy during the first decade of the 2000s. My connections with many continued until we parted ways when Erdoğan transformed into a nationalist tyrant, a repressive autocrat who suppressed fundamental liberties and violated basic human rights.

Many of my schoolmates and classmates were among the people at the highest echelons of the Turkish Foreign Ministry, ambassadors of Turkey worldwide. My close connections with the Turkish foreign policy establishment remained intact for an extended period.

Despite all, I have never been a propagandist of Turkish policy. On the contrary, I earned a reputation for its perennial critique. Notwithstanding my permanent critical outlook about the Turkish foreign policy that goes back to the Cold war period, I have also provided treatises for the foreign policy Turkey has to adopt in the post-Cold war decades of the 21st century. "Grand Politics for a New Turkey", published by *Mediterranean Quarterly* in 2001, is noteworthy among them.

One other of mine widely referenced in the international scholarly outlets was published by the primary pro-government think-tank in Turkey in 2009, titled *"Turkey's 'Soft Power Strategy': A New Vision for a Multipolar World"*. The signals and many elements of Turkey's current Eurasianist Odyssey, the leitmotif of this book, could be found in it. From 2016 Turkey entered a different era. Thus, its transformed foreign policy moving on a new trajectory needed re-evaluation.

All these might explain *why* I should have taken the assignment of writing a book on Turkey's foreign policy, evolution, ambitions, and prospects. The reason for and *how Turkey's Neo-Ottomanist Moment, A Eurasian Odyssey*, is written is easier to tell.

I had in mind to write a paper for and to be published by the Swedish Institute of International Affairs that I am a senior associate fellow at its MENA (the Middle East and North Africa) department. Its Swedish acronym, UI, is a respected institution in Sweden for its expertise in international politics. Within the context of its peculiar relations with Russia, Turkey's Syria policy would be my essay to be submitted to the UI for publication. I had already finished my research for the UI Paper during the last quarter of the year 2019. In October 2019, Turkey had undertaken its third military incursion into the Syrian territory that followed the first one in 2016 and the second in 2018. US President Trump had announced the American withdrawal from northeastern Syria, the region of confrontation between Turkey and the Kurdish-led forces of the Syrian Democratic Front.

After putting the final touches on my book *Turkey's Mission Impossible, War and Peace with the Kurds*,[2] I would settle down to writing "Turkey in Syria and the Sui-Generis Turkey-Russia Relationship". That coincided with the days of self-isolation prompted by the COVID-19 pandemic. Reading and writing would be the natural preoccupation during the pandemic period.

Observing Turkey's political and military success in Libya in June 2020 altered my plans. The Turkish foreign policy followed a militarized foreign policy by sending Syrian proxies to the Libyan battleground, confronting the Russian proxies that allied with the forces sponsored by France, Egypt, and the United Arab Emirates, and it worked. I thought of broadening the UI Paper's scope I have been working on by adding the North African dimension to the Middle Eastern one.

During its preparatory phase, the Eastern Mediterranean tensions escalated to a dangerous standoff in the summer months. In August and September 2020, we held our breath. Turkey employed gunboat diplomacy, defied France besides Greece, creating cracks in NATO. It again worked. The Libyan issue could not be taken in isolation with the situation in the Eastern Mediterranean or vice-versa.

Throughout summer 2020, I delved into subjects like international law, the UN Convention on the Law of the Seas, and concepts: maritime delimitation, Exclusive Economic Zone, continental shelf, territorial waters, and hydrocarbon exploration and drilling activities in the Eastern Mediterranean. To research on all these was a fascinating unchartered zone for me. I was engaged in correspondence to get the expert opinion and educate myself on legal and technical matters.

After a lot of reading, I prepared a new project proposal for the Swedish Institute of International Affairs (UI), almost totally different than the original one I had in mind in 2019 and the first quarter of 2020.

I was hoping to submit my oeuvre to UI before the end of the year by working hard. However, I had to postpone the project's fulfillment and even change it from top to bottom with the break of the war in the South Caucasus

---

[2] Cengiz Çandar, Turkey's Mission Impossible, War and Peace with the Kurds, Lexington Books, 2020

on September 27, 2020. The ruthless war was for Nagorno-Karabagh between Azerbaijan and Armenia, parties to the frozen conflict since the year 1994. Turkey helped Azerbaijan politically and militarily, encouraged it to turn down the international initiatives for a ceasefire, stood firmly behind it until a decisive military victory which was achieved indeed after 44 days of the war. When the fighting stopped, Turkey was in Russia's backyard with the reluctant consent of the latter. I evaluated it as an unprecedented new development, a turning point for Turkey's foreign policy.

For 44 days and nights, my focus was on the South Caucasus. I read almost all the relevant material regarding the situation, including the region's history, the origins of the conflict, and re-read the primary sources. I had been to Armenia, Azerbaijan, and Georgia several times, traveled across their territories, and had been once in Nagorno-Karabagh. While following the developments on the ground during the war, I could imagine the strategic ramifications the new balance of power in the region would entail.

Reading the terms of the trilateral deal signed by Russia, Armenia and Azerbaijan evoked memories of the past. In 1992, I had undertaken an unpublicized mission on behalf of President Özal for reaching a deal between Armenia and Azerbaijan. I could foresee the potential laid for Turkey for a Eurasianist future.

When it came to foreign policy, although I did espouse values-based foreign policy and agreed that there is nothing wrong with a foreign policy having idealist aims, I generally abided by the dictates of realpolitik and considered myself closer to the realist school.

From that standpoint, I have to admit that from North Africa to the Eastern Mediterranean and the South Caucasus, the Turkish foreign policy, which interchangeably I coined as *Erdoğanist neo-Ottomanism* or *Turkey's Eurasianist Odyssey*, looked arguably successful. Although there is nothing left to agree for me about Erdoğan's tyrannical rule in Turkey that deprived me of my beloved country, I did not let my emotions mix with sober analysis on Turkey's foreign policy. I differed with many of my peers who were vehemently against every policy position that bore the mark of Erdoğan, those who wanted to see he failed and believed so, from Libya and the Eastern Mediterranean to the South Caucasus or in the Middle East and his dealings with Russia the Western world.

I was, of course, aware of the undeniable connection between the authoritarian policies of Erdoğan's regime implemented internally and its militarized foreign policy. Extremist-nationalist pursuance of foreign policy employing populist discourse and trying to resurrect the past's imperial glory should not be seen detached from the regime's repressive practices in the domestic political scene. Being in opposition to them should not preclude the assessment of their plausibility. As much departed from the shared values with the Euro-Atlantic system and sailed on the Eurasianist trajectory, Turkey simultaneously emerged as a revisionist power in the international arena and became repressive inside.

Erdoğan's Turkey, internally and externally, did not fail. On the contrary, the country's authoritarian regime consolidated, and its assertive (to some, aggressive) foreign policy gave dividends. Whether neo-Ottomanist Turkey of Erdoğan or his successors would be sustainable? That is the big question that demanded discussion.

Inspired by the unprecedented Turkish activism that extended beyond the Middle East and performed from North Africa to the South Caucasus that made the year 2020 a milestone in the annals of history, I changed the whole substance and the scope of my study. It looked more and more, an unending work in progress.

I began writing in December 2020, with online life and self-isolation imposed by the lengthy period of the pandemic; I worked day and night. Reading, writing, modifying, discarding, re-writing has been an arduous endeavor, partly because Turkish foreign policy was a moving target.

The analysis did not confine itself to the specific region like Turkish foreign policy in Syria, Turkey and the Eastern Mediterranean, etc. It did not become a theoretical and conceptual work like the origins of the neo-Ottomanist idea and its development, or Turkey and the West, Turkey and Russia, etc. Instead, all are interwoven comprehensively. Hence, it could be read as the short history and the evolution of Turkish foreign policy and its ambitious prospects. It is equally the narrative of Turkey's transformation. Turkey was a country with a definite European vocation for centuries, firmly placed in the Euro-Atlantic system in the aftermath of the Second World War. It gradually transformed into a revisionist country on the international stage like Russia. To achieve its ambitions, Turkey navigated in the opposite direction. Especially since 2016, and with the turning year of 2020, a different Turkey emerged.

For writing this book, I have read almost every report available in English and Turkish on Turkey, which was pertinent to foreign policy and strategy issues. My sources also included those in French and other languages published in the last few years. I found precious material in numerous periodicals, daily newspapers, online sites, books, and academic publications. I let around 90 people from nearly 20 different countries speak with their voices in the book. Most of them, Turkey specialists and internationally renowned thinkers or public intellectuals, paraded in the book with their guiding, attractive, sophisticated, sharp, accurate, and thought-provoking observations, assessments, and analyses.

Assembling the subjects and topics covering a wide range from strategy and security to geopolitics, from military matters to international law and maritime disputes within a coherent manuscript made me feel like I had undertaken a mission impossible. Nevertheless, it was quite a challenge that has been a strong motivation for me to take. My references and sources provided me the ammunition, I believe.

When I put the last exclamation mark on the manuscript which I had begun to feel would never end, it has gone much beyond the limits of a paper I would submit to UI for publication.

While the writing was in progress, my wife Tuba patiently endured the dull moments of our life indoors during the long dark days of Swedish winter. Life was even more boring for her, seeing a man staring almost only at a computer on his lap 7/24. She went over quickly on the manuscript when I was done and reacted calmly: "You have told me you were writing a paper, and I was confused why it took so long to write it. Now, I see. You have written a book!"

I could not submit a book to UI to be published. There was no commitment on UI's part to publish a book I would deliver. However, if it would not be the feeling of my belonging to and obligation to UI, *Turkey's neo-Ottomanist Moment, A Eurasian Odyssey*, perhaps would never be written.

My gratitude goes to Tuba more than anything and anybody. She always stood with me, provided the excellent conditions for me to take the challenge of writing this book, and reminded me that I had written a book for publication, not a paper. Without her contribution, *Turkey's neo-Ottomanist Moment, A Eurasian Odyssey,* could never come to life.

And, in that case, I would not enjoy reading this controversial book that I would have wanted to read since nobody had taken the assignment of writing it.

June-July 2021

A NOTE ON NAMES, SPELLING AND TRANSLITERATION

The Turkish names and Arab and those with Slavic origins, whether Russian, Ukrainian, Polish, Serbian, etc., presented challenges. Many of them have no standardized spelling for transliterating into English. To solve the challenge, I applied how the names are spelled according to the English transliteration accepted where they belonged. For instance, in Russia case, I used Vladimir as it used for Vladimir Putin or Vladimir Lenin, but for the Ukrainian President Zelensky, I adopted the Ukrainian transliteration as Volodymyr. The same applied to Ukraine's capital city Kyiv, although the common English usage is Kiev. For Polish and Serbian names, I used the same principle, in the Polish spelling like Czesław Miłosz or the Serbian spelling of Slobodan Milošević.

For the Turkish names, I followed the modern Turkish spelling. In Turkish, both letters, ı and i exist, as g and ğ, s and ş, c and ç. Therefore, I spelled the surname of the president of Turkey as Erdoğan, and of the foreign minister as Çavuşoğlu. My surname begins with Ç, the Turkish equivalent of Serbian č, the English pronunciation of it is ch.

If it is not a quotation, I used ğ, ç, and i wherever they existed. If it is a quotation or in an endnote, even in my surname, which was spelled as Candar, I left it as it is in the source.

The first name of the president of Azerbaijan is İlham, but also commonly used as Ilham. If in the quotation I referred to, it was spelled as Ilham; I did not interfere.

That also applied to Nagorno-Karabagh, the disputed region between Armenian and Azerbaijan. The most standard spelling to an English-speaking audience is Nagorno-Karabagh. Nagorno is a Russian word that means mountainous, and Karabagh is Turkish and Farsi (Persian), meaning Black Garden. I used it in its most standard spelling; however, when it appeared like Nagorno-Karabakh in some quotations, albeit incorrect, I did not interfere with the author's choice.

A NOTE ON NAMES, SPELLING AND TRANSLITERATION

A REVISIONIST POWER ON THE INTERNATIONAL STAGE

The third decade of the twenty-first century began, among many other things, with the entry of a new revisionist power to the international stage: Turkey.

In the 1990s, with the end of the Cold War marked by the fall of the Berlin Wall (1989) and the dissolution of the Soviet empire (1991), many internationally-renowned experts and thinkers characterized Turkey as a newly-born "pivotal" country. In his *The Grand Chessboard* (1997), Zbigniew Brzezinski listed Turkey along with Ukraine, Azerbaijan, South Korea, and Iran to play the role of a critically important geopolitical pivot. Turkey for Prof. Paul Kennedy of Yale, one of the three editors of *The Pivotal States: A New Framework for United States in the Developing World* (1999), also was one of nine identified as a *"pivotal state"* in that important book. Geoffrey Kemp in *Strategic Geography and the Changing Middle East* (1997) confirmed Turkey's "pivotal status" in international affairs: *"The changes that brought about the end of the Cold War and the breakup of the Soviet Union radically shifted the parameters of European and Middle East strategic front lines. Turkey now finds itself at the center, rather than the periphery, of a changing environment. It remains a key Mediterranean power with a very important role in the Balkans."* Richard Holbrooke went that so far as to say, *"Turkey after the Cold War is equivalent to Germany during the Cold War, a pivotal state, where diverse interests intersect"*. [3]

However, perhaps none of them could have predicted the way Turkey would emerge as a revisionist power as it did in the year 2020. It seemed the way Turkey emerged in 2020 and carried on in 2021 confirmed what the former President of the United States, Bill Clinton, had vaguely forecast two decades ago.

In a speech at Georgetown University on November 8, 1999, a week before he visited Turkey, commemorating the 10th anniversary of the fall of the Berlin Wall, which marked the end of the Cold War and of the 20th century, Clinton said:

When I go to Turkey, I will point out that much of the history of the 20th century, for better or worse, was shaped by the way the old Ottoman Empire collapsed before and after

---

[3] Cengiz Çandar, "Turkey in the 21st Century", *United States Institute of Peace* (Unpublished Paper), Washington, D.C., presented on May 18, 2000.

World War I, and the decisions that the European powers made in the aftermath. I believe the coming century will be shaped in good measure by the way in which Turkey, itself, defines its future and its role today and tomorrow, for Turkey is a country at the crossroads of Europe, the Middle East, and Central Asia. The future can be shaped for the better if Turkey can become fully a part of Europe, as a stable, democratic, secular, Islamic nation. This too can happen if there is progress in overcoming differences with Greece, especially over Cyprus, if Turkey continues to strengthen respect for human rights, and if there is a real vision on the part of our European allies, who must be willing to reach out and to believe that it is at Turkey where Europe and the Muslim world can meet in peace and harmony, to give us a chance to have the future of our dreams in that part of the world in the new millennium.[4]

At the time I was living in Washington, D.C. Quoting Clinton's observation on Turkey, I wrote:

The important strategic implications of this message – with its ambitious theoretical overtones that contest the validity of the globally debated "clash of civilizations" postulate of Harvard scholar Samuel Huntington- were either lost in the charged political atmosphere of Washington or met with a conspicuous indifference of the American intellectual circles.

Did President Clinton's words reflect the "considered opinion" of the U.S. foreign policy? Did they reflect a bipartisan strategic outlook concerning Turkey's role 21st century? "Hopefully," was the response I received from Anthony Lake, a former National Security Advisor, when I posed these questions to him in Berlin in late January 2000. He also reminded me that he worked very hard to promote this same position during his White House years...

A week after his Georgetown speech, Clinton elaborated on his theme in an address before the Turkish parliament:

"For better and worse, the events of that time, when the Ottoman Empire disintegrated and a new Turkey arose, have shaped the entire history of this century. From Bulgaria to Albania, from Israel to Arabia, new nations were born, and a century of conflict erupted from the turmoil of shifting borders, unrealized ambitions, and old hatreds, beginnings with the First Balkan War and World War I, all the way to today's struggles in the Middle East and in the former Yugoslavia. Turkey's past is key to understanding the twentieth century. But, more importantly, I believe Turkey's future will be critical shaping the twenty-first century."[5]

At the cusp of the new century, on November 15, 1999, the President of the

---

[4] *Presidential Documents* [weekly compilation], Monday November 15, 1999, Vol. 35, No. 45, pp. 2267-2372, at p. 2290. https://www.govinfo.gov/content/pkg/WCPD-1999-11-15/pdf/WCPD-1999-11-15.pdf
[5] Cengiz Çandar, "Turkey in the 21st Century", *op cit.*

United States, Bill Clinton, had expressed a prognosis for Turkey in the speech he delivered in the Turkish capital. In contrast to the controversial "clash of civilizations" thesis that became fashionable all over the world during the 1990s, Clinton tacitly expressed his hope that Turkey would help to put the lie to *"the tired claim of an inherent clash of civilizations"*.

With a 1000-year old Western (European) vocation that started with a geopolitical impulse and attained a civilizational dimension over the last 200 years, Turkey is still a predominantly Muslim society with an imperial legacy as the standard-bearer of Islam in Europe. These Janus-type traits have led some observers to conclude that Turkey is a country suffering from a permanent "identity crisis," or as Samuel Huntington put it, that Turkey is, along with Russia and Mexico, a "torn country."[6]

Clinton's perception of Turkey at the turn of the century was a repudiation of considering it a "torn country". On the contrary, he attributed almost an extraordinary historical mission to Turkey for shaping the 21st century by referring to its Ottoman imperial legacy at the beginning of the previous century.

His statement nurtured the sentiment that already was intrinsic for numerous Turkish political activists and opinion-makers: Regenerating the imperial glory of the past.

That sentiment has been one of the underlying drives for Recep Tayyip Erdoğan, the longest-serving leader in the Turkish republic's history. Besides labels like revisionism, irredentism, expansionism, or belligerence, his ambitious foreign policy is widely marked as neo-Ottomanism. In the post–Cold War era, the most famous paradigm for Turkish foreign policy has been neo-Ottomanism. Many, including politicians from all corners of the globe and prominent international scholars, tended to see Recep Tayyip Erdoğan's assertive foreign policy as an exercise in neo-Ottomanism.

Turkey's assertive – for some aggressive and expansionist – foreign policy, increasingly reliant on hard power and militarized diplomacy deployed with an ideologically hegemonic narrative labelled as neo-Ottomanism, raised concerns in broad geopolitics during the year 2020 more than ever previously. From North Africa to South Caucasus, from the Eastern Mediterranean to the Middle East, Turkey was belligerently active in projecting its hard power.

It changed the calculus in the Libyan civil war in favour of the UN-endorsed government in Tripoli. It funnelled generous military support. It thereby turned

---

[6] Ibid.

the tables over a warlord, albeit at different levels, as the proxy of formidable players on the Libyan battleground, including Russia, France, UAE, Egypt, Jordan, and Saudi Arabia.

It challenged France, Greece, and Cyprus in the Eastern Mediterranean regarding the maritime jurisdiction and delineation as well as the East-Med Gas Forum formed by Greece, Cyprus, Israel, and Egypt (later joined by France as a member, and with the EU and UAE wishing to participate as permanent observers), to engage in the drilling and production of hydrocarbons.

Turkey provided an unprecedented level of military assistance to Azerbaijan in its war with Armenia. Azerbaijan had a stunning battlefield success in liberating its territories which Armenia had occupied for almost 30 years. It ultimately won the Nagorno Karabagh War. Turkey's role in the war, having the lion's share in the Azerbaijani victory, placed it as a regional power next to Russia in the South Caucasus, until recently considered a solely Russian sphere of influence.

Turkey and Russia, simultaneously, were embroiled in a complicated relationship of contention and cooperation in Syria. In Idlib in February 2020, the Russian air force inflicted a heavy toll on the Turkish troops that brought the two countries to the brink of a military showdown ultimately averted at a high-level meeting of Vladimir Putin and Recep Tayyip Erdoğan in Moscow. As in Libya, Turkey and Russia backed different parties in Syria, the first the opposition and the armed forces fighting against the regime, the latter the regime and the Syrian army. However, Turkey and Russia established a partnership as well, forming joint military patrols on the main highways linking Idlib to Aleppo and on the roads along the Turkish border in northeast Syria which the Kurds mainly inhabit.

In the Eastern Mediterranean, Turkey followed the policy of gunboat diplomacy, conducted drilling activities escorted by its naval forces for the prospect for gas in the contested maritime zones, and disputed the EEZs of EU member countries. With the standoff in the Eastern Mediterranean, it also defied France, which supported Greece and Cyprus.

Moreover, it deployed and tested a top-of-the-range S-400, the Russian air defense missile system, ignoring NATO warnings and to the chagrin of the U.S, which in turn decided to implement sanctions, albeit not severe, against a NATO ally, according to CAATSA (Countering American Adversaries Through Sanctions Act).

All this took place within the year 2020. Singularly, each of these acts deserves to be considered a severe international conflict, and Turkey initiated or was a party to all of them.

THE WORLD'S PANDEMIC YEAR, TURKEY'S YEAR OF BELLIGERENCE

The year 2020 is already registered in the annals of history as the year everything changed. The pandemic broke out in the early days of the year. A new coronavirus causing what was named COVID-19 caused the highest mortality rate globally since the Spanish flu that ravaged the world in 1918, almost a century ago. The world has gone through what, by every measure, is a great crisis. Therefore it is natural to assume that 2020 will prove a turning point in modern history.

For John Ikenberry, eminent theorist of international relations and best known for his work on liberal international relations theory, the spring of 2020, when the world was confronted with the COVID-19 pandemic, might be seen in the future as the end of the liberal world order. His dramatic estimation on the historical significance of the pandemic witnessed in 2020, perhaps inadvertently, gave clues for the conditions in which the illiberal forces could grow and emerge on the international stage through hard power projection.

When future historians think of the moment that marked the end of the liberal world order, they may point to the spring of 2020 – the moment when the United States and its allies, facing the gravest public health threat and economic catastrophe of the postwar era, could not even agree on a simple communiqué of common cause. But the chaos of the coronavirus pandemic engulfing the world these days is only exposing and accelerating what was already happening for years. On public health, trade, human rights, and the environment, governments seem to have lost faith in the value of working together. Not since the 1930s has the world been this bereft of even the most rudimentary forms of cooperation.[7]

Regarding the historical significance of the pandemic, Richard Haass thought just the opposite. He did not see it as a turning point and underlined that with the crisis that the pandemic would bring, the American domination of international politics would diminish. The "unipolar moment" would be even less relevant.

---

[7] G. John Ikenberry, "The Next Liberal Order", *Foreign Affairs*, July/August 2020. https://www.foreignaffairs. com/articles/united-states/2020-06-09/next-liberal-order

The world following the pandemic is unlikely to be radically different from the one that preceded it. COVID-19 will not so much change the basic direction of world history as it accelerates. The pandemic and the response to it have revealed and reinforced the fundamental characteristics of geopolitics today. As a result, this crisis promises to be less of a turning point than a way station along the road that the world has been traveling for the past few decades… If the world that follows this crisis will be one in which the United States dominates less and less – it is almost impossible to imagine anyone today writing about a "unipolar moment" – this trend is hardly new. It has been apparent for at least a decade.[8]

Nonetheless, in terms of the pandemic's expected consequences, Haass reached more or less similar conclusions as those of Ikenberry.

The pandemic is likely to reinforce the democratic recession that has been evident for the past 15 years. There will be calls for a larger government role in society, be it to constrain movement of populations or provide economic help. Civil liberties will be treated by many as a casualty of war, a luxury that cannot be afforded in a crisis. Meanwhile, threats posed by illiberal countries such as Russia, North Korea, and Iran will still exist once the pandemic does not; indeed, they may well have increased while attention was trained elsewhere.[9]

In the aftermath of the pandemic, Richard Haass predicted a world in even greater disarray.

Francis Fukuyama offered an intriguing evaluation of the historical significance of the pandemic marking the year 2020.

Major crises have major consequences, usually unforeseen. The Great Depression spurred isolationism, nationalism, fascism, and World War II – but also led to the New Deal, the rise of the United States as a global superpower, and eventually decolonization. The 9/11 attacks produced two failed American interventions, the rise of Iran, and new forms of Islamic radicalism. The 2008 financial crisis generated a surge in antiestablishment populism that replaced leaders across the globe. Future historians will trace comparably large effects to the current coronavirus pandemic; the challenge is figuring them out ahead of time…

Over the years to come, the pandemic could lead to the United States' relative decline, the continued erosion of the liberal international order, and a resurgence of fascism around the globe. It could also lead to a rebirth of liberal democracy, a system that has confounded skeptics many times, showing remarkable powers of resilience and renewal. Elements of both visions

[8] Richard Haass, "The Pandemic Will Accelerate History Rather Than Reshape It, Not Every Crisis Is a Turning Point", *Foreign Affairs*, April 7, 2020. https://www.foreignaffairs.com/articles/united-states/2020-04-07/pandemic-will-accelerate-history-rather-reshape-it
[9] Ibid.

will emerge, in different places. Unfortunately, unless current trends change dramatically, the general forecast is gloomy.[10]

Under the sub-heading Rising Fascism, Fukuyama highlighted how the pandemic would accelerate the rise of nationalist, xenophobic regimes and its ramification on the international order – as if describing Turkey's emergence as a revisionist belligerent power in volatile geopolitics during the year 2020.

Pessimistic outcomes are easy to imagine. Nationalism, isolationism, xenophobia, and attacks on the liberal world order have been increasing for years, and that trend will only be accelerated by the pandemic… The rise of nationalism will increase the possibility of international conflict. Leaders may see fights with foreigners as useful domestic political distractions, or they may be tempted by the weakness or preoccupation of their opponents and take advantage of the pandemic to destabilize favorite targets or create new facts on the ground.[11]

However, Fukuyama's direct reference to Turkey concerning the year 2020 was on its impressive use of drones in multiple conflict zones. In a striking piece in April 2021 in *American Purpose*, he tacitly attributed Turkey's rise to the introduction of its drones from Syria to Libya and the South Caucasus, yielding positive results.

Drones have done much to promote Turkey's rise as a regional power in the year 2020. The country has now decisively shaped the outcomes of three conflicts, and promises to do more of the same. The Middle East, which looked like it was being polarized along Sunni-Shia lines led by the two primary antagonists Saudi Arabia and Iran, is in fact more genuinely multipolar. Turkey has not aligned itself permanently with anyone. It has opposed its fellow Sunni powers, the Gulf States, in Libya; simultaneously sided with Russia by buying the latter's S-400 air defense system while attacking Russian forces in Syria; and has refused to align its aims with Washington despite its continuing membership in NATO. Yet it has also sold TB2 drones to Ukraine, which might help unfreeze that conflict….

This has had some good consequences. Turkey's intervention in Syria defeated what would have been a genocidal act against the refugees who had sought shelter in Idlib province. Had Assad succeeded in retaking the province, he would have provoked another massive refugee crisis with big implications for Europe. It's not clear the world would be better off had Gen. Haftar occupied Tripoli.[12]

---

[10] Francis Fukuyama, "The Pandemic and World Order", *Foreign Affairs*, July/August 2020. https://www.foreignaffairs.com/articles/world/2020-06-09/pandemic-and-political-order
[11] *Ibid*
[12] Francis Fukuyama, "Droning On in the Middle East", *American Purpose*, April 5, 2021. https://www.

2020 has indeed been identified as *Turkey's year of belligerence*. The European edition of the political newspaper *Politico* carried this as the title of an article published on December 10, 2020. *Politico*, drawing attention to how palpable Turkey's belligerence had been during the year, wrote: "*At the start of 2020, this column asked, 'How rogue can Turkey go?' If this were an end-of-year corporate performance review, the rating would have to be "exceeded expectations".* [13]

For *Foreign Policy*, 2020 was *Turkey's Year of Living Dangerously*. Its review of 2020 opened with the assertion that "*If there is one man who didn't let a pandemic stifle his quest for glory, it is Turkish President Recep Tayyip Erdogan*".

Alluding to Turkey's assertive foreign policy, Foreign Policy wrote: "In 2020, Erdogan took the wrecking ball he'd previously slammed into Turkey's domestic politics and turned it on the region. This year, Turkey's military was more active around the world than it has been in decades, or perhaps ever. From Libya to Nagorno-Karabagh, the Turkish leader has used armed force to advance Turkey's objectives."[14]

The leading columnist and the Turkey expert on Israel's opinion paper, *Haaretz*, Zvi Bar'el, saw Turkey in 2020 as a "*revisionist state*" in accordance with the ambitious objective of its leader, Erdoğan, who wanted to change the geopolitical status quo. Zvi Bar'el opined on Erdoğan as planning a new world order in which Turkey will be the rising star, will be everywhere, and will be stopped by nobody. His account of Turkey in 2020 was as follows:

Erdogan's agenda encompasses much more than mere defense and survival. His ultimate goal is to alter the geopolitical status quo in ways he believes benefit Turkey. In this sense, Turkey is now a revisionist state: It embarks upon military interventions and seeks to control foreign territory, as in Syria and Iraq; challenges land borders and maritime boundaries, as with Cyprus and Greece; engages in demographic engineering and political interference, as in Syria and Northern Cyprus; maintains bases overseas, as in Somalia and Qatar; and galvanizes dependent proxies, as in Libya, northern Syria, and Nagorno-Karabakh.[15]

Attributing "expansionist motives" for Turkey to revisionism, he proceeded with the premise that, "Revisionist undercurrents of Erdogan's worldview indicate that the Eastern

americanpurpose.com/blog/fukuyama/droning-on/

[13] Paul Taylor, "Turkey's Year of Belligerence", *Politico*, December 10, 2020. https://www.politico.eu/article/turkey-erdogan-year-of-belligerence/

[14] Allison Meakem, "The Year in Review: Turkey's Year of Living Dangerously", *Foreign Policy*, December 25, 2020. https://foreignpolicy.com/2020/12/25/turkeys-year-of-living-dangerously/

[15] Zvi Bar'el, "Analysis, Erdogan Is Planning a New World Order in Which Turkey Is the Rising Star", *Haaretz*, October 26, 2020. https://www.haaretz.com/world-news/.premium.HIGHLIGHT-erdogan-is-planning-a-new-world-order-in-which-turkey-is-the-star-1.9257381

Mediterranean crisis is not primarily about natural gas but decades-old sovereignty issues – infused with old and new geopolitical ambitions alike. Material gain has motivated Turkey's expansionism, but it is also animated by identity and ideology".[16]

Distinguished French diplomat, Gérard Araud, was among those who identified Turkey as a "revisionist power" along with Russia and China. identifying them as "revisionist powers." According to him, Russia, China and Turkey are described as *"revisionist powers which don't accept a status-quo based on a world order largely defined by the West in 1945 and 1991 by a new global balance of power".*[17]

Wall Street Journal's Yaroslav Trofimov interpreted the manifestation of Turkey's foreign policy in the year 2020 as irredentism and mentioned it as an *"irredentist power"* like Russia and China. Irredentism, he emphasized, is a belief that historic parts of one's country under foreign rule must be reunited with the homeland. He also illustriously explained the origins of the term that goes back to 1877. It was coined by the Italian politician Matteo Renato Imbriani when he pledged not to rest until all of Italy's *"terre irredente"* (unredeemed lands) under the rule of Habsburg Austria were liberated. To back his argument that Turkey is irredentist like Russia and China, Trofimov wrote:

Smaller powers are showing irredentist leanings too. Over the past three years, the Turkish military has occupied some parts of Syria and Iraq that President Recep Tayyip Erdogan has said should have remained in Turkey after the breakup of the Ottoman Empire a century ago... Turkey also came close to a military confrontation with Greece over Ankara's expansive new claims over the Eastern Mediterranean, a crisis that has prompted some senior Turkish officials to question Greece's sovereignty over Greek islands close to the Anatolian mainland such as Rhodes. "Our civilization is one of conquest," Mr. Erdogan thundered in August (2020).[18]

Prominent European political thinker and well-known French statesman Jacques Attali went so far as to make an analogy between Erdoğan and Turkey's rise in international politics, and Adolf Hitler and the Third Reich during 1930. Calling on the European Union to refrain from adopting a stance of appeasement vis-à-vis Turkey, he warned:

---

[16] Ibid.
[17] Gerard Araud, twitter.com > gerardaraud > status, August 30, 2020.
[18] Yaroslav Trofimov, "The Dangers in a New Era of Territorial Grabs", The Wall Street Journal, September 17, 2020.

We have to hear what Erdogan says, take it very seriously and be prepared to act by all means. If our predecessors had taken the Führer's speeches seriously from 1933 to 1936, they could have prevented this monster from accumulating the ways and means to do what he had announced.[19]

Some pundits likened Erdoğan to Mussolini rather than Hitler, thus somewhat disagreeing with Attali's characterization:

Although one of the world's leading political thinkers as well as a paragon of the European establishment, Attali picked the wrong '30s-era dictator to serve as an Erdogan prototype. A more apt one would have been Benito Mussolini, who proved to be nothing more than a tin-pot imperialist, rather than the monster who almost ate Europe.[20]

Notwithstanding the comparisons between Erdoğan and the doomed warmongers of the 20th century, most if not all of the arguments that described Turkey as a belligerent, revisionist, irredentist, and arguably an expansionist power were not misrepresentations. In 2020, Turkey's President Recep Tayyip Erdoğan made his intentions plain. While the world, including Turkey, was grappling with the pandemic, he said:

Turkey has become a powerful regional actor at a scale never seen in its recent history. Our country's position in global power index assessments is increasing with each passing year. We are now closer than ever to our goal of a great and strong Turkey. Once we safely carry our country to 2023 [the centennial of the Republic of Turkey], we will have made Turkey an unstoppable power.[21]

The rise of Turkey in 2020 was conceived by the president of the International Crisis Group (at the end of January 2021, President Joseph Biden named him Special U.S. Envoy for Iran), Rob Malley, as *"flexing its foreign policy muscles"* and led him to raise the intriguing question, *"Is it Neo-Ottomanism or Pan-Islamism or the combination of both?"*[22]

TURKEY: THE COUNTRY TO WATCH

Rob Malley, who had inquired whether Turkey in 2020 is to be characterized

---

[19] Jacques Attali, September 7, 2020. https://twitter.com/jattali/status/1302874004097847296

[20] David Rosenberg, "Turkey Doesn't Have the Economic Bite to Back Up Erdogan's Bark", *Haaretz*, October 28, 2020.

[21] https://www.tccb.gov.tr/en/news/542/120571/-turkey-has-become-a-powerful-regional-actor-; https://podcast.ausha.co/hold-your-fire/episode-7-turkey-flexes-its-foreign-policy-muscles

[22] https://www.crisisgroup.org/europe-central-asia/western-europemediterranean/turkey/turkey-flexes-its-foreign-policy-muscles

as Neo-Ottomanism or Pan-Islamism, positioned it among the "10 Conflicts to Watch in 2021". Following his introductory statement, *"The world will be haunted by the legacies of 2020: an ongoing pandemic, an economic crisis… and new threats emanating from wars and climate change"*, he lists the ten conflicts, in the order of Afghanistan, Ethiopia, the Sahel, Yemen, Venezuela, Somalia, Libya, Iran-United States, Russia-Turkey, and climate change. Turkey is the only country directly involved in more than one among the top ten conflicts to watch in 2021. Under the Russia-Turkey sub-heading, he presents noteworthy observations:

Paradoxically, just as Moscow and Ankara compete on an increasing number of battlefields, their ties are stronger than they have been in some time. Their "frenmity" is symptomatic of broader trends – a world in which non-Western powers increasingly push back against the United States and Western Europe and are more assertive and more willing to enter into fluctuating alliances.[23]

As it is listed as the only country involved among the top ten conflicts to watch, Turkey was the single country identified by its name among the "Top 10 Risks" forecasted for the year 2021. The influential political risk consultancy Eurasia Group, in its annual forecast for 2021, listed Turkey as "Risk 7" among the top 10 under a cynical heading "(Out in the) cold Turkey". For Eurasia Group, while Erdoğan was seeking imperial grandeur, the Turkish economy's poor performance distinguished Turkey as a risk-laden country for 2021. This was its account:

Erdogan's misadventures will boomerang painfully against the economy, because Turkey needs international goodwill to revitalize growth. It will remain dependent on predominantly Western financing, despite Ankara's best efforts to find alternative funding sources – including China.[24]

The economic difficulties aggravated by the pandemic of 2020 would not deter Erdoğan from pursuing his costly and increasingly militarized diplomacy, as long as he can portray the successful foreign policy achievements at home to reinforce the legitimacy of his autocratic rule.

Even Turkey's own economic woes do not seem to change the course of its foreign policy: in a striking example, in November 2020 Turkey volunteered to pay off Somalia's debt to International Monetary Fund. Turkey built its largest military base abroad in Somalia. The base in Mogadishu provides Turkey

---

[23] Robert Malley, "10 Conflicts to Watch in 2021", *Foreign Policy*, December 29, 2020. https://foreignpolicy.com/2020/12/29/10-conflicts-to-watch-in-2021-ethiopia-iran-yemen-somalia-venezuela/
[24] https://www.eurasiagroup.net/issues/top-risks-2021, January 4, 2021.

strategic leverage geopolitically as it is close to the entrance to the Red Sea.

Under Recep Tayyip Erdoğan, Turkey aspires to become the leader of the Islamic and non-Western world. The engagement with Somalia, a part of its broader strategy on Africa, serves that objective.

"Erdoğan's Somalia gambit is part of a larger strategy designed to enhance Turkey's influence around the world… To a degree it was easy for Erdoğan to set his sights on Africa. The continent was in many ways long-hanging fruit. The amount of investment needed to achieve the goals Turkey set for itself were modest and certainly affordable", gauged Henri Barkey, an American expert of Turkish origin.[25]

He observed that *"Ankara's interest in the region is interpreted as neo-Ottomanist imperialism by a country seen to be allied with the Islamist Muslim Brotherhood"* by Egypt and Arab Gulf states which have not happily received Turkey's military build-up and naval presence in the region. Thus, notwithstanding the economic difficulties it might encounter, Turkey's assertive foreign policy and militarized diplomacy is likely to prevail.

In this respect, a major Turkish offensive in Iraq in was predicted. French historian and professor of Middle East studies Jean-Pierre Filiu raised the possibility of Turkey's military incursion into northern Iraq in the following terms: *"Intoxicated by his successive victories in Syria, Libya, and the Caucasus, Erdogan may soon be tempted by a large-scale intervention in Iraqi Kurdistan, where his army is already carrying out occasional raids".[26]*

Soli Özel, a renowned Turkish scholar of international affairs, advanced the prognosis that Turkey, among the world's riskiest countries in the post-2020 epoch, might change its strategic trajectory. He asserted:

Turkey's recently emboldened and assertive (and for some aggressive) foreign policy has been widely noticed and even ranked as one of the top ten risks in the world for 2021. Its actions raise not totally justified concerns and cause irritation among its allies. Increasingly over-reliant on hard power, deployed with an ideologically hegemonic and even expansionist narrative, Ankara is taking advantage of the vacuum created by a retreating United States, the shambolic state of the Middle East and its own willingness to engage militarily. As an aspiring regional power whose interests are no longer parallel to those of the retreating hegemon, the United States, and feeling rejected by the European Union, Turkey is seeking the right to

---

[25] Henri Barkey, *"Turkey's Strategy to Build Influence Focuses on Africa"*, Asia Times, January 25, 2020. https://asiatimes.com/author/henri-j-barkey/-
[26] https://www.lemonde.fr/blog/filiu/2020/12/27/la-menace-en-2021-dune-offensive-majeure-de-la-turquie-en-irak/

undertake autonomous action in its surrounding regions. Mistrusting its allies Ankara is also pursuing a policy of transactional accommodation with the Russian Federation in an interesting balancing act… Ankara's need to break out of its isolation and temper its estrangement from its allies will be pressing and the relation with Russia will have to be recalibrated. Absent these, Turkey's strategic trajectory might change for good.[27]

---

[27] Soli Özel, "2021: Year of Decisions", *Observatoire de la Vie Politique Turque*, January 7, 2021. https://ovipot. hypotheses.org/15684

NEO-OTTOMANISM: A CONTROVERSY

A KALEIDOSCOPE OF HOSTILITY

There is almost a scholarly consensus to interpret Turkey's assertive foreign policy as the manifestation of neo-Ottomanism. For the Western world, the concept of neo-Ottomanism, in general, does not resonate benevolently. Less so in the immediate neighbourhood of Turkey, which is its pivotal operational ground. For the diverse actors in the geopolitics where Turkey wants to operate, neo-Ottomanism mostly has a strong derogatory connotation.

From Iran to its regional nemesis Israel, from the Caucasus – namely, Armenia – to the Balkans, Erdoğan's Turkey is looked upon as neo-Ottomanist. Such perception has nourished angst and hostility in an array of countries.

Turkey's involvement in the Armenia-Azerbaijan War and projection of itself as a formidable regional actor in the South Caucasus triggered strong resentment in next-door Iran, which lies south of Armenia and Azerbaijan and has common frontiers with both countries.

Turkish President Erdoğan recited a poem during the victory parade in Baku after the war, which ended with Azerbaijan's triumph that the Turkish troops also participated in. The poem was a lamentation of Azerbaijan's division between the Russian Empire and Iran in the early 19th century.

It caused a diplomatic spat between the two regional powers, which exhibited a certain level of (uneasy) cooperation in the Syrian conflict. Erdoğan, perhaps inadvertently, hit a very sensitive chord for Iran which has its own territory with the same name, Azerbaijan, and a fairly significant portion of Turkic-Azerbaijani speaking people among its population.

The Iranian outrage over Erdoğan's lamentation for the division of Azerbaijan was put forward in a fierce criticism published by the daily *Javan*, the mouthpiece of the IRGC (the Revolutionary Guard Corps) that controls the regime. The Iranian anger found its expression in the following:

The ambitious Turkish president, with his multiple military adventures ranging from the Horn of Africa and Mediterranean to the Caucasus, is in pursuit of creating his delusional state. This time he has taken blind aim at Iran's beloved Azerbaijan. With a recitation of a separatist-inspiring poem in Baku, the theme of which, in his view, was the violation of the territorial integrity of Iran and the seceding of Azerbaijan. He tried to include this area in his imaginary 'Neo-Ottoman' empire.[28]

---

[28] *Javanonline.ir*, December 12, 2020.

Iran's genuine outlook on Turkey's assertive foreign policy operating in the broad geopolitics was never put as bluntly as in this statement in the daily *Jawan*:

In the last decade, Erdoğan, by interfering in the domestic affairs of the regional countries, wishes to revive the Neo-Ottoman Empire with him as its leader. Meddling in the internal affairs of Syria, Libya, and the oil and gas drilling in the Mediterranean, is part of Erdoğan's project to form his empire in the region.[29]

Although the Turco-Iranian altercation was contained and appeared to be resolved, Iran's differences seem to run deeper than imagined. Almost a month after the diplomatic spat erupted in the wake of developments in the South Caucasus, Iranian foreign minister Muhammed Jawad Zarif in an interview, while refraining from mentioning Turkey by name, tacitly accused it of following an expansionist policy in Syria.

We did not try to expand our borders. One of our neighboring countries, which is present in Syria, has hoisted its flag over government buildings everywhere, even in areas where it is active as a 'peacekeeper'. Iran does not raise its flag. Iran is in Syria to support, not to order.[30]

Considering the Turkish foreign policy as "neo-Ottomanist" with expansionist motivations is not limited to the Iranian regime's hardliner power centre. The reformist opposition of the Iranian political spectrum thinks along these same lines when assessing the Turkish foreign policy of Recep Tayyip Erdoğan.

An interview with Sadeq Maleki, who is introduced as an Iranian expert on Turkish affairs, published by the Iranian reformist newspaper *Shargh* on December 15, 2020, in the wake of Turkey's extension of its sphere of influence in the South Caucasus as a result of the Armenia-Azerbaijan war, is very indicative in this respect.

For Maleki, Erdoğan *"wishes to divide Iran and to annex Azerbaijan to Turkey to form the Greater Turkistan"*. Maleki stated that Erdoğan is trying to *"establish neo-Ottomanism"*, which differentiates itself from Ottomanism in its geopolitical perception. According to Maleki, *"the old Ottomanism was looking to expand to Vienna's gates and the West, whereas Erdoğan's neo-Ottomanism has its view toward the East"*.[31]

---

[29] Ibid.
[30] https://etemadonline.com/content/460318, January 23, 2021.
[31] Sadeq Maleki (interview), "The Old Ottomanism Was Looking to Expand to the Gates of Vienna and to the West, Neo-Ottomanism Has Its View Toward the East", *Shargh*, December 15, 2020.

Interestingly, Erdoğan's foreign policy attributed to "neo-Ottomanism" was seen more or less in the same contours in Israel, Iran's regional archenemy. A paper published by the Israeli think-tank BESA (Begin–Sadat Center for Strategic Studies), affiliated with Bar-Ilan University, argued that the *"Islamist government led by President Recep Tayyip Erdoğan is pursuing an increasingly daring neo-Ottoman policy throughout the Middle East and the Eastern Mediterranean"*.[32]

The BESA paper's language mirrored the negative connotations of the term neo-Ottomanism for most of the Israeli pundits.

Over the years, Turkey's approach to the region has been increasingly driven by neo-Ottomanism, and Erdoğan's rhetoric on Israel has grown more and more hostile… Erdoğan envisions a return to the days of a Turkish sultan exercising vast political-military control over the Middle East and central Asia.[33]

Armenian perception of neo-Ottomanism, meanwhile, went so far as to allege it as not only an expansionist policy but also a genocidal policy against the Armenians. In the first week of the Nagorno-Karabagh War commenced on September 27 between Armenia and Azerbaijan, with the latter enjoying the strong military support of Turkey, Armenian prime minister Nikol Pashinyan evaluated the development as "a policy of continuing the Armenian genocide [of 1915] and a policy of reinstating the Turkish Empire". Speaking to Sky News, Pashinyan said: "Turkey has returned to the South Caucasus to continue the Armenian genocide, and Armenia was the 'last obstacle' to Turkish expansion".[34]

Pashinyan's perception of Turkish policies in the South Caucasus was echoed among diaspora Armenians. During the Armenia-Azerbaijan War on Nagorno-Karabagh, the University of South California (USC) Institute of Armenian Studies invited a select group of scholars, intellectuals, and artists to contribute short reflections and observations on the war. Avedis Hadjian, known for his 2018 book entitled *Secret Nation: The Hidden Armenians of Turkey*, contributed to the effort a short article carrying the title "Building a Neo-Ottoman Empire".

Hadjian interpreted the Nagorno-Karabagh War in 2020 as a *"historical moment propitious for Erdoğan's neo-Ottoman plans"*. According to him, Azerbaijan

---

[32] Yaakov Lappin, "As Turkey's Lira Tumbles, Erdoğan Pursues Neo-Ottoman Visions", *BESA Center Perspectives*, No. 1, 796, November 2, 2020.

[33] Ibid.

[34] https://www.thenationalnews.com/world/europe/armenian-pm-accuses-turkey-of-continuing-the-genocide-in-nagorno-karabakh-1.1089761

was Turkey's proxy in these plans and has become a de facto Turkish colony. He did not see the war as aiming at Nagorno-Karabagh itself. *"This was is not about Artsakh* [Armenian name of Nagorno Karabagh], *a 1,700 square-mile mountainous enclave. The war is part of a larger imperial design, the ultimate goal of which is, not in the very long term, the disappearance of Armenia itself"*.[35]

Similar negative connotations of neo-Ottomanism were widely resonated in the Balkans, especially among nationalist Serbs and Macedonians. For them, neo-Ottomanism is akin to Turkish imperialism and Islamic irredentism. For influential Serbian nationalist ideologist Darko Tanasković, neo-Ottomanism is an *"imperialist ideological cocktail of Islamism, Turkism, and Ottomanism…less ideology and more psychic mentality with regard to Turkish leadership"*.[36] A former diplomat and academic, Tanasković served as Serbia's ambassador in Turkey during the 1990s, is fluent in Turkish, and is the author of a book entitled *Neo-Ottomanism and Islamism*.

In his book Nostalgia for the Empire, The Politics of Neo-Ottomanism, Turkish scholar Hakan Yavuz quotes the prominent Serbian historian Miroslav Svirčević who contended that "although the framing of neo-Ottomanism fluctuates from time to time, its goal always has been the same: the strengthening of Turkey's political, economic and military influence on the countries in her 'broader neighborhoods'; in fact those that once formed part of the Ottoman Empire, most of all those in the Transcaucasus, Central Asia, the Near East and the Balkans".[37]

Yavuz devotes a full chapter of his book to "The Balkan and Arab Responses to Neo-Ottomanism". In this context he presents the views of Srdja Trifković, a well-known Serbian-American publicist and historian who argues: "Turkey's *neo-Ottomanist policy is responsible for nearly all the problems and conflicts in the Balkans, and this policy has supported the independence of Bosnia and Herzegovina and the Republic of Kosovo"*. For Trifković, Turkey pursues an expansionist policy just like the Ottoman Empire, and *"Islamism is the same as neo-Ottomanism. Islamism is the body, and neo-Ottomanism is the cloth for this body".[38]*

The Serbian nationalists' resentment concerning Turkey's alleged neo-

---

[35] https://armenian.usc.edu/voices-on-karabakh/#avedis-hadjian
[36] Darko Tanasković, *Neo-Ottomanism: Turkey's Return to the Balkans* [in Serbian], Belgrade: J. P. Službeni Glasnik, 2010, 19-20.
[37] M. Hakan Yavuz, *Nostalgia for the Empire, The Politics of Neo-Ottomanism*, Oxford University Press, 2020, Kindle Edition, 220.
[38] Ibid.

Ottomanism goes back to the early 1990s when Serbs fought against Muslim Bosnians in a bloody war during the breakup of Yugoslavia. Paradoxically and in contrast to the prevailing adversarial mood against Erdoğan's Turkey in some corners of its periphery, Erdoğan managed to establish a partnership with Serbia's Aleksandar Vučić in 2017.

In his very interesting reportage, Dimitar Bechev illustrates the profound shift in Turkey-Serbia relations in contrast to those years of Serbian resentment against anything that could be identifiable with neo-Ottomanism.

The return of historic empires has long been a favorite theme in Western pundits' writings on the Balkans. The crisis-ridden EU is losing ground, we are told, and Russia and Turkey are filling in the gap. "Neo-Ottomanism" is on everyone's lips... But in President Recep Tayyip Erdogan's visit to Serbia, it is difficult to find neo-Ottoman "ambitions"... It is remarkable that Erdogan has found a partner in Aleksandar Vučić. Serbia's president cut his teeth in the ultranationalist Radical Party in the 1990s and served as Slobodan Milosevic's minister of information. But now he is the voice of pragmatism: "This is not 1389. Serbia and Turkey are friendly countries," he said, referring to the year of the Battle of Kosovo between Serbian forces and the invading Ottoman army...

The cost of engaging Turkey is minimal. Nationalists in Serbia cheer at Erdogan's disputes with the US and EU and the blooming friendship with Putin. Those who point at the unsettling parallels between Vucic's strongman tactics and Erdogan's authoritarian ways are simply ignored.[39]

Notwithstanding the amelioration in Turkey-Serbia relations, Ankara's assertive foreign policy has remained a source of concern in the greater Balkans region. More than any other country, Turkey's immediate neighbour in the Aegean and southeastern Balkans, Greece, displayed discomfort. This is revealed for instance in the New Years Message for 2021 sent by the Foreign Minister of Greece, Nikos Dendias, to his Turkish counterpart Mevlût Çavuşoğlu. He wrote, *"Aspire to become more European, Less Neo-Ottoman. This will best serve the Turkish people"*. Almost two weeks later, in his interview with Greek daily *Kathimerini*, Dendias was asked about the agreements signed with the UAE, waiting to be signed with Saudi Arabia, and strengthening Greece's relations with Israel – while relations with Egypt are flourishing. To the question of whether all these serve to contain "Turkish provocations", Dendias responded:

---

[39] Dimitar Bechev, "Erdogan in the Balkans: A neo-Ottoman Quest?", Aljazeera, October 11, 2017. https://www.aljazeera.com/opinions/2017/10/11/erdogan-in-the-balkans-a-neo-ottoman-quest

My answer is, yes, but under certain conditions. The countries you mentioned have, at some level, difficult relations with Turkey. But this is exclusively due to Turkey's aggressive and expansionist policy. More than 100 years ago, the West viewed the then Ottoman Empire as the "sick man." Now, Turkey aims to impose itself in the area formerly ruled by the Ottoman Empire as "the great revisionist."[40]

CONTESTATION

Nicholas Danforth, a Washington-based Turkey expert, almost single-handedly contested the neo-Ottomanism concept. He entitled an article "The Non-Sense of Neo-Ottomanism". At the end of the year 2020, his self-satisfied reflection in his social media account on this piece of writing was *"Forget 2020, this may be my favorite professional accomplishment of all time"*.[41]

In the article in question, Danforth argued that neo-Ottomanism does not explain modern Turkey, and represents a misreading of Turkish foreign policy. With some grain of truth, he wrote:

For over a decade, discussions of contemporary Turkey have often referred to the idea of 'Neo-Ottomanism.' Left undefined, it often serves as a convenient short-hand for anything aggressive, authoritarian, irredentist, overly Islamic, or anti-Western about Erdogan's actions... It is in the realm of foreign policy that the term neo-Ottoman has created the greatest confusion. Here, paradoxically, commentators have used it somewhat interchangeably as a synonym for Islamism, nationalism, and virtually anything anti-Western. In short, whatever Turkey does that Washington doesn't like... can be casually attributed to neo-Ottomanism. The result is a misunderstanding of how Turkey's anti-Westernism has evolved, and the risks posed by the deepening fusion of Islamist and nationalist policies, particularly amidst a series of interlocking conflicts across the Eastern Mediterranean in Libya, Syria and Cyprus.[42]

To acknowledge neo-Ottomanism, Danforth had a precondition that he disclosed in sarcastic terms:

---

[40] Vassilis Nedos, "Comment: Dendias: Turkey Not the Same as in 2000 or 2016", *Kathimerini*, January 12, 2021. https://www.ekathimerini.com/261135/article/ekathimerini/comment/dendias-turkey-not-the-same-as-in-2000-or-2016

[41] Nicholas Danforth, "Forget 2020, This May Be My Favorite Professional Accomplishment of All Time", December 28, 2020.

[42] *Nicholas Danforth, "The Non-Sense of Neo-Ottomanism", War on the Rocks, March 29, 2020.*

The day Erdogan leads his army on a campaign to capture Vienna, by all means call it Neo-Ottoman. Until then, describing contemporary Turkish politics in contemporary terms will make for better analysis – and hopefully, better policy.[43]

Nicholas Danforth conceded that the impulses called neo-Ottoman – aggressive nationalism, religious chauvinism, and anti-Western hostility – are genuine in Turkey. Yet, according to him, there are also real albeit various other pragmatic geopolitical, economic factors driving Turkish decision-making that neo-Ottomanism ignores. Therefore, he asserts, it is inappropriate to define Turkish foreign policy according to such a paradigm. Quite sure of his piece hitting the last nail in the coffin of the neo-Ottomanism paradigm, he concluded his article under the sub-heading "The End of Neo-Ottomanism" with the cynical note mentioned above.

NOSTALGIA OR RESTORING IMPERIAL GLORY

What analysts like Danforth might be oblivious to in today's Turkey is the prevalent craze for the Ottoman Empire. Thus, the neo-Ottomanism paradigm is more than mere politics. It is a social imaginary, a bundle of historically rooted emotions, a form of behaviour, and an identity.

Hakan M. Yavuz, a political scientist and historian who runs the Turkish Studies Project at the University of Utah, departs from his peers in Washington in his analysis of neo-Ottomanism. In his book *Nostalgia for the Empire–The Politics of Neo-Ottomanism*, introduced as the result of 20 years of research, he reached different conclusions than Danforth.

According to Yavuz, neo-Ottomanism by no means refutes Erdoğan's Islamism. On the contrary, it is interpreted as the foreign policy manifestation of Turkey's Islamization. The relevant argument is formulated as follows:

For Erdoğan, having been in government since 2002, Islam and the Ottoman past are not only the core elements of his identity but are also important sources of motivation for his foreign policy. In fact, the foreign policy manifestation of Turkey's domestic Islamization process was neo-Ottomanism. There is a mutually constitutive relationship between Islamization and Ottomanization. Neo-Ottomanism or restoring the grandeur of the Ottoman past has meant the Islamization of society and foreign policy. The Republican project of Europeanization and the civilizational shift have been under attack as never before. There is a tectonic shift away

---

[43] *Ibid.*

from the republican orientation and back to the conservative and autocratic Ottoman tradition.[44]

Neo-Ottomanism aggregates the nostalgia for Ottoman grandeur, which is a public psychological need, and searches for a new "old" identity of the self by re-imagining the Ottoman past as a justification for Turkish autocracy. As Yavuz sees it, *"the debate over the Ottoman past under Erdoğan's leadership is an attempt to inspire the youth and justify the current president's autocratic rule"* and Neo-Ottomanism that has become *"the most powerful discourse in today's Turkey, especially as it is since nostalgic as it is utopian".*[45]

In his Nostalgia for the Empire–The Politics of Neo-Ottomanism, Hakan Yavuz postulates that Recep Tayyip Erdoğan has instrumentalized Turkey's Ottoman past for his authoritarian domestic political agenda. Neo-Ottomanism thus can be envisaged as a reflection of that phenomenon in his foreign policy.

At the hands of Erdoğan, this Ottoman past has turned into an instrument to create an authoritarian place for him – and just for him. Neither politicians nor academics invented Neo-Ottomanism as a routine ethical and political discourse. Rather, it originated as a confluence of intellectual and sociocultural trends shaped by domestic and international events.[46]

The scholarly outlook defines neo-Ottomanism, structured with its ethno-nationalist and Sunni-Islamist pillars like Turkification and Sunnification, as an instrument for Erdoğan's revisionist and assertive foreign policy. It is a significant transformation that looks to be a lasting phenomenon in Turkey's prospects, inevitably impacting a vast geopolitical region.

The axial dislocation in Turkey's foreign policy is far from being insignificant and merely tactical. Under the AKP's directive, Turkey has been turning away from Europe in particular and the West in general, at both discursive and implementation levels. Retiring from the Western world at the discourse level and the use of foreign policy as an instrument in domestic politics could be seen as a return to a coercive version of a neo-Ottoman mentality, using a top-down approach. The AKP's new understanding of neo-Ottomanism is revisionist in two aspects: reframing Ottoman history by Turkification (ethno-nationalist) and Sunnification (prioritising Sunni Islam), and sorrow for the lost lands that were once under 'Turkish' domination... The AKP's formulation of the new Turkish foreign policy... include a desire to become the supreme leader of the Muslim world (read Erdoğan)... Finally, it would be deficient to read Turkish foreign policy without comparing it with the Ottoman period, since

---

[44] Yavuz, Nostalgia for the Empire, op. cit., 181.
[45] Ibid., 8.
[46] Ibid., 5.

the Republic inherited not only relatively modern institutions from the Ottomans but also the very idea of modernization itself.[47]

---

[47] Ahmet Erdi Öztürk, *Religion, Identity and Power: Turkey and Balkans in the Twenty-first Century*, Edinburgh: Edinburgh University Press, 2021, 51-52.

NEO-OTTOMANISM: A METAMORPHOSIS
(FROM ÖZAL TO ERDOĞAN VIA DAVUTOĞLU)

GENESIS OF NEO-OTTOMANISM

It is important to note that neo-Ottomanism emerged well before the rise of the AKP (Justice and Development Party) and Recep Tayyip Erdoğan. It was often used to describe the foreign policy of Turkey's President Turgut Özal at the beginning of the 1990s.

Özal was Turkey's prime minister between 1983 to 1989, and then the president until 1993. As an advisor on foreign policy issues, I worked closely with him from 1991 until he died in 1993, and my name became a point of reference concerning the discourse on neo-Ottomanism, as the person who first coined the term.[48] [49]

Nick Danforth referred to my name in an article published in 2008:

Neo-Ottomanism was used both by Turkish writers like Cengiz Çandar, for whom it had positive connotations, and by writers from the Balkans and Middle East, for whom the Ottomans were associated with imperial rule... Özal's activism was aimed at taking advantage of the new possibilities that the Soviet collapse had brought while simultaneously minimizing the negative consequences that it might also bring.[50]

Similar references can be found in various other publications by Turkish and non-Turkish academicians and researchers.[51]

As the person behind the neo-Ottomanist stance attributed to President Özal's foreign policy, I can attest to the astounding accuracy in two separate assessments: one in a dissertation paper submitted in Budapest, which exhilarated me, and the other by a Turkish academician who, seemingly, perceived the central tenets of my *"Özalian neo-Ottomanism"*.

---

[48] I must also recognize and pay tribute to the late David Barchard (1947–2020), a British journalist and an acquaintance, as the first to coin neo-Ottomanism back in 1985. I learned this a few days before his tragic death on Christmas eve of 2020, a result of an accident. Nostalgia for the Empire–The Politics of Neo-Ottomanism referred to him as follows: "In 1985, David Barchard, a British journalist, coined the term neo-Ottomanism as one of several options for Turkey's possible future orientation. He offered the aptest definition of the term as "a consciousness of the imperial Ottoman past," which is "a more potent force in Turkey than Islam, [and] as Turkey regains economic strength, it will be increasingly tempted to assert itself." Yet, while David should be commended for his clairvoyance, that does not alter the fact that his premonition has gone largely unnoticed, because the neo-Ottomanism paradigm regarding Turkish foreign policy was related to post–Cold War circumstances that emerged with the fall of the Berlin Wall and the dissolution of the Soviet Union. All these events were beyond the scope of David Barchard's prediction.
[49] David Barchard, *Turkey and the West,* Routledge, Chatham House Papers, 1985.
[50] Nicholas Danforth, "Ideology and Pragmatism in Turkish Foreign Policy: From Atatürk to the AKP", *Turkish Policy Quarterly,* Vol. 7, No. 3 (Fall 2008).
[51] *Robert Cenzon, "Geopolitics in a Post-Historical World: A Comparative Analysis of the Foreign Policies of Germany and Turkey",* Cosmopolite, Vol. 4 No. 1 (Fall 2010), 85, 86; Lerna K. Yanik, "Constructing 'Turkish Exceptionalism': Discourses in Liminality and Hybridity in Post-Cold War Turkish Foreign Policy, Political Geography, No. 30 (2011).

In 2018, Zoltán Egeresi, a Hungarian research fellow, put it in a concise form:

Özal did promote a foreign policy focusing rather on Turkic people in the Caucasus and Central Asia, he opened a debate about Turkish identity including ex-Ottoman Muslims. This was linked to some advisors, like the influential Turkish intellectual, journalist and political advisor of Turgut Özal, Cengiz Çandar. At the beginning of the Post-Cold War period, when Turkey met the problem of repositioning itself in the new world order, and a relative decline in its previously appreciated role as a bastion against the Soviet Union, Çandar proposed to reconsider the country's foreign policy on the basis of Neo-Ottomanism. His 'invention' has become well-known as well as much criticised in Turkey and abroad, too. In his interpretation the notion was a reflection to the new geopolitical circumstance of the country after the collapse of the huge neighbour and dramatic changes in the Middle East and the Balkans. Accordingly, Neo-Ottomanism as a foreign policy paradigm has a rather peaceful approach that aimed at helping the decision makers to reposition Turkey and find a new role in the global turmoil. It intended to use the cultural and historical heritage of the country as a base for creating bridges towards the neighbours, something that can be seen as a common without redrawing the current political borders and boosting Turkish dominance.[52]

The Turkish political scientist Prof. Yılmaz Çolak defined it from a different angle, but in an equally concise and accurate way:

Cengiz Çandar, one of the main leading figures in the formulation of neo-Ottomanism, mentioned 'imperial vision' in order to express the new direction of the Republic of Turkey, moving from 'monocultural and closed' nation-state form to multicultural and multiethnic structure. Neo-Ottomanists rejected the ethnic version of Turkish nationalism and reinterpreted Turkish identity on the basis of regional and religious grounds (multiethnic and multireligious bases) and cosmopolitan liberal values. Thus, for Çandar, the premises of neo-Ottomanism are free enterprise, human rights and cultural and ethnic pluralism.[53]

He based his reference on my 1993 article entitled "*21. Yüzyıl'a Doğru Türkiye*" (*Turkey Towards the 21st Century*), published in the periodical Türkiye Günlüğü (*Turkey Chronicle*). Türkiye Günlüğü is described in the Nostalgia for the Empire–The Politics of Neo-Ottomanism *as the place* where groups of liberals, conservatives, and nationalists gathered to fill in the content of neo-Ottomanism in 1992.[54]

---

[52] Zoltán Egeresi, Neo-Ottomanist Hegemonic Order and Its Implications on Ankara's Foreign Policy in the Balkans, PhD thesis submitted to Corvinus University of Budapest, 2018.
[53] Yılmaz Çolak, "Ottomanism vs. Kemalism: Collective Memory and Cultural Pluralism of 1990s Turkey", Middle Eastern Studies, Vol. 42, No. 4 (July 2006), 587-602.
[54] *Türkiye Günlüğü* [Turkey Chronicle], No. 19 (1992).

I had in fact coined the concept neo-Ottomanism a little earlier, in an op-ed piece in 1992, which subsequently became a matter for public debate.

THE CONTOURS OF ÖZALIAN NEO-OTTOMANISM

Concerning the genesis and the evolution of the Neo-Ottomanism paradigm, and to perceive how Özal's Neo-Ottomanism differs from the current Erdoğanist one, the name Igor Torbakov is a vital source of reference.

In 2017, Igor Torbakov, a Russian-Ukrainian historian, a Senior Fellow at the Institute for Russian and Eurasian Studies at Uppsala University, and the Swedish Institute of International Affairs (UI) made a unique contribution on the matter with his seminal essay "Neo-Ottomanism versus Neo-Eurasianism".

Torbakov highlighted the peculiar international circumstances that had begun to mold the minds of Turkish thinkers and decision-makers like President Turgut Özal in a new matrix.

In the early 1990s, with the end of the Cold War and the collapse of the Soviet Union, Turkey's leadership sensed that the new geopolitical situation brought about new strategic challenges and even greater opportunities… The tectonic geopolitical shifts accompanying the end of the communist era in Eastern Europe and Eurasia also helped the Turks see themselves once again at the center of a world reemerging around them on all sides rather than at the tail-end of a European world.[55]

Torbakov resonated with Eric Rouleau's astute observation penned in 1993. A dear friend to me, the legendary Middle East expert-journalist of *Le Monde* during the 1960s, 70s, and 80s who also served as French ambassador in Turkey from 1988 to 1991, Eric Rouleau (1926–2015) captured the imperatives of the post–Cold War Turkey in his seminal essay:

Today, Turks speak with pride of their Ottoman heritage even while retaining a certain critical distance… Former President Özal, who died earlier this year, contributed a great deal to reconciling the Turks with their past and promoting the synthesis between Kemalism and what he considered to be the positive aspects of Ottomanism. He believed that diversity in unity could contribute to strength and stability, just as it had under the empire.

Özal's convictions were well suited to the geopolitical needs of a new international situation. The fall of the Berlin Wall ended Turkey's long-standing strategic role in a bipolar world.

---

[55] Igor Torbakov, *"Neo-Ottomanism versus Neo-Eurasianism? Nationalism and Symbolic Geography in Postimperial Turkey and Russia",* Mediterranean Quarterly, Vol. 28, No. 2 (June 2017).

Meanwhile, the collapse of the Soviet Union and the consequent independence of the Central Asian republics opened Turkey's eyes to a vast territory inhabited by some 150 million fellow Muslim Turkic-speakers on its northern borders. The years of claustrophobia abruptly ended.[56]

Drawing on a treatise I had co-authored in the 2001 March edition of *Mediterranean Quarterly*, Igor Torbakov presented a sharp observation:

It appears that the term neo-Ottomanism was coined by the prominent Turkish journalist Cengiz Çandar, who was Özal's foreign policy advisor in the early 1990s. Together with a leading US Middle East analyst, Graham Fuller, Çandar co-authored a programmatic article titled 'Grand Geopolitics for a New Turkey'… Çandar and Fuller boldly proclaimed in the article's opening section. "The narrow geopolitical perspectives of a Soviet-dominated region have been replaced by a brand new geopolitical reality that leaves Turkey as the emerging great power in the region. The piece seems to have contained some key tropes, concepts, ideas, and principles (beginning with the 'new Turkey' mentioned in the title) that Davutoglu and other like-minded Turkish strategists would later elaborate on."[57]

Torbakov has reiterated the two key characteristics that the initial idea of neo-Ottomanism entailed: an endeavour to overcome the Ottoman period's negative features – particularly imperial attitudes toward the non-Turkish elements – and as a new cultural identity for the country as part of a globalizing world. These suggested a premise devoid of nationalism, territorial expansionism, and aggressive political posture.

In his very true formulation, also essential to mention is that "*notwithstanding all the talk about 'imperial vision,' Özalian neo-Ottomanism 'used the new Ottoman cultural identity not as counter-hegemonic, but as being part of a globalizing Western world. This particular feature distinguished it from various strands of Russian Eurasianism. Whatever differences these strands of thought might have among themselves, however, there is one thing they all have in common: all Eurasianists view Russia and the globalizing US-dominated West as being worlds apart*".[58]

That is contrary to Erdoğan's neo-Ottomanism, which in essence is a unique blend of extreme Turkish nationalism and Sunni Islamism, is inherently anti-Western, and veritably a version of Turkish Eurasianism. Erdoğan's neo-Ottomanism categorically incarnates the third wave of neo-Ottomanism. Its

---

[56] Eric Rouleau, "The Challenges to Turkey", *Foreign Affairs*, November/December 1993. https://www.foreignaffairs.com/articles/europe/1993-12-01/challenges-turkey
[57] Cengiz Candar and Graham E. Fuller, "Grand Geopolitics for a New Turkey", *Mediterranean Quarterly*, Vol. 12, No. 1 (Winter 2001), 22-38.
[58] Igor Torbakov, Neo-Ottomanism versus Neo-Eurasianism, op. cit.

debut, arguably, could be traced back to 2016, when Erdoğan emphatically established his absolute power and consolidated it further in coalition with vehemently anti-Kurdish nationalists and Eurasianists in the military in the wake of a dubious coup attempt in July of that year.

It is crucial to bear in mind that the original conceptualization of neo-Ottomanism – the practice of the new Turkish foreign policy in the 1990s – was geared toward seizing opportunities for new ties and connections, the development of new relationships in a context in which the old Cold War barriers had fallen, rather than any assertion of Turkish expansionism or foreign policy adventurism.

DAVUTOĞLU: NEO-OTTOMANIST OR NOT?

However, neo-Ottomanism could not go further than a burgeoning thought which, with Özal's early death in 1993, could not actualize in the Turkish foreign policy. The political instability and the economic crises that dominated the remaining period of the 1990s prevented this from happening. Nevertheless, it did leave a legacy for Ahmet Davutoğlu.

For Igor Torbakov, Ahmet Davutoğlu and those who shared his ideas on Turkey's place in the world at the dawn of the 21st century constituted a "second wave" of neo-Ottomanism. According to Torbakov, in developing such a vision they *developed the ideas advanced during the Özal era and brought their theoretical construct, in terms of its overall political philosophy, much closer to views broadly shared by Russian Eurasianists*". Notably, first wave neo-Ottomanism had characteristics running contrary to Russian Eurasianism – and synchronously, by definition, to Turkish Eurasianism. The second wave neo-Ottomanism attributed to Ahmet Davutoğlu diverges from it in this respect, thus constituting a link bridging the Özalian first wave and the Erdoğanist third wave which possessed an unquestionable anti-Western, "Eurasianist" aspect.

Ahmet Davutoğlu put his indelible mark on Turkish policy from the very beginning of the AKP government in 2002 until May 2016, the date when President Erdoğan sacked him. Erdoğan handpicked Davutoğlu in 2014 to be his successor, both as the prime minister and the chairman of the ruling AKP. From 2002 until 2009, he was the influential foreign policy advisor to prime ministers Abdullah Gül and Tayyip Erdoğan, virtually formulating and running the Turkish foreign policy. In 2009 he became the foreign minister, and in 2014 the prime minister. Losing Erdoğan's favour and pushed to oblivion in mid-2016, he formed a party called Gelecek (Future) in December 2019, and engaged in fervent opposition against Erdoğan.

A pious Muslim, before he began to shine in the international political scene Davutoğlu was an obscure academician who in the 1990s taught political science at the International Islamic University Malaysia. His magnum opus *Stratejik Derinlik* (*Strategic Depth*) published in 2001 went largely unnoticed. But as his reputation rose as the architect of Turkey's new and unconventional foreign policy in the first decade of the 21st century, the work has been translated into many languages with more than 100,000 copies. Over the years, his vision and the strategy propounded in *Strategic Depth* initiated a wide-ranging debate. Many people identified his vision as neo-Ottomanism. A Turkish academician depicted it as "A Neo-Ottomanist Interpretation of Turkish Eurasianism". The article, published by Mediterranean Quarterly in April 2014, had the following abstract:

> *The change in Turkish foreign policy in the twenty-first century's second decade has its origin in the approach referred to by Turkish foreign minister Ahmet Davutoglu as Strategic Depth. Because it aims to give Turkey status as a Eurasian power, this approach has been described as neo-Ottomanism, referencing the geographic extent of the Ottoman Empire.*[59]

> *However, Davutoğlu never identified his views as neo-Ottomanist.* Hakan Yavuz in his *Nostalgia for the Empire–The Politics of Neo-Ottomanism* notified that "*Although Davutoğlu relentlessly declares that he is 'not a Neo-Ottoman,' his name has become synonymous with neo-Ottomanism*". Yet, Yavuz did not hesitate to describe Davutoğlu as "*the architect and rigid ideologue of the neo-Ottomanist foreign policy*".[60]

TURKEY-CENTRED ISLAMISM OR ARAB REVENGE ON TURKEY

Soner Çağaptay, director of the Turkish Research Program at the Washington Institute, an American think-tank, was keen on grasping the implicit Turkish nationalist element in Davutoğlu's outlook. He observed:

> *Davutoglu views the Ottoman legacy from the perspective of the Turks, not from the perspective of nations once ruled by the Ottomans. Davutoglu's plan was not one that was*

---

[59] Göktürk Tüysüzoğlu, "Strategic Depth: A Neo-Ottomanist Interpretation of Turkish Eurasianism", *Mediterranean Quarterly*, Vol. 25, No. 2 (April 2014), 85-104.
[60] Yavuz, Nostalgia for the Empire, op. cit., 182-185.

predicated on equal partnerships, but rather on Turkey reaching out to Arab capitals, building influence over them, and then having them follow its lead.[61]

Ahmet Davutoğlu, not mistakenly, saw the Middle East's frontiers drawn by partitioning the Ottoman lands in the aftermath of World War I as an unacceptable colonial legacy that fed anachronic local nationalisms. In a speech in 2013, he proposed an ambitious mission for Turkey to overcome the divisions in the region and to unite it:

[Middle Eastern] states first emerged on the maps of [the Sykes–Picot agreement that broke apart the Ottoman Empire], then by colonial methods, and finally on maps that were artificially drawn. You cannot build a future based on these states, which are at enmity with each other due to nationalism. We shall break the mold shaped for us by Sykes–Picot.[62]

Hakan Yavuz elaborated on Davutoğlu's Turkey-centred strategic proposition:

Davutoğlu contends that Turkey should become a powerful player in the international system due to its geographical location and historical importance as the heir to the Ottoman Empire. He seeks to utilize cultural and religious affinities and its common Ottoman history with the Caucasus, Middle East, Balkans, and North Africa to promote the influence of Turkey. Davutoğlu presents Turkey with multiple identities: In terms of geography, Turkey occupies a unique space. As a large country in the midst of Afro-Eurasia's vast landmass, it may be defined as a central country with multiple regional identities that cannot be reduced to one unified character. Like Russia, Germany, Iran, and Egypt, Turkey cannot be explained geographically or culturally by associating it with one single region. Turkey's diverse regional composition lends it the capability of maneuvering in several regions simultaneously; in this sense, it controls an area of influence in its immediate environs.[63]

For Davutoğlu, the Turkish foreign policy activism in the broad geopolitics where Ottomans once reigned is legitimate and an emotional obligation. When the winds of change of the so-called Arab Spring reached Libya in 2011, the centenary of the loss of the then Ottoman territory of Tripolitania (Trablusgarp[64] in Turkish), he made a speech at a conference held by the ultra-

---

[61] Soner Cagaptay, "Turkey's Imperial Foreign Policy: Vision vs. Reality", *Washington Institute*, March 6, 2020. *https://www.washingtoninstitute.org/policy-analysis/turkeys-imperial-foreign-policy-vision-vs-reality*

[62] Turkish Ministry of Foreign Affairs, "Büyük Restorasyon: Kadim'den Küreselleşmeye Yeni Siyaset Anlayisimiz", 15 March 2013. http://www.mfa.gov.tr/disisleri-bakani-ahmet-davutoglu_nun-diyarbakir-dicle-universitesinde-verdigi-_buyuk-restorasyon_-kadim_den-kureselleşmeye-yeni.tr.mfa

[63] Yavuz, Nostalgia for the Empire, op. cit.,186, 187.

[64] In Ottoman times, its territory that lies in today's Libya was called Trablusgarp, which means Tripoli of the West, to distinguish it from the city of Tripoli in today's Lebanon, which was hailed as Trablusşam, meaning Tripoli of Sham, in other words Tripoli of Syria. The North African port city of Tripoli (Trablusgarp) was conquered by the Ottomans in 1551 and remained in the Empire until 1911. The Syrian-Lebanese port of

nationalist organization Turkish Hearths (Türk Ocakları) with the title *"Towards Great Turkey"* and said:

We see Libya's problems as our own problems... We carry the legacy of broad horizons, at every corner lie our buried martyrs. Next year will be the centennial anniversary of the Balkan Wars. 2014 is the centennial anniversary of the WW I, in other words, the emergence of these borders between Turkey and Syria, Iraq and the Caucasus has no geographical, cultural, and demographical foundation. Just as the state [meaning the Ottoman Empire], which was the political center of an ancient civilization, was torn apart in twelve years from the Tripolitanian War in 1911 to 1923 and foundational elements of this state were psychologically and historically divided, only to be replaced by a new Republic founded in 1923... now we need to unify the elements of this broken and fragmented nation again. The question is how do we unify this geography? How do we build a new generation, who can shape the flow of history marching towards the future with a great hope from these divided histories? Therefore, "Towards the Great Turkey" is the right title.[65]

Whether or not he should be considered a neo-Ottomanist, an identification he chose not to accept, an interesting and scathing comment on Davutoğlu's understanding of the past was presented by Yavuz, who labelled him as *"the Arab revenge on Turkey"* and judged his views on Ottomans to be ahistorical.

Davutoğlu did what Atatürk feared his successors would do – ignore realities and the capacity of Turkey and romanticize the Ottoman imperial dream in the Middle East. Davutoğlu has emerged as the Arab revenge on Turkey by destroying Turkey's Western orientation, along with the widely respected institution of the foreign ministry. Davutoğlu's nostalgia for the Ottoman state as the "golden age" is not commensurate with history. The past he presents never existed except as a post-Ottoman utopian narrative.[66]

DAVUTOĞLU VERSUS ÖZAL: PRELUDE TO ERDOĞAN

The most comprehensive critique of Davutoğlu's views on strategy and his foreign policy was made by Turkish academician Behlül Özkan, his former student. After thorough research of Davutoğlu's work spanning from his student dissertation to over 300 articles published mostly in not very well known pro-Islamist journals, periodicals, and newspapers, and his book *Strategic Depth,*

Tripoli (Trablusşam) was an Ottoman city from 1516 to 1918.
[65] Ahmet Davutoğlu, "Turkey's New Foreign Policy Vision", *Insight Turkey*, Vol. 10, No. 1 (2008), 78. http://www.mfa.gov.tr/disisleri-bakani-sayin-ahmet-Davutoğlu_nun-turk-ocaklari_nin-kurulusunun-100_-yilini-kutlama-etkinlikleri-kapsaminda-duzenlenen.tr.mfa
[66] Yavuz, Nostalgia for the Empire, op. cit.,187.

Özkan identified Davutoğlu as a pan-Islamist ideologue. He alleged that the imperial geopolitical theories developed in the first half of the 20th century by Western strategists like Alfred Thayer Mahan, Harold Mackinder, Karl Haushofer, and Nicholas Spykman shaped Davutoğlu's views.

In an interview concerning his research on Davutoğlu, which was conducted in August 2014 with *Al-Monitor*, the online Middle East journal for which I am a columnist, Behlül Özkan commented:

Their effect is obvious in the articles that I scanned and that were written when Davutoglu was a young doctoral candidate. Many of his ideas are not original but imported. He simply grafted them onto his pan-Islamic worldview. What inspired him [Davutoğlu] though was not the West's liberal humanitarian ideals and its advocacy of individual rights, but rather the kind of geopolitical thinking that prevailed in Germany in the early 20th century; one that saw politics as more of a power struggle in which the ends justify the means. Few are aware of this and he was long regarded as a star, a poster boy for political Islam in Turkey.[67]

Özkan's research results published in the bi-monthly journal of IISS (International Institute for Strategic Studies) in July 2014 became a significant contribution. The paper's title was *"Turkey, Davutoglu, and the Idea of Pan-Islamism"*. Behlül Özkan expressed his conviction that Davutoğlu should be identified as a pan-Islamist, and rejected considering him a neo-Ottomanist. According to Özkan, Davutoğlu found neo-Ottomanism too Western-oriented and therefore opposed it.

The neo-Ottomanist label that is frequently attributed to Davutoglu is misleading. He criticizes neo-Ottomanism in his articles for being too Western-oriented. Davutoglu is a pan-Islamist... He believes in a Sunni Muslim hegemonic order led by Turkey that would encompass the Middle East, the Caucasus and Central Asia, and include Albania and Bosnia as well.., he wants to go back in time to an order based on Islamic unity, on which Turkey expands its power not through military power but by creating spheres of influence.[68]

From Behlül Özkan we also learn Davutoğlu's appraisal of Turgut Özal. In an op-ed piece in 1999, Davutoğlu criticized the neo-Ottomanist approach of Turgut Özal for being *"theoretically insufficient, superficial and journalistic"*.[69]

Cognizant of being targeted personally with the employment of the word

[67] https://www.al-monitor.com/pulse/originals/2014/08/zaman-davutoglu-ideologue-behlul-ozkan-academic-akp-islamic.html#ixxzz6jmuVh5
[68] Davutoğlu'nun Özal eleştirisi Ahmet Davutoglu, "Yakın Tarihimizin Ana Akımları ve Seçim Sonuçları", *Yeni Şafak*, 23 April 1999.
[69] Behlül Özkan, "Turkey, Davutoğlu and the Idea of Pan-Islamism", *Survival,* published online July 23, 2014.

"journalistic", in hindsight I should admit that there is a grain of truth in Davutoğlu's criticism because in advocating neo-Ottomanism, I and a few other intellectuals did not present a profound and coherent outline. Our neo-Ottomanism, which later was referred to as *"Özalian"*, was theoretically insufficient, indeed. We all were under the strong impact of extraordinary historical developments that led Francis Fukuyama to go so far as to raise the concept *"The End of History"*. The great historian Eric Hobsbawm considered the 20th century to have ended with the end of the Cold War.

The neo-Ottomanism premise in the early 1990s was coherent with the Zeitgeist and, to a large extent, was driven by pragmatic impulses, as correctly observed by Hakan Yavuz:

> *The discourse of neo-Ottomanism entails the configuration of Turkey's international position and its identity… Özal's understanding of neo-Ottomanism comprised a strategic recalculation to promote nation's interests and capitalize on previously unforeseen geopolitical opportunities.*[70]

Behlül Özkan added the European Union component in Özal's political thought, which has to be considered an essential aspect of his foreign policy. The credentials of Turgut Özal, whose influence on Turkish politics lasted until he died in 1993, is deftly described in Özkan's lines:

> *He [Özal] cherished the ideal of neo-Ottomanism as a means of integrating with the European Union through modernisation, and of adopting a supranational identity that went beyond ethnic allegiance. His enthusiasm was reflected in Turkey's 1987 application for European Union membership; its attempts to expand its sphere of influence in the Caucasus and the Balkans; its efforts to solve the Kurdish issue through reforms; and his dream of bringing northern Iraq under the control of Ankara, after Baghdad's power was diminished by the First Gulf War.*[71]

In his research Behlül Özkan, using quotations from various articles mostly unknown to the Turkish public, illustrated how Davutoğlu directed his criticism to Turgut Özal for being pro-West. He commented:

> *Davutoğlu treasures Islamism as the only valid ideological legacy of the Ottoman Empire, however, and likens Özal to the "Tanzimat pashas who tried to protect the internal integrity*

---

[70] Yavuz, Nostalgia for the Empire, op. cit., 118.

[71] Özkan, "Turkey, Davutoğlu and the Idea of Pan-Islamism", *op. cit.*

[72] *Tanzimat* in the old Ottoman-Turkish language meant reorganization. In the Turkish historiography, the Ottoman modernization and Westernization process inaugurated in 1839 is called *Tanzimat*. Several Ottoman statesmen carrying the honorary title of "Pasha" were identified with the history-making undertaking of *Tan-*

of the Ottoman State via friendships developed with strong Western countries".[72][73]

Therefore, even as some scholars see Davutoğlu as the political philosopher and strategist who developed the ideas advanced during the Özal era, he is considered the main person to have steered Turkey somewhat off course from its Western orientation. Davutoğlu laid the groundwork – albeit unintentionally, and in a much more nuanced fashion – for the belligerent, irredentist, expansionist neo-Ottomanist version widely identified with the autocratic rule of Recep Tayyip Erdoğan.

FROM OBSCURE ISLAMIST SCHOLAR TO HIGH-PROFILE STRATEGIST

Irrespective of his trademark self-indulgence and self-portrayal as a great strategic mind with a consistent *weltanschauung*, Ahmet Davutoğlu's posture in foreign policy and performance as foreign minister and prime minister varied. Davutoğlu, the self-styled thinker, was privileged to be in the rare position of being able to put his ideas to practice. From 2009 to 2014, he was the foreign minister, and from 2014 to 2016 the prime minister, replacing Tayyip Erdoğan who had acquired the mantle of the presidency. Erdoğan pushed him out in May 2016, two months before the botched coup that radically changed the history of Turkey.

In the wake of the coup, Erdoğan consolidated his power by the repression that transformed Turkey into an autocracy, undertook military forays into Syria, and launched an aggressive Turkish foreign policy. Davutoğlu withdrew from the public eye and emerged again in 2019, forming an opposition party called Gelecek (the Future Party).

Abdullah Gül formed the first AKP government in November 2002 following the elections that catapulted into positions of power those who claimed they had changed their Islamist outfits into what they described as "democratic conservatism".

Ahmet Davutoğlu, an obscure Islamist academician, was introduced to politics by Abdullah Gül and was appointed as a special adviser to the prime minister on foreign policy. His old friend Gül accorded him the title of

---

zimat, which, according to some historians, is seen as the precursor of modern Turkey. However, in the Turkish Islamist lexicon, Tanzimat is synonymous with a spiritual and cultural betrayal to the Muslim nation and the state. Therefore, Davutoğlu's likening Özal to Tanzimat pashas can be interpreted as an irreverent metaphor.

[73] Ibid.

ambassador. Davutoğlu had no prior acquaintance with Tayyip Erdoğan but kept him when he took over the portfolio of prime minister for Gül in March 2003. Abdullah Gül became the foreign minister in Erdoğan's cabinet, a post he held until elected as president in 2007.

Davutoğlu was well-positioned to be close to both leaders, but his title did not provide enough influence to shape Turkish foreign policy. He would eventually be able to do so, however, beginning from 2009 when Erdoğan made him foreign minister.

From 2002/2003 to 2011, the apex of the Arab Spring, Turkey's accession to the European Union took precedence in foreign policy. It was Abdullah Gül who should be credited for spearheading Turkey's drive towards the EU. In December 2003 the EU decided to start the accession negotiations, and in 2004, Turkey's odyssey to Brussels was inaugurated.

During that period, Davutoğlu's main contribution to foreign policy concerned Turkey's relations with the Middle East. Under his guidance, ties with all the countries in Turkey's southern proximity were developed. Davutoğlu pursued a pragmatic policy vis-à-vis the neighbouring countries, introducing Turkey's *soft power* in the context of the concept coined by the renowned American political scientist Joseph Nye at the end of the 1980s. In the Turkish version, soft power involved active diplomacy, offering mediation for resolving the conflicts in the region, economic assistance, and increasing trade over the former Ottoman territories to consolidate Turkey's sphere of influence.

"SHAMGEN" VERSUS SCHENGEN

Thanks to its opening to the region with the projection of soft power, Turkey's annual foreign trade with the Middle East and North Africa increased by more than five times in 2011, the year in which the Arab Spring unfolded, compared to 2002, the year when the AKP took the reins of the Turkish government. It jumped from $10 billion to $54bn.

Visa-free travel was established with almost all Middle Eastern countries, including Syria, Lebanon, Jordan, Egypt, and Libya. In line with Davutoğlu's strategy of not having a single destination in Turkey's hinterland that is not covered by flights, Turkish Airlines opened routes to all major cities in the Middle East. 50 Turkish companies' construction investments in the region exceeded $ 10 bn due to the increase in the oil revenues of the Middle Eastern states and post-war development in Iraq.

Turkey's soft power projection to the Middle East maintained its re-entry into the zone and the markets that were once the territory of Turkey's predecessor state, the Ottoman Empire. Ahmet Davutoğlu coined the "zero problems with the neighbours" doctrine to that end.

One ambitious project as a by-product of the zero problems with the neighbours strategy has been the aspiration to form a free trade zone and economic union initially among Turkey, Syria, Lebanon, and Jordan but aiming to culminate in a larger economic and political union in the Muslim Middle East region. The historical referent was the Iron and Steel Union formed among Germany, France, and Benelux countries, which is considered the nucleus of today's European Union. Turkey's then Prime Minister Tayyip Erdoğan likened it to the Schengen Zone of the European Union, tagged somewhat jokingly as Shamgen. Sham is the name given to the territory in history that encompasses today's Syria, Lebanon, Jordan, and Palestine.

The Lebanese Prime Minister Saad Hariri enthusiastically told me in person what Erdoğan told him, "*If they* [implying the Europeans *have their Schengen, why don't we have our Shamgen!*" Later on, Erdoğan's Shamgen-Schengen connotation widely circulated in the Turkish media community.

Erdoğan and Syrian President Bashar Assad had developed warm personal relations that included their family members. Istanbul and Turkish resort towns had become regular venues for the Assad family to spend their vacations. Those days that preceded the Arab Spring were the honeymoon period reached between Turkey and many of its Arab neighbours due to following the zero problems with the neighbours concept.

NEO-OTTOMANS VERSUS NEO-SAFAVIDS

Refraining from regime change in the region was the *sine qua non* for the success of the pseudo-doctrine of zero problems with the neighbours. It poised Turkey to rival Iran at the regional level as a status-quo power that did not question the legitimacy of the authoritarian regimes in the Middle East, whose interests lie in the region's stability. In contrast, Iran is perceived as a revisionist power, pursuing policies for regime change.

The different tracks – the Turkish one introduced by Davutoğlu – to penetrate the Arab Middle East represented by the two main Muslim power centres in the region, namely Iran and Turkey, implicitly reflected the Sunni-Shia chasm. They invoked the historical memory that goes back to the 16th century, regarding the antagonistic rivalry between the Sunni Ottoman Empire and the Shiite Safavid Iran, contesting the hegemony over the Middle East.

A 19th century painting depicting the Battle of Chaldiran. The battle took place on 23 August 1514 and ended with a decisive victory for the Ottoman Empire over the Safavid Empire.

Soft power projection and zero problems with the neighbours worked to the advantage of Turkey, and the prestige of Davutoğlu soared particularly in the Western world. Turkey's activism in the region, as long as it functioned as a check against Iran, met with tacit approval in the Western world. Turkey was seen as a stabilizing power in the volatile Middle East.

Thus, Davutoğlu's identification with neo-Ottomanism was not a matter of real concern. Turkey's international standing was good. For a while, Turkey was the only country accepted as a fair broker for the plethora of belligerents from Israel to Syria, from the Sunni resistance in Iraq to the United States, which was occupying Iraq, and able to address with the same ease everybody from Iran to Saudi Arabia.

That was the period when secular Turkey with an acceptable pro-Islamist government was advertised as a role model for the Muslim world, a source of emulation. This was in contrast to Islamic Iran, which was continuously perceived as a threat to stability in the Middle East, the Gulf, and the Arabian Peninsula, especially in American minds. Turkey's Sunni-Muslim government, thought to be firmly bonded to the West, would also serve as a panacea against the appeal of Sunni extremism in the Middle East, which manifested in Salafi-jihadi trends.

U.S. President Barrack Obama's first official visit after taking office was to Turkey in April 2009. The visit naturally signified the high point of Turkish foreign policy for which Davutoğlu could claim the credit.

From different azimuths, Turkey looked like the rising star of international politics. Those were the glory days for Turkey, utilizing soft power and promoting the motto "zero problems with the neighbours".

ARAB SPRING, THE GAME CHANGER

Less than two years later, everything changed with the Arab Spring and its aftermath. The status quo enabling Turkey to implement its zero problems pseudo-doctrine ended as the region where Turkey had emerged as a pro-stability player destabilized. The winds of change engulfed the MENA region and radically changed Turkish foreign policy, with Ahmet Davutoğlu at its helm.

Per Özkan, "Davutoğlu was convinced that Turkey's long-awaited opportunity came with the upheaval that began in Tunisia in late 2010 and continued into Egypt, Yemen, Libya, and Syria… In line with Davutoğlu's views, Turkey supported An-Nahda in Tunisia and the Muslim Brotherhood in Egypt and Syria".[74]

Turkey rapidly moved from the pro-status quo regional power position to that of a revisionist power pushing for regime change in the MENA. Prime Minister Erdoğan's call to Egypt's leader Hosni Mubarak at the peak of the upheaval in Cairo was noteworthy in this respect. Erdoğan's call was broadcast live by the demonstrators at Tahrir Square in the Egyptian capital a week before the eventual fall of Mobarak.

With the Arab Spring, Turkey was transformed from a pro-status quo regional power into a revisionist one and emerged as the Muslim Brotherhood movement's primary sponsor with branches in the MENA geopolitical zone.

The Arab Spring arrived as a blessing for Erdoğan's foreign policy at a

[74] Ibid.

moment when Germany and France had obscured Turkey's EU vision. Turkey's EU anchor has been dragging since the change of guard in Germany and France. Following the electoral victories of Angela Merkel in 2005 and especially of Nicolas Sarkozy in 2007, it became clear to the Turkish leaders that the EU had had no intention to negotiate in good faith with Turkey's accession.

During the 2006–07 presidential campaign, opposition to Turkey's joining the EU was Sarkozy's main foreign policy theme. He revived the view of one of his predecessors, Valery Giscard d'Estaing, who had publicly stated that Turkey's admission would mean "the end of the EU" and therefore Turkey should be denied. Sarkozy also rejected Turkey's full membership in the EU on the basis of cultural and religious differences. His German partner Merkel insisted on offering Turkey a "privileged partnership" instead of full membership which she rejected in 2009.

The changed and negative attitude of these two prominent EU countries' leaders, who replaced Gerhard Schröder and Jacques Chirac known for their pro-Turkey stance, came as a shock to Tayyip Erdoğan. With no Western educational upbringing and always suspicious of Islamophobia attributed to the Europeans, he believed that Europe would never accept Turkey in its family.

Step by step, Erdoğan's feeling of betrayal by Europeans accumulated. The Greek Cypriots' rejection of the Annan Plan for uniting Cyprus was a milestone in this respect. The referendum on the Annan Plan was held in the Republic of Cyprus (Greek Cyprus) and the non-recognized Turkish Republic of Northern Cyprus (TRNC) on April 24, 2004. Erdoğan spent his political capital working against the "no" campaign led by a historical figure, the ultra-nationalist TRNC President Rauf Denktaş. Consequently, the Annan Plan was approved by 65 percent of Turkish Cypriots. However, 76 percent of Greek Cypriots rejected it. But, conforming to the EU enlargement schedule, it had already been agreed that the Republic of Cyprus would become a member regardless of the referendum's result. So on May 1, 2004, Cyprus joined the European Union together with nine other countries. The UN Secretary-General Kofi Annan said a unique and historic chance to resolve the Cyprus problem had been missed. The European Commissioner for Enlargement Verheugen added that he felt cheated by the Greek Cypriot government. For his part, Erdoğan felt he was cheated by the European Union as the referendum decision did not hinder the Republic of Cyprus' entry into the EU while leaving the Turkish Cypriots out in the cold.

The obstacles Turkey met on the road to accession were seen by Erdoğan as changing the goalposts and the rules of the game even as the game was being played. Turkey has been linked to the EU by an Association Agreement since 1964, and a Customs Union was established in 1995. The European Council granted the status of candidate country to Turkey in December 1999, and accession negotiations were opened in October 2005. Within the framework of accession negotiations, 16 of 35 chapters had been opened, and one of these was provisionally closed. In his mind, even before the Arab Spring Erdoğan had already concluded that Turkey's road to the European Union was irredeemably blocked.

While Turkey almost lost its EU vision and Erdoğan was in deep disappointment concerning the Western world, with the Arab Spring the hopes of projecting Turkey's power to its Muslim "near abroad" blossomed. The regime changes in Tunisia and Egypt, and later in Libya, strengthened Turkey's international standing at a time when its fortunes had declined in Europe.

The period between Turkey's alienation from the EU and its involvement in the Syrian crisis was appraised succinctly by Soli Özel:

The strategic ambitions of Turkey were not just the brainchild of the AKP governments either. Different schools of thought since the end of the Cold War had pushed for a more expansive view of Turkey's strategic interests. At the turn of the 21st century the ascending view of Turkey's national interest, despite a deep sovereigntist streak in strategic thought, was membership of the EU. The fact that the European Union misled Turkey first by admitting Cyprus as a member and then following the will of the German Chancellor and French President, by effectively opting not to make Turkey a member, contributed to the estrangement of Ankara.

Later on, as the financial and economic crisis of the EU diminished its lure economically and the Arab revolts presented an ideologically defined geopolitical opening for Ankara and also because the taming of the military and the secular elites was almost concluded by 2011, Turkey assumed a more assertive regional power posture. At the beginning, it pursued this through the deployment of its soft power, however as the Syrian situation deteriorated and began to present a major national security problem, there was a swift turn to hard power.[75]

When the tremors in the region reached Syria, Turkey's next-door neighbour, Ankara departed from its traditional policy of non-involvement in the neighbours' domestic affairs. It assisted in the formation of the Syrian

---

[75] Özel, "2021: Year of Decisions", *op. cit.*

opposition in exile. Istanbul became the birthplace of the Syrian opposition body that brought diverse anti-regime groups and individuals together under the name of the Syrian National Council. The Syrian wing of the Muslim Brotherhood was the backbone of the Council.

In March 2011, I had a confidential conversation with President Tayyip Erdoğan on Turkey's possible position, only a week after the turmoil in Syria. In April of that year, I participated in Foreign Minister Davutoğlu's impromptu visit to Damascus. I had been to Egypt and Tunisia when Muslim Brotherhood and an-Nahda established power in the wake of the Arab Spring. Thanks to my involvement in all these events, I was well positioned to attest to the Turkish foreign policy's new trajectory.

The Muslim Brotherhood affiliation attributed to the Turkish government has widely been speculated about and circulated by various protagonists of the Middle East conflict, from Israel to Syria. A BESA report in Israel maintained that the ruling AKP chaired by Erdoğan is *"guided by a Turkish variant of Muslim Brotherhood philosophy, making it natural ideological partner to Hamas – the Brotherhood's Palestinian offshoot"*.[76] Interestingly, Syrian President Bashar Assad's confidant and advisor Buthaina Shabaan confided to me in 2014 how Damascus saw the regime in Turkey, alleging that *"Erdoğan's government is Turkey's Muslim Brotherhood"*.[77]

FROM ZERO PROBLEMS WITH NEIGHBOURS TO NO NEIGHBOURS WITHOUT PROBLEMS

Turkish foreign policy gradually adopted militarized diplomacy and developed problematic relations with almost every country in its neighbourhood after being involved heavily with the Syrian crisis and civil war in 2011. "Zero problems with the neighbours" was replaced by a state of affairs that critics of Turkish foreign policy sarcastically referred to as "no neighbours without problems".

Before the end of 2013, Turkey's relations deteriorated with Egypt when a military coup overthrew the Muslim Brotherhood led by President Muhammed Morsi. Relations with Israel and Syria had already deteriorated, and Iran and Iraq were not in good shape. At the time, Ahmet Davutoğlu was still holding

---

[76] Yaakov Lappin, **"As Turkey's Lira Tumbles, Erdoğan Pursues Neo-Ottoman Visions"**, *BESA Center Perspectives*, No. 1, 796, November 2, 2020.
[77] Çandar, Turkey's Mission Impossible, War and Peace with the Kurds, op. cit., 187.

the reins of Turkish foreign policy. The architect of the zero problems with the neighbours, Davutoğlu, presided over the foreign policy that left Turkey with no neighbours without problems, stranded in diplomatic isolation in the region.

İbrahim Kalın, Davutoğlu's successor as Tayyip Erdoğan's chief advisor on foreign policy, who later became the presidential spokesperson, defended Turkey's isolation as *"precious loneliness"*.

Kalın, a theologian by education rather than a historian or political scientist, apparently confused the 19th-century British diplomatic practice of avoiding permanent alliances in continental Europe, termed *"splendid isolation"*, and the unenviable diplomatic situation of Turkey during the second decade of the 21st century. Instead of *"splendid isolation"*, he inadvertently coined the senseless term *"precious loneliness"*.

His confusion and the diplomatic failures of the AKP government subjected him – along with certain other colleagues – to my continuous criticism and sarcasm in the Turkish print media and on air, which set me further apart from those holding power. Erdoğan and his loyalists set out along the road to authoritarianism. That was the period from 2011 to 2016 when there was nothing to suggest any differences between Erdoğan and Davutoğlu regarding Turkish foreign policy's philosophy and practice.

Turkey's involvement in the Syrian conflict put a definite end to its primary foreign policy asset in the region: soft power. As the civil war intensified, Turkey adopted a sectarian position and formed a Sunni axis with Saudi Arabia and Qatar. These countries provided ideological support and financial assistance to various Salafi/jihadist extremist organizations. Thanks to its geographical proximity to the Syrian theatre of operations, Turkey hosted most of those organizations, supplying vital logistical support and equipping weaponry, including shelter and medical treatment.

SUNNI-SECTARIAN AND ANTI-KURDISH IMPULSES

Until its heavy involvement in the Syrian conflict, Turkey maintained a non-sectarian stand in regional affairs, in contrast to Iran which took the approach of allying with Shia groups in Mesopotamia, the Levant, and the Arabian Peninsula. Consequently, as a partner in the trilateral Sunni axis with Qatar and Saudi Arabia, Turkey confronted Tehran, Baghdad, the Syrian regime in

Damascus, and Lebanon, which was largely under the control of Iran's proxy Hezbollah.

At the instigation of Iran and with the participation of Lebanese Hezbollah, the Syrian regime confronted the peaceful mass protests at the initial stages of the conflict with sectarian violence and brutal suppression. Tens of thousands of people were killed, maimed, and jailed, while hundreds of thousands were internally displaced and millions fled the country. Syria was devastated. One of the biggest refugee problems of history, with all its tragic humanitarian aspects, had been created.

In that respect, the blame for the wrongdoings of sectarianism should not fall solely on Turkey. The hapless refugees, whose number climbed nearly to four million and who were mostly Sunni, took shelter in Turkey. It would not be difficult to anticipate that the Syrian conflict's extraordinary circumstances would trigger sectarian sentiment among Turkey's Sunnis.

The intensification of the Syrian civil war revealed the Sunni sectarian impulses of Davutoğlu, which were basically in accord with Erdoğan. He described Bashar al-Assad's regime as a "Nusayri regime" referring to the Syrian leader's religious sect. Nusayri is a derogatory name used by Sunnis instead of calling these people Alawi, the proper name of the sect's adherents. Syrian Alawites or their kin in Turkey never call themselves Nusayris. That is the Sunni defamatory usage.

The Sunni sectarian position Davutoğlu maintained against the Damascus regime with an Alawite sectarian core had also been instrumentalized against the Syrian Kurds who mainly inhabited the northern and northeastern swathes of Syria stretching across the common frontier. In July 2012, the Syrian regime pulled back the Syrian army from the majority Kurdish-populated areas adjacent to Turkey. The vacuum left was immediately filled by the Kurdish PYD (Democratic Unity Party), the Syrian affiliate of the PKK (Kurdistan Workers Party), which has waged a two-decade-long insurgency in Turkey. The PYD established de facto Kurdish self-rule in July 2012. On July 19, the founding of the YPG (People's Defense Forces), the Syrian Kurdish administration's military arm of the PYD, was announced.

In 2011 and even in 2012, guided by the Foreign Minister Ahmet Davutoğlu, Turkish leaders firmly believed that the days of the Damascus regime were numbered. Therefore, Turkey's focus was primarily to strengthen the Syrian opposition, namely the Syrian National Council based in Istanbul, to preparing it to replace Bashar Assad. In 2011 and 2012, Turkey leaned toward Damascus and was not particularly concerned with any Kurdish threat contiguous with its southern borders.[78]

Turkey and Syria share the longest border compared to those they have with their respective neighbouring countries. Almost 400 kilometres of the 911 kilometre frontier is formed by a railroad line stretching across flat terrain. The Kurds inhabit both sides of the railroad line. They had been living as Ottoman subjects for centuries, only to be divided between Turkey and Syria when the frontier was drawn in 1921. In the aftermath of World War I, Turkey lost the Ottoman land Syria to France.

Turkey, which was proclaimed a republic in 1923 and Syria, which became an independent sovereign state in 1943, denied their citizens' Kurdish identity, and subdued them. Kurdish aspirations were translated as threats by both countries and were squashed.

That changed beginning from July 2012. Turkey realized that the Syrian regime was no longer in complete control of its Kurds. Turkey saw the establishment of autonomous rule in Syria and rising Kurdish fortunes as a serious threat to its national security. Under the influence of Davutoğlu's arguments, Turkish leadership opted to undo the Kurdish "threat" by relying on the Arab Sunni armed groups mushrooming in northern Syria.

With Salafi ideological backgrounds and jihadist perspectives, financed primarily by Qatar and various other Gulf sources, they ranged from the Muslim Brotherhood to al-Qaeda (which adopted the name al-Nusra in the Syrian theatre) to their breakaway factions. They enjoyed the logistical support and assistance of Turkey.

The case of the al-Nusra-YPG fight for control of the predominantly Kurdish-inhabited Syrian border town of Ras al-Ayn in November 2012 took place before the eyes of international media based in Ceylanpınar on the Turkish side of the border. In a dialogue between the two of us in December 2012, Davutoğlu defended Turkish support for the Islamic groups against the Syrian Kurds in the battle for Ras al-Ayn, alleging that the latter were cooperating with the Damascus regime.

In 2014, even after Mosul was captured and ISIS took the Turkish Consulate personnel hostage, Davutoğlu would go so far as to offer some justification for

---

[78] *Ibid.*, 187, 188.

the efforts of the Islamic State. He claimed that ISIS militants are the bereaved Sunni youth who emerged as a consequence of Iraq's American occupation.

Many Western media outlets labelled Turkey, embarrassingly, as the "Jihadist Highway" for the logistical support provided to Sunni armed factions taking part in the Syrian civil war. As long as Turkey could not send its military into Syria to prevent Kurdish self-rule from rooting and extending contiguously all along the Turkish border, the Turkish leadership did not shy away from a transactional relationship with the Sunni Arab extremists who provided the force to undermine the Syrian Kurdish groups. Being perceived as the Jihadist Highway did not alter Turkey's priorities in its demeanour regarding the Syrian war.

From 2014 on, President Tayyip Erdoğan was also unequivocal in explaining Turkey's priority in Syria as prohibiting the Kurds from self-rule. He had statements reported in the Turkish media several times on this issue. I quoted his statement of January 26, 2015, in my book *Turkey's Mission Impossible, War and Peace with the Kurds*, which was very telling:

[Implying Syria's north] *What would happen there? What has happened in Iraq would happen. We do not want the repetition of what happened in Iraq. What do I mean? North Iraq... Now, North Syria would be born! We cannot accept this. I am aware that for Turkey, it is burdensome [to prevent the birth of North Syria]. But we have to keep our posture against such a happening. Otherwise, after Northern Iraq, we will be facing Northern Syria. Such developments will create big troubles in the future.*[79]

Erdoğan's statement indicated that Turkey prioritized the threat perception of a Kurdish entity on its doorstep over the presence of the Islamic State in its proximity. It would not hesitate to undo such an entity established even beyond its borders. The timing of these statements was particularly significant, reflecting the *volte-face* Erdoğan made at the end of 2013 to integrate himself with anti-Kurdish arch-nationalists. That alignment in Turkish politics was related to the developments in Syria, which mirrored the longstanding strategic obsession of the Turkish establishment, as follows:

Formation of a Kurdish corridor adjacent to Turkey's southern borders, stretching from the Mediterranean to Iran, is in clear conflict with the Turkish state's geopolitical outlook that envisages using the same route to extend its influence to the Mediterranean — and this is a fact

---

[79] *Ibid.*, 194.

known by all those who have the privilege of inside information about Turkey's strategic choices.[80]

Years later I encountered with a similar appraisal in a review of Turkish foreign study:

Turkish concern about the creation of a Kurdish belt separating Turkey from the rest of the Middle East, which in the worst scenarios included a Kurdish state with access to the sea independent of Turkey, was a result not only of developments in northern Syria, but also of developments in northern Iraq. Had they not been thwarted by countries in the region, the Kurds in northern Iraq would have wanted to declare independence following the independence referendum in the autonomous Kurdish region in 2017.[81]

Turkey's military involvement in Syria could only be assessed in broader strategic thinking and geopolitical vision.

---

[80] *Ibid.*, 193.
[81] Gallia Lindenstrauss and Remi Daniel, "The Erdoganian Amalgam: The Ottoman Past, the Ataturk Heritage, and the Arab Upheaval", *Strategic Assessment*, Vol. 24, No. 1 (January 2021). https://strategic assessment.inss.org.il/en/articles/the-erdoganian-amalgam-the-ottoman-past-the-ataturk-heritage-and-the-arab-upheaval/

TURKEY IN SYRIA, EURASIANISM IN ACTION

ERDOĞANIST NEO-OTTOMANISM IN PLAY

To forestall the perceived or alleged threats from Syria, Turkey sent in its military and created a Turkish-ruled enclave in northern Syria beginning in August 2016.

Turkey's military expeditions into Syria began less than a month after the controversial coup on July 15, 2016. This date is the milestone event in modern Turkish history that led to an unprecedented crackdown, especially on the Kurdish opposition, steering the country towards authoritarianism and further from the West. Concurrently, Turkey's growing partnership with Russia illustrated a Eurasian turn in Turkey's vocation.

Using every means possible, from the summer of 2016 Turkey entered into an era of assertive (for some aggressive and expansionist) foreign policy that genuinely can be defined as neo-Ottomanism in the Erdoğanist sense.

An article in the Iranian daily *Entekhab* published on March 1, 2020 in striking truthfulness described the Erdoğanist neo-Ottomanism as a Turkish nationalist ideology. Outlining when and how the approach was established, it simultaneously summarized all the Turkish military campaigns in Syria in chronological order:

Ahmet Davutoğlu's resignation from the position of prime minister on May 5, 2016 can be regarded as the starting point of Erdoğan's one-man rule in Turkey and of the unbalanced implementation of neo-Ottomanism there. In the years after 2003, Davutoğlu's strategic-depth doctrine and his [other] ideas informed Turkey's domestic and foreign policy... Although Davutoğlu's ideas often described as the neo-Ottomanist road-map, his approach was never based on extremism and military aggression. After deposing the ideologue of the AKP (Justice and Development Party), Erdoğan operating on a belligerent rationale, adopted the strategy of reinforcement by the sword. Three months after Davutoğlu's ouster as prime minister... on August 24, 2016, Turkey launched Operation Euphrates Shield in the Aleppo governorate [Syria] against ISIS and the Kurds...

After expanding in the Levant, Erdoğan did not confine himself to the northern parts of the Aleppo governorate, but took control of the entire area by joining forces with the extremist groups in the Idlib governorate. Furthermore, on January 20, 2018, the Turkish military and militias under its command launched an attack on the Kurdish-controlled Afrin governorate, as part of the Operation Olive Branch, and 58 days later, on March 18, they managed to gain control of the area. But Erdoğan's expansion in northern Syria did not end there. On October 9, 2019, despite widespread international opposition, he launched an offensive on the

Kurds and Syrians east of the Euphrates and managed to take over several additional areas.[82] [83]

Entekhab, a reformist daily in Iran, banned several times in Iran for drawing the ire of the Supreme Leader Khamenei, claimed that Turkey's President Erdoğan sees himself as the Islamic world leader or, to be more precise, leader of the world's Sunni Muslims. Examining his tone and actions, it reached the judgment that Erdoğan has the appetite for the Ottoman sultans' glory and might. According to Entekhab, Recep Tayyip Erdoğan considers himself the equal of Mehmed the Conqueror of Istanbul in 1453 and Suleiman the Magnificent, who ruled for 46 years in the 16th century, signifying the apex of the Empire.

The Iranian newspaper sarcastically labels Turkey's president as Sultan Recep and sees him in the eye of a big storm that will sweep him from office in 2023. Turkey's next presidential elections will be held on the centenary of the republic founded in the wake of the Ottoman Empire's demise.

Illustration accompanying the Entekhab article, Erdoğan as Sultan Recep. The same image was the cover of The Economist's issue June 8-14, 2013, with the rubric Democrat or Sultan inscribed over it. The original is a painting of Ottoman Sultan Selim III, who reigned from 1789 to 1807, replaced by Erdoğan's head drawn with a turban.

---

[82] Memri, an Israeli press monitoring organization believed to be close to Israeli military intelligence, published excerpts from an article of the Iranian daily *Entekhab* from March 1, 2020 that, according to Memri, came out against the expansionist ambitions of Turkish President Recep Tayyip Erdogan, who, it said, wishes to restore the political and territorial glory of the Ottoman Empire. Titled "When Sultan Recep [Tayyip Erdogan] Fantasizes that He Is the Equal of the Ottoman Sultans and Can Tell the Word What to Do: How Erdogan Thinks and Analyzes the World".

[83] Memri (Middle East Media Research Institute), Iran, *Turkey Special Dispatch* No. 9078, December 9, 2020.

Speculative foretelling on Recep Tayyip Erdoğan's ultimate downfall in 2023 aside, *Entekhab* presents a remarkable assessment of the timeline of events signalling Tayyip Erdoğan's neo-Ottomanism in domestic and foreign policy. It is arguably the most concise in the countless papers, reports, and research material I went over. The only caveat is that it did not refer to July 15, 2016, the date of the failed coup.

Erdoğan blamed the masterminding of the coup attempt on his erstwhile ally, the Sunni cleric Fethullah Gülen, the background of which claim remains shrouded in mystery. Nevertheless, the attempt stimulated a dramatic leap towards consolidation of an autocratic nationalist regime in Turkey. It concurrently signified an unexpected rapprochement with Russia to the detriment of Turkey's traditional Western ties and commitments on security, and opened the way for Turkey's Eurasianist shift away from its historic European allies. That became one of the most significant geopolitical realignments of our age.

In their review of Turkish foreign policy in the Middle East since 2003, which corresponds to the beginning of the AKP rule under Erdoğan, two Israeli experts highlighted the year 2013 as notable for drastic changes. The decisive developments in 2013 in Egypt and Turkey's domestic political scene defined Turkey's new trajectory in foreign policy, an amalgam that is unique in history.

The factors behind the changing patterns in Turkey's foreign policy in the Middle East, regarding both the extent of Ankara's activism and the shifting direction of that activism— from a country making extensive use of soft power tools to a country making greater use of hard power tools... the contribution of geopolitical interests, the "neo-Ottoman" factor, constraints resulting from domestic Turkish politics and economics, and ideological motives in Turkey's foreign policy in the Middle East... since 2013: One is the fall of Egyptian President Mohamed Morsi in 2013, which was a blow to the vision of an axis of countries dominated by the Muslim Brotherhood movement, an axis that Turkey had hoped to lead. The second reason is the Gezi Park demonstrations that year. Furthermore, as part of the escalating struggle between religious leader Fethullah Gulen and then-Turkish Prime Minister (and current President) Recep Tayyip Erdogan and his supporters, extensive corruption was revealed that same year that changed Erdogan's perception of the internal threat... The geopolitical changes resulting from the Arab upheaval and domestic trends in Turkey have led Erdogan to create a foreign policy amalgam that is unique in Turkish history. From the Turkish Republic's traditional foreign policy, he has adopted nationalism, militarization, and suspicion toward the rest of the world. From the Ottoman past, he has assimilated the religious dimension, the element of territorial expansion, and revisionism. Since this is an amalgam, the relative weight of the respective dimensions varies over time, depending on the issue and the period.[84]

The unorthodox – but nevertheless accurate – argument they put forward is remarkable and notable, indeed. I agree with it, but in terms of Turkey adopting an assertive foreign policy, moving away from the Euro-Atlantic system, and navigating with Eurasianist winds, the year 2016 has to be registered as the turning point.

The timeline of developments indicates how Erdoğan steered Turkey away from the West in establishing a partnership with Putin's Russia and how the botched military coup in July 2016 has become a significant turning point in that sense. Years later, *Financial Times*, in a series described as *"looking at Recep Tayyip Erdoğan's geopolitical ambitions"* under the title *"Erdoğan's Great Game"*, acknowledged the historical significance of the 2016 coup for Turkey-Russia rapprochement. That rapprochement later translated into partnership in Syria and enabled the Turkish military incursions with Moscow's green light or tacit endorsement.

A bloody attempted coup by rogue military factions in 2016 marked a rupture in Turkey's dealings with the rest of the world, analysts say. It left Mr Erdogan even more suspicious of the west, pushed him closer to Russia's Vladimir Putin, forced him to forge new political alliances at home and enabled him to take unprecedented control of the Turkish state.[85]

Without Russian acquiescence, if not outright endorsement, Turkey could not have stepped into Syria militarily. The opportunity was due to the improvement between Ankara-Moscow relationship.

The relationship began to improve in the summer of 2016, when Mr Putin commiserated with the Turkish president after an abortive coup in Turkey that killed some 270 people… Since 2016 Mr Erdogan has held more face-to-face meetings with Mr Putin than with any other leader. Russia has turned from being Turkey's opponent in Syria's civil war into its most important partner there. Turkey has been able to carry out its military operations in northern Syria only with Russian consent. Meanwhile, Russian news outlets have made inroads among Turkish audiences. Mr Erdogan's inner circle now includes a group of "Eurasianists", who are open to co-operation with Russia and China and hostile towards Europe and NATO.[86]

[84] Lindenstrauss and Daniel, *op. cit.*
[85] *Financial Times*, "Erdogan's Great Game: Soldiers, Spies and Turkey's Quest for Power", January 12, 2021.
[86] *The Economist*, "The odd couple: Putin and Erdogan have formed a brotherhood of hard power", February 27, 2021. https://www.economist.com/europe/2021/02/23/putin-and-erdogan-have-formed-a-brother

As foreign policy always begins at home, Turkey's Eurasianist drive, manifested in extraterritorial military forays, went hand in hand with its repressive anti-Kurdish nationalism and the introduction of authoritarian rule. Sinem Adar analysed this phenomenon in her brilliant piece, "Understanding Turkey's Increasingly Militaristic Foreign Policy":

Scholars and experts have offered numerous explanations for Turkey's increasing use of military power... A focus on domestic factors is a useful lens for understanding Turkey's foreign policy choices. Domestic events can strongly shape perceptions of threat, attitudes toward alliances, and definition of interests. The 2016 coup attempt shows how such domestic events bring familiar characteristics of Turkish politics into sharper relief, not only providing the ruling elites with the justification for a shift to hard power but also triggering a re-configuration of intra-state alliances in ways which placed narrow interests in the driving seat of foreign policy.[87]

THE EURASIANIST DIVERSION: TURKEY MARCHES TO SYRIA

The consolidation of Erdoğan's power in the wake of 15 July 2016 was celebrated as the birth of the "New Turkey" by his loyalists. What was mostly seen and interpreted as establishing one-man rule in Turkey, likening Erdoğan to an imperial Sultan rather than a president of a modern country, concealed the real nature of Turkish power configuration: a coalition of nationalists of different stripes gathered around Erdoğan, the strongman.

To decipher Erdoğan's autocratic "New Turkey" code with its militarized and activist foreign policy, the unusual alliance between the Young Turks' reincarnation and the neo-Hamidians needs to be understood. These are representations of different versions of Turkish nationalism. Without reference to the late Ottoman imperial period and lacking knowledge and understanding, it is almost impossible to correctly assess the current Turkish power equation.

The Ottoman Empire's late period was marked by the rule of the secretive Committee of Union and Progress (CUP) having roots extending back to the 1880s and the origins of the Young Turk movement. The CUP gained power in the Young Turk Revolution of 1908. In the following year, it dethroned Sultan

hood-of-hard-power?itm_source=parsely-api
[87] Sinem Adar, "Understanding Turkey's Increasingly Militaristic Foreign Policy", Centre for Applied Turkey Studies at the German Institute for International and Security Affairs (CATS-SWP), *MENA Politics Newsletter*, Vol. 3, No. 1 (Spring 2020). https://apsamena.org/wp-content/uploads/2020/06/apsa-mena-politics-newsletter-spring-2020-final.pdf

Abdulhamid II, who had reigned for 33 years.[88] *The CUP administration established its autocratic one-party rule… which eventually brought the end of the Ottoman Empire… While the CUP upheld the façade of being an open party committed to parliamentary government and the rule of law, its members maintained a secret parallel system of control over the country. The CUP era led to the development of culture and conspiracy and subversion within the Turkish state's ranks.*[89]

In other words, the CUP's influence, the mindset of the Young Turk movement, survived in the ranks of the Turkish state, mainly in the upper echelons of the military and security establishment. The armed forces, given their role in the Young Turk movement and the foundation of the modern Turkish nation-state, regarded themselves as the guardians of the nation's republic and as its saviours. The security establishment constituted the parallel system of control in the state structure perceived as the "deep state". This is a concept that originated in modern Turkey and became Turkey's contribution to the lexicon of political science.

Sultan Abdulhamid II, who the Young Turks overthrew, is regarded as the last great statesman of the Ottoman dynasty, revered by the Turkish Islamists, including Recep Tayyip Erdoğan.

Contrastingly, one of the most brilliant historians of Turkey, Edhem Eldem, a scion of the Ottoman royal family, gives credit to Sultan Abdulhamid II as the founder of the deep state:

Abdulhamid's contribution to authoritarianism cannot be underestimated. By creating his autocratic regime as an alternative, not only to constitutionalism, but also to the bureaucratic and legalist tradition of Tanzimat, he paved the way to a form of modern personal rule that eventually play a crucial role in late Ottoman and Turkish politics. He can thus be credited what is today called the 'deep state'… an unaccountable and uncontrollable "core" that will guarantee the survival of the state. In that sense, while there is no doubt that the ideological foundations of modern Turkey was established by the Young Turks and Unionists after the 1908 Revolution… it seem that Abdulhamid can be credited with the paternity of the structure of the modern Turkish state, including its darkest components.[90]

The unthinkable and unprecedented happened in Turkey, and the ideological and political descendants of the late Ottoman period's antagonists, whom I

---

[88] Çandar, Turkey's Mission Impossible, op. cit., 247.
[89] Ryan Gingeras, "How Deep State Came to America: A History," *War on the Rocks*, February 4, 2019. https://warontherocks.com/2019/how-the-deep-state-come-to-america
[90] Edhem Eldem, "Sultan Abdulhamid II: Founding Father of the Turkish State," *Journal of the Ottoman and Turkish Studies Association*, Vol. 5, No. 2 (Fall 2018), 44.

name as "neo-Unionists" and "neo-Hamidians", forged a nationalist coalition.[91]

Since 2015, Turkey is governed by a nationalist coalition that is an amalgam of neo-unionists, traditional ethnic Turkish right-wing nationalists and Islamist nationalists... After Erdoğan's volte face in 2014, the deep state nationalists have made a come-back in grand style. They were not only released from prison but were in many cases returned to their key positions in the security establishment. They have been instrumental in masterminding the rapprochement between Turkey and Russia that had begun on the eve of the 2016 coup attempt and which has been pursued in its aftermath. These nationalists within the Turkish state establishment are also referred to as Eurasianists, and they are strongly present within the military. They espouse anti-American and anti-NATO views, and advocate an eastward strategic realignment that would make Turkey the partner of Russia, Iran and China.[92]

A prolific writer and old friend and colleague of mine, Washington-based expert Ömer Taşpınar shared the essential contours of my characterization of the "new" Turkey's power configuration, but chose to describe it in a somewhat more benign fashion as "Turkish Gaullism":

Despite the important differences between the "secularist nationalism" of Kemalism and the "religious nationalism" of neo-Ottomanism (seeking to project soft power in formerly Ottoman territories) both strategic visions are strongly attached to Turkish national interests. Neo-Ottomanism and, especially, the "Eurasianist" wing of Kemalism (well-represented among officers who now have upward mobility in the army) are in favor of regional strategic alliances to boost Turkish leverage against Western partners in the transatlantic alliance. At the end of the day, both neo-Ottomanism and Kemalism share a state-centric view of the world with the primacy of Turkish national interests. In that sense, both ideologies share Turkish nationalism as a common denominator.

If current trends continue, what we will see emerging in Turkey is not an Islamist foreign policy but a much more nationalist, defiant, independent and self-centered strategic orientation – in short, a Turkish variant of "Gaullism." As in the case of Charles de Gaulle's anti-American and anti-NATO policies in the 1960s, a Gaullist Turkey may in the long run question Ankara's membership within the military structure of NATO or the logic of waiting for the elusive EU membership. In search of full independence, full sovereignty, strategic leverage and, most importantly, "national prestige, glory and grandeur," a Gaullist Turkey may opt

---

[91] Cengiz Çandar, "New Turkey: Neo-Nationalist or the Reincarnation of the Old?", *Turkey Analyst,* December 20, 2017. http://www.turkeyanalyst.org/publications/turkey-analyst-articles/item/592-new-turkey-neo-nationalist-or-the-reincarnation-of-the-old?.html

[92] *Ibid.,* 276, 277.

for its own "force de frappe" – a nuclear deterrent – and its own "Realpolitik" with countries such as Russia, China, and India.

One should not underestimate the emergence of a "New Turkey" that transcends the Islamic-secular divide, because both the Turkish military's Kemalism and the AKP's neo-Ottomanism share the primacy of national interests against Western influence. Turkey's current military offensive in northern Syria, the growing anti-Americanism at home, the rapprochement with Russian and Iran, the frustration with the EU over visa liberalization, and the war against the PKK are all factors that will contribute to the growth of Turkish Gaullism.[93]

Hercules (Herkül/Iraklis) Millas, a respected cultural historian and a Greek (Rum) of Istanbul with dual citizenship in Turkey and Greece, presents a similar analysis in terms of the components of the current power equation in Turkey but from a different vantage point and with a different emphasis:

An unproductive way to start an analysis on Turkey is to give precedence to prior knowledge. Turkey has changed so much the last few years that knowledge of the recent past may prove deceptive in leading one's judgment astray... There is now a strong man in power with unrestricted authority. The once (so called "Islamist Democratic") Justice and Development Party (AKP) of the first decade of the century, which was in favour of a rapprochement with the West through the EU, is at present in close collaboration with its old phobic opponents: the Nationalist Movement Party (MHP) and the "military". This alliance has a special image of the West: it is perceived and presented as a "negative" block... What is new is not the negative image of the West; "Christianophobia" in the East is as old as the Ottomans and it is the flip side of "Islamophobia" of the West. These prejudices are the historical legacies of centuries-long crusades and jihads...There is also a high probability that Erdoğan's extreme anti-West rhetoric is not a tactical choice, but a sincere conviction.[94]

A quite recent observation by two Israel experts about the new power configuration in Turkey is also noteworthy. What makes it even more interesting that it is published as the product of joint research conducted for the first time ever between Israeli and Emirati institutions following the Abraham Accords:

The "deep state" political culture is still evident in Erdoğan's empire. However, it has been turned from a tool of Kemalist and secularist repression into an ambitious vehicle for the neo-Ottoman agenda, and as tool meant primarily for internal matters to a tool for achieving

---

[93] Omer Taspinar, "Foreign Policy after the Failed Coup: The Rise of Turkish Gaullism", September 2, 2016. https://lobelog.com/foreign-policy-after-the-failed-coup-the-rise-of-turkish-gaullism/

[94] Hercules Millas, "Rediscovering and Re-evaluating the New Turkey", *Ahval*, December 5, 2020. https://ahvalnews.com/turkish-politics/rediscovering-and-re-evaluating-new-turkey

external ambitions… Today, President Erdoğan's AKP and its MHP ally rule the Turkish state without any significant opposition. The two parties dominate all state organs and mechanisms, including the deep state and its covert tools. To strengthen his position at home, Erdoğan continues to pursue a hardline Islamist, nationalist, and increasingly blunt neo-Ottoman stance in Turkey's foreign policy.[95]

SYRIA: THE FIRST MOVE ON THE NEO-OTTOMANIST CHESSBOARD

The Ottoman Empire entered the Middle East from today's Syria and gained controlled of it as far as Yemen, during the reign of Sultan Selim I in 1516. Acquiring Mecca and Medina, the two holiest places of Islam, enabled the Ottoman sultans to bear the title of Caliph. For four centuries, until partitioned between the victors of World War I, the Middle East remained as Ottoman territories. Syria has become the launching pad for the return of Turkish power to the region, albeit through "soft power", at the turn of the 21st century.

From the year 2016 on, the military activism of neo-Ottomanist Turkey has been performed on Syria. In a sense, for Turkey, the Middle East starts with Syria. The move also reflected the growing concentration of power in Erdoğan's hands. An IISS comment titled "Turkey's Increasingly Assertive Foreign Policy" published at the end of September 2020 identified this connection manifested in Turkey's first military move into Syria following the coup attempt in July 2016:

For example, the first Turkish military operation in Syria in August 2016 came after Erdogan had declared a domestic state of emergency and initiated a massive purge of the officer corps following the failed coup attempt in July, the origins of which are still largely unexplained. In June 2015, even though its once considerable political influence was already waning, the Turkish armed forces had defied an order from Erdogan to draw up plans for a military incursion into Syria.[96]

The first Turkish military incursion, *Operation Euphrates Shield*, which began in August 2016, ended in March 2017 with Turkey establishing control of the Syrian territory from the frontier town of Jarablus on the north side of Al-Bab,

[95] Hay Eytan Yanarocak and Jonathan Spyer, *Turkish Militias and Proxies*, Jerusalem Institute for Strategy and Security, TRENDS Research & Advisory of Abu Dhabi, UAE, January 27, 2021. https://trendsresearch.org/research/turkish-militias-and-proxies; Hay Eytan Yanarocak and Jonathan Spyer, "Erdoğan's Private Armies", *Middle East Forum*, January 27, 2021. https://www.meforum.org/61963/turkish-militias-and-proxies

[96] "Turkey's Increasingly Assertive Foreign Policy", *IISS*, Vol. 26, No. 6, Comment 24, 30 September 2020.

a triangular area in the vicinity of Aleppo. The second Turkish military operation, *Olive Branch*, unleashed in January 2018 and continuing until March 2018, ended self-rule in the Kurdish enclave in the northwestern area of Afrin where Turkish and allied Syrian groups took full control. The third Turkish military campaign, *Operation Peace Spring*, captured the area between the towns Tel Abyad and Ras al-Ain and penetrated nearly 30 kilometres in depth. Turkey also militarily took control of the Idlib province of Syria on the northwest bordering Turkey's southernmost province of Hayat (formerly Liwa al-Iskenderun of Syria under the French Mandate).

Before the last Turkish military incursion, the US Presidential Envoy to Syria and also the person in charge of coordinating the war against ISIS, Brett McGurk, unveiled Erdoğan's designs on Syria. In a *Foreign Affairs* article under the sub-title "Ottoman Dreams", referencing President Erdoğan, McGurk wrote that in several meetings he heard from Erdoğan that the Turkish president envisages Turkey's security zone as extending from Aleppo in Syria to Mosul in Iraq.[97]

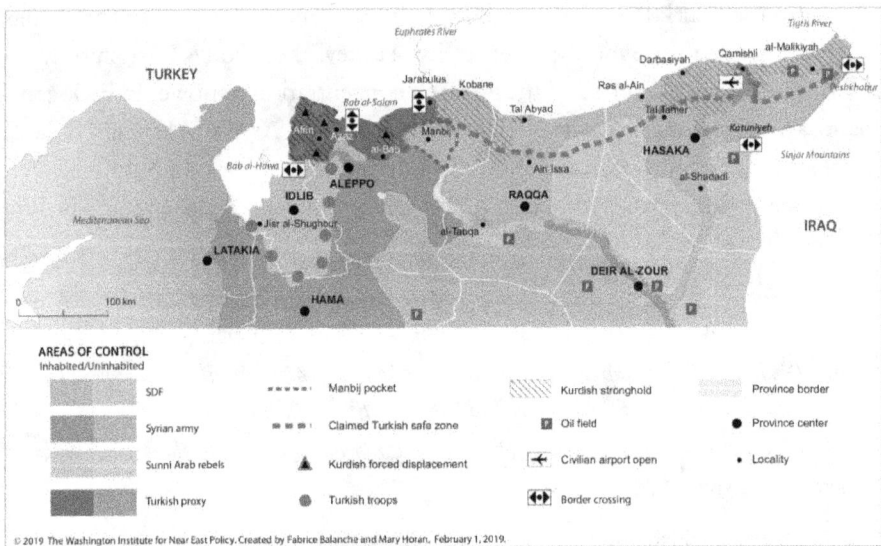

When the year 2021 arrived, Turkish control in Syria was fairly close to what Brett McGurk had referenced. The area controlled by Turkey or its Syrian proxies is larger than Turkey's province of Hatay or the Turkish Republic of Northern Cyprus – the entity recognized only by Turkey and that covers 37

---

[97] Brett McGurk, "Hard Truths in Syria", *Foreign Affairs*, Vol. 98, No. 3 (May/June 2019). https://www.foreignaffairs.com/articles/syria/2019-04-16/hard-truths-syria

percent of Cyprus's territory. Almost a quarter of Syria's population lives in the area under Turkey's direct and indirect control.

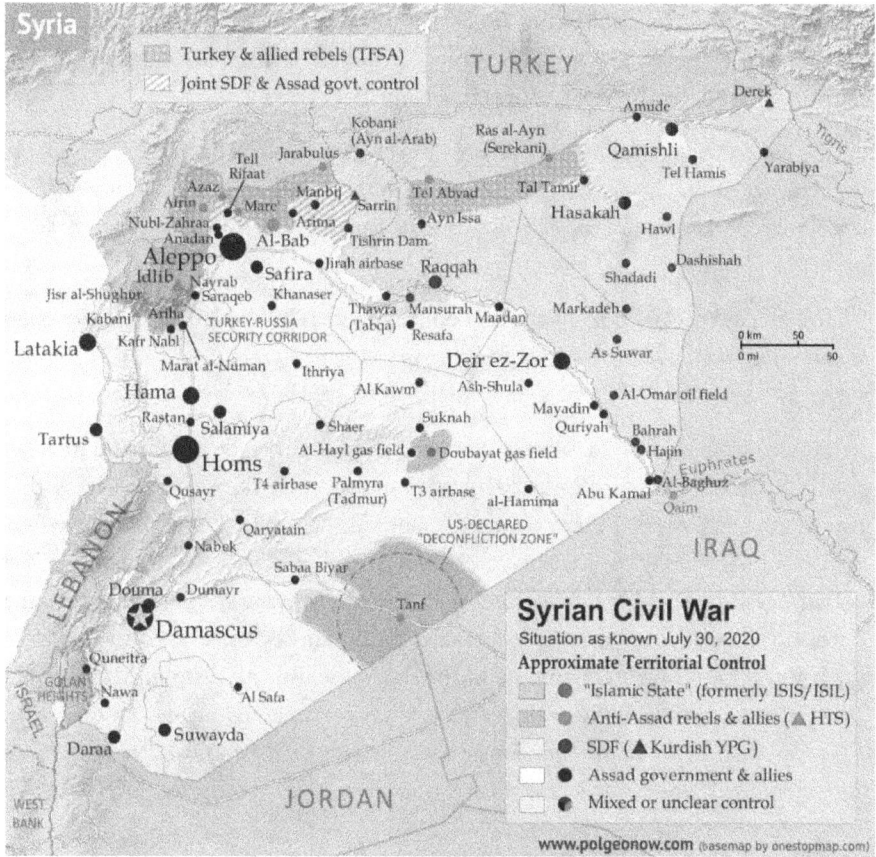

Base map by Koen Adams of onestopmap.com, with territorial control by Evan Centanni and Djordje Djukic.

There is ongoing demographic engineering in the Turkish-controlled parts of Syria, aiming to depopulate the Kurdish inhabitants and create a Sunni Arab and Turkmen belt to serve as a buffer zone. The buffer zone was envisaged between Turkey's Kurdish-inhabited southeast and Syria's predominantly Kurdish northern and northeastern regions.

In a well-documented piece Sinem Adar observed:

Besides these attempts at demographic engineering, Ankara is extending Turkish administrative structures and practices into northern Syria, particularly in the areas of education, health and humanitarian aid.

Turkey's demographic, administrative and military practices in northern Syria indicate that Ankara is planning for a long-term presence.[98]

Iran, another stakeholder in the Syrian imbroglio, sees it as a manifestation of Turkey's expansionist motives. Iran's Foreign Minister Mohammad Javad Zarif expressed denunciatory notes implying Turkey:

We did not try to expand our borders. One of our neighboring countries, which is present in Syria, has hoisted its flag over government buildings everywhere, even in areas where it is active as a "peacekeeper". Iran does not raise its flag. Iran is in Syria to support, not to order.[99]

In her *Turkey's Gains in Syria,* Adar emphasized that *"Turkish war-making efforts in northern Syria are catalysts of rising authoritarianism in Turkey and of Syria's potential further Balkanization".[100]*

However, her unique observation regarding Turkey's militaristic foreign policy in the aftermath of the 2016 coup attempt, as she describes it, is that important sectors in Turkey stand to benefit: *"The Turkish military-industrial complex has been one of the primary beneficiaries of Ankara's shift toward an increasingly militaristic foreign policy in the aftermath of the 2016 coup attempt"*. She adds that the Turkish construction sector also benefits from Turkey's presence in northern Syria. Recalling heavy investments in the domestic industry, she underlines that *"the Syrian war provided Ankara a golden opportunity to test and improve its homegrown defense products. They enabled Turkey to become an exporter of defense products that increased its volume from $248 million to over $3 billion between 2002, the year the AKP formed its first government to 2019."[101]*

The Turkish defence industry grew rapidly and considerably during the second decade of the 2000s. Between 2010 and 2019, Turkish military expenditures increased almost two-fold from $11 billion to $20.5 billion. The drones that have been produced domestically by Turkish Aviation Industries and Bayraktar, a firm owned by the family of the son-in-law of President Erdoğan , played a decisive role in changing the balance of power in the Libyan civil war. They also have the lion's share in Turkey's increased defence exports.

---

[98] Sinem Adar, "Turkey's Gains in Syria, Turkish Intervention in Syria Heightens Authoritarianism in Turkey and Fragmentation in Syria", *MERIP,* July 14, 2020.
https://merip.org/2020/07/turkish-intervention-in-syria-heightens-authoritarianism-in-turkey-and-fragmentation-in-syria/
[99] https://etemadonline.com/content/460318, January 23, 2021.
[100] Adar, "Turkey's Gains in Syria", *op. cit.*
[101] Ibid.

The Turkish drones, a source of pride for the Turkish defence industries, attracted international attention and stimulated high demand following their deployment in Syria and Libya.

For instance, in March 2020 Tunisia awarded a $240 million contract to Turkish Aerospace Industries for six Anka-S drones plus three ground-control stations and associated technologies.

The development of the Turkish defence industry and the increase in the export of its products cultivated assertiveness in Turkish foreign policy and infused self-confidence into Turkey's military undertakings abroad.

The Turkish military operates around 130 armed drones of several types, including five versions of the Anka produced by the TAI plus the Karayel and the Bayraktar TB2… Turkey's drones have helped to lead the country's aerial campaign targeting forces loyal to the regime of Syrian president Bashar Al Assad… Turkish drones and manned warplanes have made quick work of many of the regime's Russian-supplied Pantsir air-defense vehicles. Videos that have circulated on-line depict Turkish drones firing precision-guided missiles to destroy idling Pantsirs. The Turkish military's drones represent an "asymmetric" force in Syria. Damascus's forces lack the technology reliably to defeat attacks by unmanned aerial vehicles.[102]

In an enticing argument, the renowned political scientist and internationally acclaimed democracy theorist Francis Fukuyama, reflecting on the changing nature of land warfare in our day, compared the role of drones in undermining existing force structures to how the introduction of the dreadnaught made earlier battleships obsolete in naval warfare. For the development of Turkey's military industries, drones being the jewel on the crown, he gave the credit to Erdoğan.

The main actor in this development is Turkey under its autocratic president Recep Tayyip Erdogan. The country has developed its own domestic drones and has used them to devastating effect in several recent military conflicts: Libya, Syria, in the Nagorno-Karabakh war between Armenia and Azerbaijan, and in the fight against the PKK inside its own borders. In the process, it has elevated itself to being a major regional power broker with more ability to shape outcomes than Russia, China, or the United States.

Turkish drones like Bayraktar TB2 and Anka-S were developed by the Turkish defense firm Baykar Makina, led by MIT-educated designer Selçuk Bayraktar, who was to later marry Erdogan's daughter. The impetus to create a domestically-produce drone was driven by

[102] David Axe, "Guess Who's a Drone Power Now. Turkey", *The National Interest*, February 6, 2021. https://nationalinterest.org/blog/reboot/guess-who%E2%80%99s-drone-power-now-turkey-177801

the U.S. military embargo in 1975, and Washington's reluctance to sell the country its advanced Predator and Reaper drones. Turkey bought Heron drones from Israel but found that relationship problematic as well. Drones are, however, not that hard to manufacture, and the most recent Turkish ones are quite impressive. TB2 can stay aloft for 24 hour and can perform both reconnaissance and attack missions.

The effectiveness of these weapons was first demonstrated beyond Turkey's borders in Syria in March 2020, where in retaliation for a Russian-backed Syrian attack that killed 36 Turkish soldiers, Ankara launched a devastating attack on Syrian armored forces that were moving into Idlib province along the Turkish border. Video footage showed them destroying one Syrian armored vehicle after another, including more than 100 tanks, armored personnel carriers, and air defense systems.

The Syrian offensive was brought to a complete halt, and Idlib province secured as a haven for refuges. Then in May, Turkish drones were used to attack an air base in Libya used by UAE-backed Libyan National Army of General Khalifa Haftar, which ended the LNA's offensive against Tripoli. Finally, during the Nagorno-Karabagh war in September, Turkish drones intervening for Azerbaijan against Armenia destroyed an estimated 200 tanks, 90 other armored vehicles, and 182 artillery pieces, forcing the latter to withdraw from the territory. This has become a point of nationalist pride in Turkey.

It seems to me that Turkey's use of drones is going to change the nature of land power in ways that will undermine existing force structures, in the way that the Dreadnaught obsoleted earlier classes of battleships, or the aircraft carrier made battleships themselves obsolete at the beginning of World War II.[103]

In addition to the drones, the Turkish navy reached an operational capacity to simultaneously perform on multiple fronts in the Eastern Mediterranean, the Aegean waters, and the Black Sea. With its naval modernization projects and upgrades, Turkey felt it could project its power across the Eastern Mediterranean, challenging and confronting its adversaries.

In 2020, Libya and the Eastern Mediterranean became entangled as Turkish spheres of interest and conflict, demonstrating that Turkey's expansionism was not confined to Syria and pockets in northern Iraq.

With its military involvement in the Libyan conflict and muscle-flexing against Greece, Cyprus, and to a certain extent Israel, Egypt, and the UAE – and even against France – Turkey's self-confidence was sufficiently established to defy multiple adversaries in broad geopolitics.

---

[103] Fukuyama, "Droning On in the Middle East", *op. cit.*

If Turkey's assertive foreign policy and military activism had remained confined to Syria and the Kurdistan region of Iraq, to describe it as "neo-Ottomanist" would not sound particularly persuasive, as the Turkish actions could be fittingly seen within the framework of security imperatives. They could well be interpreted as defensive moves against the security threats from across the border. However, neo-Ottomanism could serve as an appropriately inclusive term to define Turkey's assertive foreign policy with its ideological underpinnings when it comes to Turkey's involvement with the war in Libya that is situated more than 2,000 kilometres away.

BLUE HOMELAND: TURKISH MARE NOSTRUM
(REACHING NORTH AFRICA, GUNBOAT DIPLOMACY IN THE EASTERN MEDITERRANEAN)

EXPANDING TO LIBYA AND THE EASTERN MEDITERRANEAN

Turkey's direct military engagement in Libya materialized almost eight years after the civil war began in 2011. The United Arab Emirates and Egypt had a military presence in Libya from the year 2014.

Turkey sided with the UN-sponsored Government of National Accord (GNA) in Tripoli in its entry into the Libyan battlefield. Thus, Erdoğan's Libya policy, at least on the paper and from the beginning of the Turkish military support to the GNA, enjoyed a certain legitimacy from the angle of international law and legality. It also salvaged Tripoli from succumbing to General Khalifa Haftar who besieged the city and was 7 kilometres away from the center and maintained the GNA's survival. Moreover, it brought to Erdoğan's Turkey self-confidence and prestige.

Between April and December 2019, the Emirates carried out more than 900 airstrikes in the Greater Tripoli area using Chinese-made combat drones and, in some instances, French-made fighter jets. The Emirati military intervention… wasn't enough to propel Haftar's men into downtown Tripoli. Mere weeks after Abu Dhabi started its bombing campaign, Ankara followed suit by sending its own drones and several dozen Turkish personnel, who carried out about 250 strikes in 2019. It is important to acknowledge that, before January 2020, the Emirati intervention in Libya was dramatically larger than the Turkish one. And still, that failed to suffice.[104]

A report penned by a group of experts affiliated to CATS (Centre for Applied Turkish Studies) at SWP (Stiftung Wissenschaft und Politik – German Institute for International and Security Affairs) lucidly illustrated the connection between the foreign policy choices regarding Libya and the Eastern Mediterranean.

The Eastern Mediterranean has become a flashpoint for maritime boundary conflicts, competing drilling activities, international naval exercises, and bellicose statements in recent years. Because of Turkey's ambitious aspirations and strong military footprint, its actions are indicative of new security imperatives and shifting balances of power in the region…

Turkey's interest in protecting the legitimate GNA government in Libya is deeply connected with its ambitions in the Eastern Mediterranean. Isolated in the Eastern Mediterranean, Turkey found an ally in the beleaguered Tripoli government. The two parties

---

[104] Jalel Harchaoui, "The Pendulum: How Russia Sways Its Way to More Influence in Libya", *War on the Rocks*, January 7, 2021. https://warontherocks.com/2021/01/the-pendulum-how-russia-sways-its-way-to-more-influence-in-libya/

signed a Memorandum of Understanding regarding the maritime borders in November 2019 in exchange for Turkish military support for the GNA government.[105]

In a perceptive essay "How Did the East Mediterranean Become the Eye of a Geopolitical Storm?" Michaël Tanchum expressed a similar assessment:

In a bid to break out of its regional isolation, in November 2019 Turkey signed its own maritime demarcation agreement with the Tripoli-based Government of National Accord (GNA) in war-torn Libya. The deal was an attempt to gain greater legal standing to challenge the maritime borders Greece had established with Cyprus and Egypt, upon which their eastern Mediterranean natural gas development plans depend. The Ankara-Tripoli maritime boundary agreement was accompanied by a military cooperation pact providing the GNA a security guarantee against the efforts of General Khalifa Haftar's forces, backed by France and Egypt, to topple the Tripoli-based government. The GNA formally activated its military pact with Ankara in December, linking the already tense maritime stand-off in the Eastern Mediterranean to the Libyan civil war.[106]

In summary, Turkey's decisive role in shaping Libya's future began with signing a Memorandum of Understanding (MoU) at the end of November 2019. The MoU declared Turkey and Libya as maritime neighbours, a controversial move with regard to international law. Relying on that document, Turkey's overt intervention in the conflict in the first half of 2020 turned the tide of the Libyan civil war.

INTERCONNECTION

Turkey emerged as a power to reckon with in the North Africa–East Mediterranean geopolitics, concurrently and overtly challenging France, Russia, Egypt, UAE, Greece, and Cyprus, and indirectly Israel and Saudi Arabia.

The East-Med Gas Forum, which formally brought together Greece, Egypt, Israel, Cyprus, Jordan, and the Palestine Administration, was established as an international body on 16 January 2020, less than two months after Turkey and Libya signed the MoU. France joined in 2021, and the European Union, UAE, and United States have permanent observer status. The EMGF does not

---

[105] Sinem Adar, Hürcan Aslı Aksoy, Salim Çevik, Daria Isachenko, and Moritz Rau, "Visualizing Turkey's Foreign Policy Activism", *SWP-CATS*, 17 December 2020. https://www.cats-network.eu/topics/visualizing-turkeys-foreign-policy-activism/

[106] Michaël Tanchum, "How Did the Eastern Mediterranean Become the Eye of a Geopolitical Storm?", *Foreign Policy*, August 18, 2020. https://foreignpolicy.com/2020/08/18/eastern-mediterranean-greece-turkey-warship-geopolitical-showdown/

recognize the legitimacy of the Turkish-Libyan MoU that claimed the EEZs of each respectively. In that sense, the EMGF was more than merely continuing the informal forum among Greece, Cyprus, Egypt, and Israel whereby major companies such as Total, Eni, and Exxon had signed exploration and production agreements concerning gas with those governments. It was a geopolitical alignment against Turkey that firmly positioned itself in Libya and assumed gunboat diplomacy in the Eastern Mediterranean.

Steven Cook was astute on the overriding geopolitical dimension of the developments in Northern Africa and the Eastern Mediterranean:

Ankara's moves in Libya are actually countermoves to the burgeoning ties among Greece, Egypt, Cyprus, and Israel. Officially, there is no security component to what is intended to be a consortium to exploit gas deposits in the Eastern Mediterranean, but given each of these countries' strained – at best – relations with Turkey, it is hard not to see in these ties what international relations scholars call "bandwagoning." In addition, when the Turks looked at the combination of these growing ties, which have American support, and the interlocking nature of Greek, Egyptian, Cypriot, and Israeli exclusive economic zones, they could reasonably conclude that their freedom of navigation in the area could be choked off.[107]

In addition to its priceless usefulness for Turkey's geopolitical ambitions, Libya is also a place where Turkey can challenge its two most ardent regional adversaries – Egypt and the UAE. Turkey is considered a leading supporter of the Muslim Brotherhood. The Muslim Brotherhood members in exile set up a parliament in Istanbul, which has become a sanctuary for the Egyptian opposition. Turkey and Egypt are in covert competition claiming the leadership of Sunni Islam. The UAE, as Egypt's formidable ally and occasionally acting on behalf of Saudi Arabia, has been at odds with Turkey which forged a strong financial and military relationship with Qatar in the Gulf. Turkey's military base in Qatar is a deterrent not only for Iran but for the Arab monarchies – above all, the UAE – in the Gulf.

Libya turned out to be the nexus for the geopolitical game pulling in the United Arab Emirates and Egypt, pitting them against Turkey.

Libya, in this sense, represents an extraordinary possibility for Abu Dhabi to see its medium-power aims realized, as well as for Cairo to expand its area of influence westward. In fact, Libya's eastern, coastal region of Cyrenaica has always been a land of trade and deep tribal ties with Egypt. Lately, Cairo has aimed to play a central role in crisis scenarios in the

---

[107] Steven A. Cook, "Erdogan Is Libya's Man Without a Plan", *Foreign Policy*, July 9, 2020. https://foreignpolicy.com/2020/07/09/erdogan-is-libyas-man-without-a-plan/

broader Mediterranean, where the problems of the Palestinians intersect with those of the Syrians and Libyans, and where the energy resources are enormous interests that go well beyond the Mediterranean basin.[108]

The flow of history ever since civil war erupted in Libya in 2011, and massive gas fields were discovered in the Egyptian maritime territory in 2015, means that Libyan and the Eastern Mediterranean developments have become enchained. The Eastern Mediterranean suddenly proved to have marketable volumes of natural gas, bringing in Italian and French energy majors Eni and Total, followed by the American global giant Exxon. Egyptian, Israeli, Greek-Cypriot, and Greek interests converged to the detriment of Turkey.

Turkey's activism in Libya was the harbinger of the tensions that rose in 2020. The volatility in the Eastern Mediterranean and its connection with Turkey's activism in Libya was discernible even in 2019. In a salient report, the Eastern Mediterranean was described as a geopolitical zone sitting on a dormant volcano:

The strident objections voiced recently by Greece and Egypt to the deals signed between Turkey and the UN-backed Libyan government is but the latest example of a series of incidents that point to rising tensions in the Eastern Mediterranean... In the current scheme of things, the Eastern Mediterranean is sitting atop a dormant volcano. Developments in other hot spots in the Middle East, such as the carnage in Syria, the conflict and humanitarian crisis in Yemen, the Saudi-Iranian standoff in the Gulf and the civil war in Libya, have diverted the attention away from a latent yet perilous conflict. If triggered, such a conflict could have tremendous ramifications for countries in North Africa, West Asia and Southern Europe as well as for the stability of shipping transportation and energy markets worldwide.

Eastern Mediterranean stability is predominantly undermined by Turkey's pursuit of an aggressive foreign policy in the region. Evident in both fiery rhetoric and coercive diplomacy, this policy seems to reflect its legal weakness and military might. Turkey's legal posture is not congruent with the tenets of international law, and the UN Convention on the Law of the Sea (to which it is not a signatory). Instead, the Turkish government provides a novel interpretation of maritime boundaries, arguing that ownership of offshore waters should be governed by the continental shelf and that the exclusive economic zone (EEZ) of an island, such as Cyprus, is limited to only twelve nautical miles of territorial waters. Further, while Cyprus has bolstered its legal posture by signing maritime border agreements with Egypt, Lebanon and Israel, in

---

108 Federica Saini Fasanotti, "Order from Chaos: The New Great Dangerous Game in the Eastern Mediterranean", *Brookings Institute*, August 28, 2020. https://www.brookings.edu/blog/order-from-chaos/2020/08/28/the-new-great-dangerous-game-in-the-eastern-mediterranean

2003, 2007 and 2010, respectively, Turkey reached no such agreements with its Mediterranean neighbors.

Politically, Turkey's motives are numerous. Having the longest shoreline in the Eastern Mediterranean, it considers the sea to be vital for both its internal security and its power projection plans in the entire Middle East. However, facing a group of allied adversaries, especially the fledgling Greek-Egyptian-Cypriot partnership, it feels marginalized and threatened.[109]

In addition, Turkey's pipeline infrastructure to Europe and its plans to become a regional energy hub seemed to be undermined by its exclusion from the Eastern Mediterranean grouping of natural gas-producing countries.

However, there is disputing informed analysis concerning Turkey's real motivations to do with its gas demand. Accordingly, drilling for the discovery of gas resources should not explain Turkey's Eastern Mediterranean policy.

In the complex chessboard of the Eastern Mediterranean, energy undoubtedly plays a leading strategic role, which however tends to be misrepresented. The huge natural gas resources present in the region are in fact often described as one of the triggering causes of the conflict between Turkey and the other coastal countries… This is not the case… It is necessary to shed light is that energy interests do not explain the Turkish actions of destabilization in the eastern Mediterranean. Finding new gas fields shouldn't be a priority for Turkey and probably isn't. Gas is therefore not the bone of contention, but the victim of a geopolitical instability whose roots must be sought elsewhere.[110]

Irrespective of Turkey's genuine motives in the Eastern Mediterranean, France entered into the fray in 2018 through its energy giant Total, the EU's third-largest company by revenue, partnered in all of the firm's gas development operations in Cyprus. Besides its very close relations with Egypt, which went so far as to decorate the dictatorial head of the military regime General Sisi with its highest French order of merit, *Legion d'Honneur*, France projected its influence on the Gulf through its exclusive relationship with the UAE. In addition, it emerged as the primary sponsor of Greece within the EU. Fundamentally, France placed itself at the centre of the Eastern Mediterranean maelstrom as the leading contender against Turkey.

---

[109] Nael Shama, "The Geopolitics of a Latent International Conflict in Eastern Mediterranean", *Aljazeera Centre for Studies*, December 23, 2019. https://studies.aljazeera.net/en/reports/2019/12/geopolitics-latent-international-conflict-eastern-mediterranean-191223074025635.html

[110] Luca Franza, "EU-Turkey 5 Years Later: The Relaunch of Cooperation Passes through Energy", *Istituto Affari Internazionali*, March 18, 2021. https://www.affarinternazionali.it/2021/03/ue-turchia-5-anni-dopo-dallenergia-passa-il-rilancio-della-cooperazione/

The Eastern Mediterranean alignment – including France, Greece, Cyprus, and Egypt, with Israel taking part tacitly and "the import from the Gulf", the UAE, as an auxiliary – led Turkey's confrontational posture. Sending exploration and drilling vessels into Cypriot waters under naval escort, it engaged in gunboat diplomacy.

Turkey refuses to recognize Cyprus's maritime boundaries, raising the argument that the Cyprus issue remains unresolved, disregarding the existence of the Turkish Republic of Northern Cyprus extending over the northern half of the island. For Turkey, the maritime boundaries of Cyprus were drawn illegally at Turkey's expense.

TURKEY AND GREECE: DISPUTE ON MARITIME DELIMITATION AND EEZ'S

From Turkey's viewpoint, not only are the maritime boundaries of Cyprus unacceptable but also, as a whole, the Eastern Mediterranean's de facto maritime boundaries. Turkey sees the Eastern Mediterranean de facto maritime boundaries as unjust and even illegal: in violation of the equity principle as stipulated in the UNCLOS (United Nations Convention on the Law of the Sea), denying Turkey its rightful maritime territory.

Thus, the arrangements for offshore natural gas exploration depending on these de facto boundaries have no legitimacy from the Turkish legal viewpoint. Paradoxically, according to the UNCLOS, which was concluded in 1982 and came into force in 1994, Turkey has a point about the demarcations of the Eastern Mediterranean's maritime boundaries being unfair.

Even though, having the longest coastline, being entitled to a larger maritime zone per the principle of equity and international case law under the UN Convention on the Law of the Sea, Turkey nevertheless refrained from signing. The main reason is that the ambiguity of some articles of the Convention, if interpreted by Greece literally, could cause Turkey to lose its rights irretrievably.

According to Article 121 of the UN Convention on the Law of the Sea, islands generate an EEZ like any other land territory. The Aegean Sea, a subdivision of the Mediterranean that separates Turkey's mainland and Greece, has a peculiarity: it has around 200 inhabited Greek islands. Some of these are close to the Turkish coast, less than 12 miles, and hundreds of miles away from the Greek mainland.

The differences between Turkey and Greece on maritime issues are deftly outlined by an expert on maritime conflicts and the law of the seas in the following passage:

In the Eastern Mediterranean, Turkey and Greece both have excessive and maximalist maritime claims over their EEZs. The massive differences between these claims mainly emanate from different interpretations of the role played by islands in maritime delimitation. Greece claims to accord full effect to these islands and Cyprus, while Turkey attempts to restrict them with a territorial sea zone, but nothing more. On the one hand, if these islands are given the same effect as given to coastal mainland, which Greece claims for, the result of the delimitation would be devastating for Turkey and it would lose almost two thirds of its claimed maritime area. A contrary interpretation, on the other hand, would cut Greece's claimed maritime zone almost into half.[111]

The Turkey-Libya Memorandum of Understanding became the tangible result of that "contrary interpretation". Michaël Tanchum offers an elaboration on this matter:

Turkey's method for drawing the Ankara-Tripoli map is specious. Most egregiously, the map ignores the presence of Crete, which is 3,219 square miles and between these coasts. UNCLOS Article 121, an article dealing with the legal status of islands, affirms that island coastlines generate continental shelves and EEZs the same as any coastal land formation, except those that "cannot sustain human habitation or economic life of their own." Crete, with a population of almost 650,000 (nearly the same as Athens), would unquestionably generate an EEZ.[112]

Almost nine months after the Turkey-Libya agreement, on August 6, 2020, the signing of a similar maritime delimitation agreement between Greece and Egypt added to the Eastern Mediterranean controversies. The Turkish-Libyan and the Greek-Egyptian exclusive economic zones overlap and lay the ground for a dangerous confrontation among the main players in the Eastern Mediterranean geopolitics.

Developments in the region created fissures in NATO and exposed the European Union's weaknesses in terms of intervening effectively on behalf of its members Greece and Cyprus. French President Emmanuel Macron did not conceal his frustration at NATO's reluctance to stand in Turkey's way and

---

[111] Yunus Emre Açıkgönül, "Turkey's East Med Policy: Victory at Home, Isolation Abroad", *Heinrich Böll Stiftung*, September 12, 2020. https://tr.boell.org/en/2020/09/12/turkeys-east-med-policy-victory-home-isolation-abroad

[112] Tanchum, "How Did the Eastern Mediterranean Become the Eye of a Geopolitical Storm", *op. cit.*

accused the Alliance of "brain death".

Territorial disputes in the Eastern Mediterranean
Maritime boundaries and energy competition between Turkey, Greece, and Cyprus

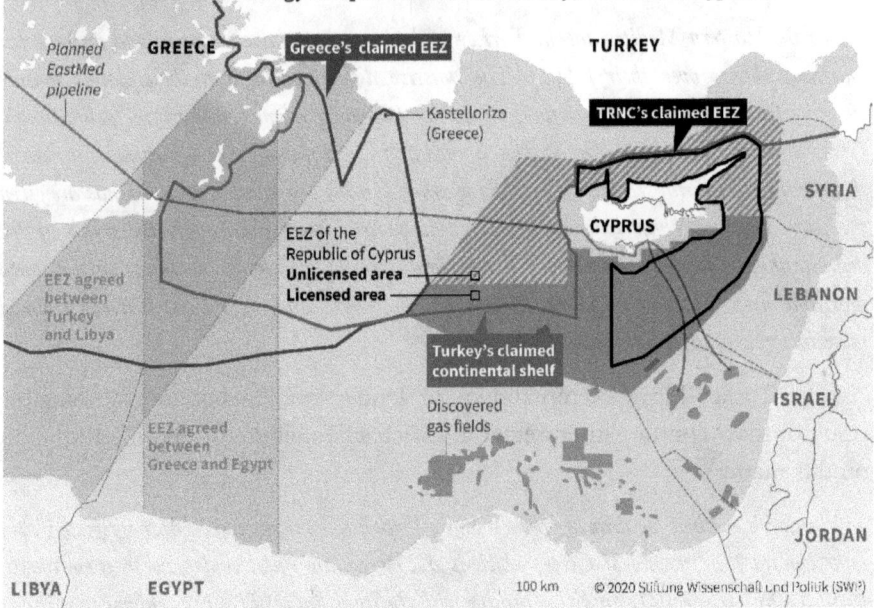

GREECE Greece's claimed EEZ TURKEY

Planned
EastMed
pipeline

Kastellorizo
(Greece)

TRNC's claimed EEZ

SYRIA

CYPRUS

EEZ of the
Republic of Cyprus
Unlicensed area
Licensed area

LEBANON

EEZ agreed
between
Turkey
and Libya

Turkey's claimed
continental shelf

ISRAEL

Discovered
gas fields

EEZ agreed
between
Greece and Egypt

JORDAN

100 km   © 2020 Stiftung Wissenschaft und Politik (SWP)

LIBYA   EGYPT

Reprint: Centre for Applied Turkey Studies (CATS), Visualizing Turkey's Foreign Policy Activism, December 16, 2020, https://www.cats-network.eu/topics/visualizing-turkeys-foreign-policy-activism/

GREEK RESENTMENT, GERMAN "APPEASEMENT"

A similar frustration on the Greek side pushed Athens, which has been in the grip of acute economic problems, into an arms race. The frustration likely led to self-deception, as the following argument can demonstrate:

There is widespread disappointment because most European governments are not willing to confront Erdogan's neo-Ottoman ambitions and his brinkmanship strategy in the region. The Greek government has repeatedly called for the imposition of sanctions against Turkey… In addition, Athens has formulated a regional balancing strategy by collaborating with key neighbouring countries like Israel and Egypt. Both Jerusalem and Cairo have shared Greek concerns about Turkish assertiveness in the Eastern Mediterranean. Ankara's support for Hamas and the Muslim Brotherhood has infuriated Israel and Egypt, respectively. Moreover, the new Greek government has reached out to pro-Western Arab countries, such as Saudi

Arabia and the United Arab Emirates, that have their own problems with Turkey's neo-Islamist leadership.

In this context, Athens is constructing a new geopolitical identity as a bulwark of the West in the Eastern Mediterranean…Thus, Greece can become a security provider that will protect Western interests in a perennially volatile region.[113]

The unpleasant fact for Greece and its backers, and above all for France, was that Turkey's gunboat diplomacy and brinkmanship policy paid off in the Eastern Mediterranean.

Tanchum conceded the facts, and illustrated the reasons:

Despite backing Greece, neither Egypt nor Israel can afford to be drawn into a war with Turkey in the Eastern Mediterranean. The EU has expressed its unequivocal support for members Greece and Cyprus, but the bloc is divided on how to handle the current crisis. The six Mediterranean EU countries are evenly split. Greece, Cyprus, and France advocate strong action against Turkey while Italy, Malta, and Spain – which all share significant commercial interests with Turkey in the central and western Mediterranean – have refrained.[114]

More importantly, Turkey has the strongest nation of the EU on board: Germany. Germany under Angela Merkel, despite measured and occasional critical salvos fired for the sake of showing solidarity with France and other EU members, which are apprehensive about Turkey, always stood against seriously punishing Erdoğan for his policies.

Germany's tacit sponsorship – which for some equates to appeasement of Erdoğan's belligerency – of Turkey caused resentment in Greece more than anywhere else. Greek criticism was also directed against the EU for its inconsistency regarding the Eastern Mediterranean issues. Distrust about the change in German outlook was expressed, citing various reasons for Berlin's dependence on Erdoğan's complacency.

The EU's strategic thinking on Turkey is inconsistent. Greece and Cyprus, backed by France, spent the past few weeks pushing for new and wider sanctions to show that a threat to the sovereignty of one EU member state will trigger the intervention of the entire bloc. Germany, however, worries that a new raft of sanctions would exacerbate tensions with Mr. Erdogan, who in Chancellor Angela Merkel's eyes has played a helpful role in limiting migration into

---

[113] Emmanuel Karagiannis, "The Silent Rise of Greece as a Mediterranean Power", *RUSI*, November 16, 2020. https://rusi.org/commentary/silent-rise-greece-mediterranean-power
[114] Tanchum, *op. cit.*

Europe. Berlin's stance is also influenced by the large Turkish-speaking minority in Germany and by the close economic ties between the two countries.[115]

Similar views were underlined in February 2021, much later than the dangerous escalation in the Eastern Mediterranean defused in the summer of 2020.

Germany sees Turkey as belonging to its traditional sphere of influence. It deems that the two countries share a large number of key interests. The way in which the mass influx of refugees/migrants destabilized Germany has left a mark on Chancellor Angela Merkel and her aides. Germany gets frustrated with the French when they push things with Ankara.

It does not understand why Greece has to spend so much on defense, particularly on non-German systems, as it considers Greece a small, bankrupt country. It would like Athens to accept a comprehensive compromise settlement in the Aegean and the Eastern Mediterranean without going into much detail about which side is right. It is a square, inflexible logic.

And it will not change until the end of Merkel's tenure, and certainly not in view of elections where the Turkish minority has a role to play in the final outcome.[116]

The Foreign Minister of Greece, Nikos Dendias, was explicit in sounding out the Greek frustration about Germany's appeasement of Turkey. Accusing Germany of failing to live up its leadership role in the EU by rejecting pleas from Athens to impose an arms embargo on Turkey, he underscored *"Germany's reluctance to use the enormous power of its economy to set a clear example to countries that they must obey international law"*. Dendias was straightforward in highlighting how German economic interests are served by arms sales to Turkey. He said, *"I understand the financial issue, but I am sure Germany also understands the huge contradiction of providing offensive weapons to a country that threatens the peace and stability of two EU countries"*, and noted that the deal for the submarines dates back to 2009 when the Turkish government and its foreign policy were very different.

Greece specifically called on Germany not to allow the delivery of six Type 214 submarines ordered by Turkey. Athens argued the vessels would upset the balance of power in the Eastern Mediterranean.

With a measure of disbelief that Germany and the EU could play a positive role in redressing the balance of power in the Eastern Mediterranean, Dendias

---

[115] Yannis Palaiologos, "Europe Fails to Contain Turkey", *Wall Street Journal*, September 30, 2020. https://www.wsj.com/articles/europe-fails-to-contain-turkey-11601507708
[116] Alexis Papachellas, "From Bismarck to Merkel", *Kathimerini*, February 7, 2021. https://www.ekathimerini.com/opinion/262093/from-bismarck-to-merkel/

emphasized the military comeback of America to the regional strategic equation: *"I believe that the region needs the presence of the United States and particularly its military presence, in a way that would offset the lack of European military presence in the region."*[117]

The change of guard in the Turkish half of Cyprus in October 2020, and its radical departure from Turkey's traditional Cyprus policy, further exacerbate the complexity of Eastern Mediterranean issues. The presidential elections held in October 2020 in the breakaway Turkish Republic of Northern Cyprus, which saw a heavy-handed interference by Erdoğan, ended with the election of Erdoğan loyalist Ersin Tatar by 51 percent of the vote, replacing the incumbent Mustafa Akıncı. Akıncı was for a reunified, federal Cyprus. In February 2021, Erdoğan, in response to the Greek Prime Minister Kyriakos Mitsotakis, bluntly declared the radical change in Turkey's Cyprus policy. He stated that a two-state solution is the only way forward, and said, *"Whether you accept it or not, there can no longer be such a thing as a federation… That business is finished now"*.

Implying that he intends to walk away from the exploratory talks[118] underway with Greece, he addressed the Greek prime minister in a threatening tone, alluding to the idiom "crazy Turks", a self-congratulatory remark fancied by Turkish nationalists:

"Mitsotakis challenged me. How can we sit down with you now? Know your limits first. If you really seek peace, don't challenge me. Know your limits. If you don't know your limits, it means you've kicked the (negotiation) table. We cannot sit with you at the table if you carry on like this. To whom you trust? Those you trust are gone. You (Greece) will not get any help from anyone. Now, you will get to know the "Crazy Turks!"[119]

An op-ed piece in the influential Greek daily *Kathimerini* commented:

Recep Tayyip Erdogan's habit of lashing out at foreign leaders, including Greek ones of course, is hard to understand sometimes; the Turkish president obviously feels that he is invincible and has the right to insult and threaten whomever he chooses… Drunk on the notion

[117] Nektaria Stamouli, "Greece Blasts Berlin for Shunning Plea for Turkey Arms Embargo", *Politico*, November 28, 2020. https://www.politico.eu/article/greece-blasts-berlin-for-shunning-plea-for-turkey-arms-embargo/
[118] Exploratory talks have been an exercise that brought together Greek and Turkish officials to decide how negotiations about the bilateral disputes on the Aegean, ranging from maritime delimitation to the continental shelf, can be conducted. They started in 2002 and after 60 rounds which did not yield any results, were interrupted in 2016. Encouraged by the EU to defuse the tensions in the Eastern Mediterranean, the 61st round began in January 2021. The Turkish side was interested in the undertaking to impress the European Commission and to prevent the possible sanctions against Turkey that could be brought into force at the EU summit in March 2021.
[119] https://www.yenisafak.com/gundem/cumhurbaskani-erdogandan-micotakise-tepki-cilgin-turkleri-iyi-tani yacaksin-3598463; https://tr.sputniknews.com/turkiye/202102101043775932-erdogandan-micotakise-cilgin -turkleri-iyi-taniyacaksin/

of a grand Turkey that is not limited to its present borders, the leadership in Ankara feels justified in his criticism of Greek officials for visiting Greek islands. Referring to Mitsotakis' recent visit to islands in the eastern Aegean, Erdogan "warned" that no one will help Greece and sent a message to the Greek prime minister that he'll get to know the "crazy Turks" well.[120]

REASONABLE PROPOSITIONS FOR MARITIME DELIMITATION

From 2020 to 2021 and perhaps even in its aftermath, the Turkish-Greek disputes in the Aegean look far from being resolved, therefore unlikely to restore the Eastern Mediterranean's status quo ante. Turkey's arguably best maritime delimitation expert, Yunus Emre Açıkgönül, a former diplomat who is in exile following the purges in the wake of the 2016 coup attempt, observed the situation realistically:

In light of the current direction of developments, the resolution of the Turkey-Greece maritime dispute in the Eastern Mediterranean in the near future is unlikely. Both parties have extreme and excessive claims against each other and are not making meaningful efforts to resolve the issue amicably nor through bilateral diplomacy. Particularly the neo-nationalist and adventurous Turkish maritime concept of "Mavi Vatan-Blue Homeland", which involves quite ambitious claims, does not bring further optimism to a settlement of the conflict.[121]

The following map illustrates the maritime delimitation and the EEZs for Turkey and Greece, presumably according to the international law proposed by Açıkgönül, former Turkish diplomat and an expert on the law of the seas. The red-dotted line indicates the maximalist Greek position depriving Turkey of having a reasonable and legitimate EEZ. The green-dotted line reflects Turkey's maximalist position denying EEZs to the large inhabited Greek islands like Rhodes and Greece. The blue-dotted line is what Açıkgönül claims is equitable and in conformity with the principles of international law.

---

[120] Tom Ellis, "Erdogan Threatens Mitsotakis", op-ed, *Kathimerini*, February 11, 2021. https://www.ekathimerini.com/opinion/262241/erdogan-threatens-mitsotakis/
[121] Açıkgönül, "Turkey's East Med Policy", *op. cit.*

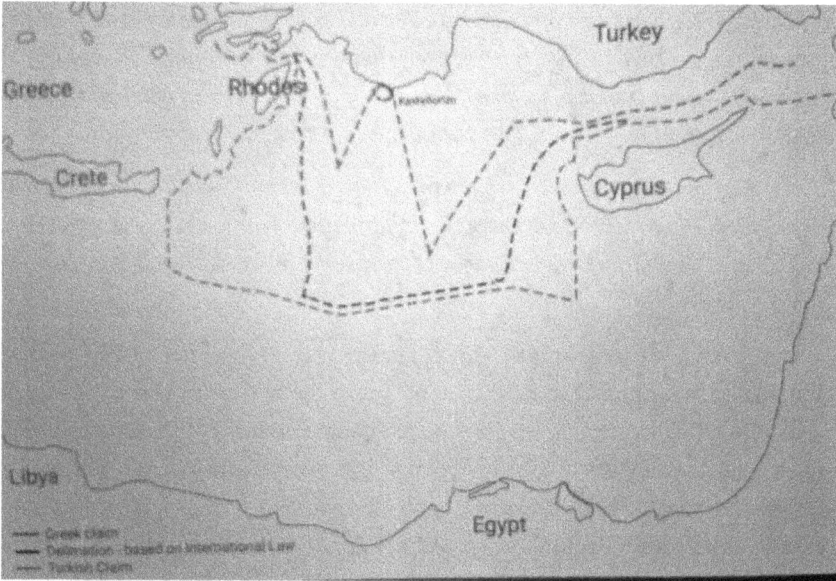

Açıkgönül has the recipe for settlement of the Turkish maritime disputes that have a long and complicated historical and legal background in the Aegean and Eastern Mediterranean seas. The Aegean Sea, especially, is a *sui generis* case that provides substantial legal and legitimate grounds for the Turkish position. If the equitable principles of international law of the sea and the relevant court decisions can be observed with goodwill and in the spirit of good neighbourliness, a settlement between Turkey and Greece is not beyond reach. In a very brilliant treatise, Açıkgönül wrote:

> *Due to the particularities of its unique geography, there is no other coastal state that has been so grossly and negatively impacted by the evolution of international law of the sea as Turkey. The Aegean Sea is the only maritime area where thousands of islands belong to one state in a semi-closed narrow sea, encroaching upon a 1,000-km long coastline of another state. Some of these islands are only a few km from the Turkish shoreline…*

> *Greece and Turkey freely settled their land borders with the Treaty of Lausanne and sustained a maritime balance. No authority or third party has the right to dictate otherwise. Turkey has indeed been trying to argue this case, but it has been going about it incorrectly. Instead of resting on these solid legal principles, it declared that Greece's TS expansion would be a casus belli, questioned the sovereignty of Greek islands, and brought about maximalist claims that lack legal ground, including those enclosed in the Turkey-Libya maritime agreement…*

If the parties commence international adjudication for the delimitation of EEZs in the Aegean Sea, courts would apply equitable principles. The generosity that Article 121 of UNCLOS grants to islands would not prevail, and the vast majority of Greek islands in the Aegean Sea would be deemed to have partial to no effect on the Anatolian coast.

Having said that, even were such a favourable judgment to be passed, the vast majority of the maritime area would still fall under Greek jurisdiction. Turkey should not expect to control half of the Aegean Sea in any scenario. At the end of the day, thousands of Aegean islands belong to Greece.[122]

To reach a settlement both sides, Turkey and Greece, need to lay aside their maximalist positions. Turkey should abandon the zero-sum-game approach vis-à-vis Greece in its dealings on the Aegean and Eastern Mediterranean disputes. With a belligerent discourse, wrong policy formulations, and unconvincing arguments wrapped in fraudulent patriotic rhetoric, Turkey has undermined its strong legal and legitimate position against Greece. Pseudo-patriotism developed by an expansionist maritime doctrine, Blue Homeland, well serves Turkey's neo-Ottomanist moment but, for domestic political purposes, pushes back any possibility of a peaceful settlement of maritime disputes concerning the East Mediterranean.

BLUE HOMELAND: TURKISH MARITIME CLAIMS LARGER THAN SWEDEN

The concept that evolved to be a doctrine, Blue Homeland (Mavi Vatan in Turkish), began to be circulated following the Turkey-Libya MoU at the end of 2012. Rear Admiral Cihat Yaycı, who was the chief of staff of the Navy at the time of the signing, is hailed as the mastermind of the Turkey-Libya deal. He rested the legitimacy of the MoU on the map he presented showing Turkey's maritime zone extending to Libya's shores.

Yaycı labelled his map as the "Blue Homeland". The concept was originated in 2006 by Rear Admiral Cem Gürdeniz, who was superior to Yaycı at the time, in reaction to the Seville Map. The Seville Map refers to EU-commissioned research conducted by the two marine geography experts at the University of Sevilla, Juan Luis Suarez de Vivero and Juan Carlos Rodriguez Mateos, in the year 2006, following the EU enlargement. The map drawn by the Spanish

---

[122] Yunus Emre Açıkgönül, "Untold Legal Principles Favoring Turkey in Aegean Maritime Disputes", *FeniksPolitik*, February 26, 2021. https://fenikspolitik.org/2021/02/26/untold-legal-principles-favouring-turkey-in-aegean-maritime-disputes/

scholars as part of their research was not certified as an official EU document, but was nonetheless widely seen by the Turkish nationalist milieu as an EU plot against Turkey. It reflected the literal interpretation of Article 121 of the UNCLOS, which stipulates that islands generate an EEZ like any other land territory. In drawing the Seville Map, the Spanish scholars did not consider the peculiarities of the Aegean. Consequently, their study reinforced the Greek and (Greek) Cypriot claims. More than the resentment it caused, especially among Turkish nationalist flag officers in the Navy, it served as a source of inspiration for the subsequent Turkish Blue Homeland map.

Prepared by Admiral Yaycı, the Blue Homeland map became a referent for the legitimacy of the deal with Libya that he masterminded. The map illustrates the claimed maritime zones, thus the EEZ of Turkey, and comprises 462,000 square kilometres, an area larger than the entire land of Sweden, the biggest country of Scandinavia with 435,000 square kilometres of territory.

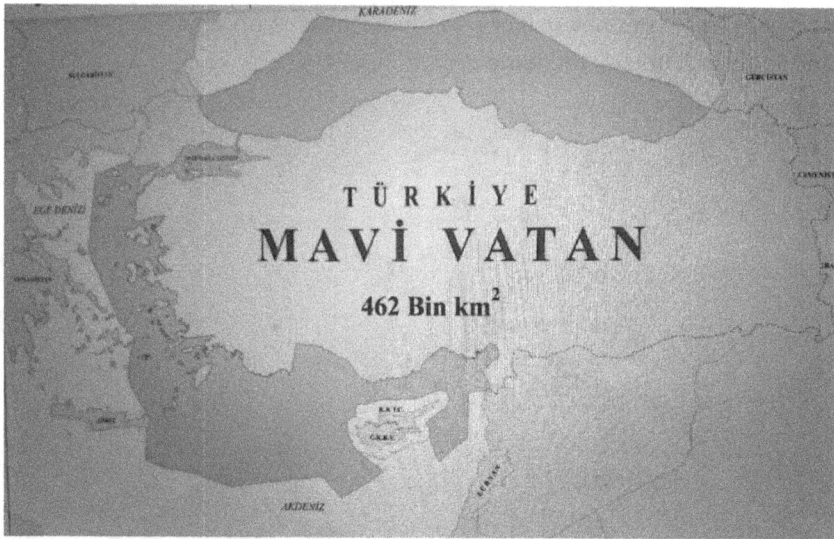

https://www.savunmasanayi.org/doc-dr-cihat-yaycinin-cizdigi-mavi-vatan-haritasi/
(Defense Industries website, the Blue Homeland map drawn by Cihat Yaycı)

The proponents of the Blue Homeland doctrine are obsessed with Greece and Cyprus. For them, Greece is a tool used by the West (the United States and Europe) against Turkey's legitimate aspirations in the Aegean and the Eastern Mediterranean.

Blaming Greece is core to Yaycı's political and strategic thinking. In his estimation, Greek behavior in the Aegean and the Mediterranean constitutes a grave challenge to Turkey's integrity and ambitions. He has characterized Greece as a "revisionist" state, one unswervingly committed to seizing and holding territory rightly belonging to Turkey.

To combat what he characterizes as Greece's assertiveness, *"Yaycı has gone so far as to abandon using the term Aegean (Ege in Turkish and Aigaio in Greek) for a Turkicized phrase, the Islands Sea (Adalar Denizi)".*[123]

In reference to the Turkey-Libya MoU and introducing Cihat Yaycı as the *"architect of the illegal Erdogan-Sarraj agreement"*, the UAE-funded Libyan newspaper *Al Marsad* reminded readers that Yaycı had written a *"controversial book,* Libya Is a Neighbor of Turkey, *in which he stated that Libya has a maritime border with Turkey in the Mediterranean Sea based on Turkey's maritime jurisdiction areas which are defined according to a unilateral interpretation of Article No. 74 of the UNCLOS"*. The Libyan paper, citing the Israeli media, asserted that relying on Yaycı's arguments, Israel like Libya is also Turkey's maritime neighbour. Turkey is trying to reach out to conclude a maritime delimitation agreement with Israel as well. The Libyan newspaper published a map of how Yaycı envisaged Libya and Israel as Turkey's maritime neighbours.[124]

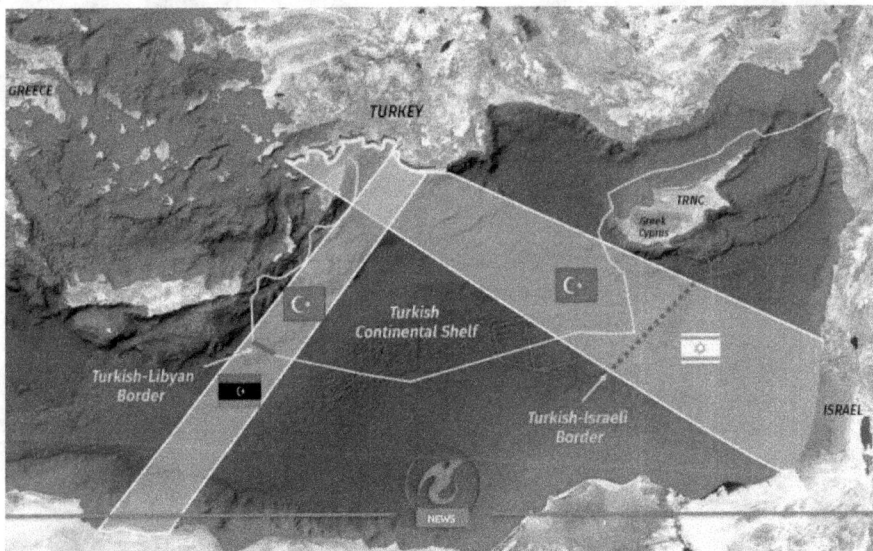

Libyan weekly Al Marsad illustrating the EEZs according to the Turkey-Libya MoU and suggested by the ideologues of the Blue Homeland to Israel.

---

[123] Ryan Gingeras, "What Can a Retired Sailor Teach Us About Turkey", *War on the Rocks*, October 21, 2020.
[124] *Al Marsad*, "Turkey Makes Maritime EEZ to Israel as Extension of the Border Drawn with Sarraj for Libya", December 7, 2020.

To bypass Greek and Cypriot opposition, he advocates signing bilateral economic zone agreements, with Egypt, Lebanon, Israel, and the Palestinian Authority. Such agreements, he argues, would appeal directly to the self-interest of each of these states. In disregarding the claims of Greece and Cyprus, each signatory would enjoy larger chunks of the seafloor. To date, however, no one within the Turkish government has endorsed such a plan. Given Ankara's poor relations with Egypt and Israel, as well as signs the two states have grown closer to Greece in recent months, the likelihood of Turkey signing multiple economic zone agreements with its Mediterranean neighbors appears slim.[125]

The Eastern Mediterranean section of the Blue Homeland drawn by Cihat Yaycı bypassing the EEZs of Greece and Cyprus, claiming that Turkey's EEZ, besides Israel, neighbours with Syria (Suriye), Lebanon (Lübnan), and Palestine (Filistin) EEZs. The Palestinian EEZ is presumed to stretch from Gaza. The map was published by Bahcesehir University Maritime and Global Strategies Center chaired by Yaycı on its social media account, @BAUDEGS, on March 6, 2021.

Yaycı was demoted in 2020 and resigned from the Navy. Nevertheless, he left his map of the 462,000 square kilometre Blue Homeland as the legacy of ultra-nationalist-Eurasianist allies of neo-Ottomanist Erdoğan, who endorsed it and made it a point of reference.

---

[125] Gingeras, "What Can a Retired Sailor Teach Us About Turkey", *op. cit.*

Yaycı's demotion did not spell the end of the Blue Homeland concept. In 2020, the dangerous escalation between Turkey and Greece and its supporters in the Eastern Mediterranean gained priority in Turkey's foreign policy agenda. The Blue Homeland was promoted to become a doctrine. The inventor of the Blue Homeland, former Rear Adm. Cem Gürdeniz, came to the fore alongside a group of his colleagues, all former flag officers of the Navy. During the summer of 2020 Gürdeniz, through his presence in the Turkish public media, his writings, and frequent television appearances, suggested the ascendancy of a more aggressive and antagonistic strain of thought within Turkish security circles, dominating the public debate in advocating the Blue Homeland doctrine.

Ryan Gingeras, the brilliant historian of the late Ottoman period and an expert on modern Turkey, described Cem Gürdeniz *"as an adherent of Turkey's nationalist left appears to represent a growing contingent of influential figures, including several former flag officers"*. Gingeras qualified Gürdeniz as *"a presumptive visionary when it comes to matters of foreign policy"*. He went further in portraying former Rear Adm. Gürdeniz as *"the most glaring exception to the trend of several individuals who have yet to offer a comprehensive strategic vision for the country's future"* after Davutoğlu's marginalization.[126]

Cem Gürdeniz was arrested in 2011 along with many other senior officers accused of belonging to putschist networks in the military. Although sentenced to 18 years, he was released in 2015 under the Faustian pact that Erdoğan made with those imprisoned officers whose support he thought was necessary to win the power struggle against his erstwhile ally, Fethullah Gülen.

Erdoğan's alliance with the Eurasianist faction within the Turkish military – among whom Gürdeniz stood out as the faction's foremost ideologist and ultra-nationalist – signified the neo-nationalist power structure that transformed Turkey. Under such a power configuration, Turkey turned into an autocracy and followed a militarized foreign policy. Gürdeniz, in his frequent television interviews during 2020, was candid in espousing authoritarian rule in Turkey on the premise that if Turkey were a democracy with the standards of the West, the United States and its European allies would not allow Turkey's gunboat diplomacy in the Eastern Mediterranean.

Cem Gürdeniz blamed what he termed *"the imperialist powers of the West"* for his and fellow officers' arrest in 2011, following his creation of the concept of a

---

[126] Ryan Gingeras, "Blue Homeland: The Heated Politics Behind Turkey's New Maritime Strategy", *War on the Rocks*, June 2, 2020.

Blue Homeland, which stood up against the designs of those imperialist powers against Turkey. Gürdeniz explained the reason for their arrest as *"a new warning from the European Union and the United States to Turkey; not to push too hard in the Aegean Sea and the Mediterranean"*.

In a long exclusive interview he gave to a French publication on geopolitics, he said:

> They [the United States and the European Union] believed that beheading Turkish admirals and naval officers would persuade Turkey to surrender in defense of its maritime rights, thus pushing Turkey into Anatolia and cutting it off from the Mediterranean geopolitics, from Mediterranean civilization. The message was clear: stay where you are and don't move forward.[127]

In the numerous TV talks he delivered throughout the year 2020, former Rear Adm. Cem Gürdeniz usually emphasized that the imperialist powers of the past dared to partition the Ottoman Empire following World War I by imposing the Sèvres Treaty (1920) because the latter was not a maritime power. In the Gürdeniz narrative, the Western imperialist powers, by manipulating Greece, are pursuing the same objective: to confine Turkey to Anatolia and deprive it of access to high seas in order to suffocate it. Gürdeniz referred to these powers as the Atlantic framework or Atlantic front, implying NATO.

> The Greeks want more of the Aegean Sea; they want more of the Mediterranean Sea… they refuse Turkey to reach international waters, to reach oceans… We are talking here about half of the Mediterranean, the eastern Mediterranean. And the Greeks, along with the European Union and the United States, tell us that we can only have 40,000 square-kilometers in the Mediterranean while stealing almost 150,000 square-kilometers…They [Greeks] still consider Anatolia to be theirs. Without taking into account that the Aegean Sea is, for them, a Greek lake. They have a sick mind. For over a thousand years, the Turks lived in Anatolia, but they still regard Ionia as their property. They live in the imaginary land of Sophocles or Aristotle.[128]

Therefore, the response to such "imperialist machinations" to deprive Turkey of the opportunity to emerge as a maritime power is the Blue Homeland doctrine. Its copyright-owner Gürdeniz described it as follows:

---

[127] Matthieu Cailleaud interview with Cem Gürdeniz, "Qu'est-ce que la 'Patrie Bleue'? Une Conversation avec l'idéologue de la doctrine géopolitique Turc [What Is the "Blue Homeland?" A Conversation with the Ideologue of the Turkish Geopolitical Doctrine], *Le Grand Continent*, Geopolitical Study Group, Paris, October 26, 2020.
[128] Ibid.

Blue Homeland is first and foremost a symbol. A symbol of the maritimization of Turkey. Turkey wishes to return to the seas to become a maritime nation... Secondly, Mavi Vatan (Blue Homeland) is a definition. It was born as a definition of areas of maritime jurisdiction. Third, it is a doctrine to safeguard, protect, and develop Turkey's maritime rights and interests, not only in areas of Turkish maritime jurisdiction but also in areas of interest, effect, and impact.[129]

From the definition of the chief ideologist who coined it, it will be accurate to define the Blue Homeland Doctrine as the strategic principle of Turkey's irredentism and expansionism within the all-embracing context of neo-Ottomanism. Gürdeniz claimed however that it has nothing to do with neo-Ottomanism. Describing himself as a "Kemalist" and associating neo-Ottomanism with the perceived Islamism of Erdoğan, Gürdeniz said, *"I have nothing to do with the government, nor any relation"*.[130]

Gürdeniz nonetheless gave credit to the Erdoğan government and added: *"But the government is protecting the interests and rights of our Mavi Vatan"*.[131]

---

[129] Ibid.
[130] Ibid.
[131] Ibid.

BLUE HOMELAND: "EURASIANISM VERSUS THE IMPERIALIST POWERS OF THE WEST AND GREECE"

President Recep Tayyip Erdoğan in front of the Blue Homeland map at the National Defense University, August 31, 2019.

The unconventional alliance among Erdoğanist Islamists, Muslim ultra-nationalists, and the Eurasianist elements of the military with secularist-nationalist tendencies – a faction that Gürdeniz belonged to – found its expression in his remarks. Implying the coup attempt that forged and consolidated Erdoğan's authoritarian power and signalled the drift from the West to Eurasianism, Cem Gürdeniz said, *"The fight for 'Mavi Vatan' started after 2016"*. He blamed the US and the EU for the wrong they had allegedly committed against Turkey:

"They tried to create a civil war in Turkey. Ultimately, their main objective was the submission of Turkey to the Euro-Atlantic design, which includes the withdrawal of troops from Northern Cyprus… as well as the creation of a puppet state from Kurdistan, with maritime access… and submission to Turkish maritime withdrawal in the Aegean Sea and the Mediterranean."[132]

What is especially noteworthy in this assessment is his reference to the perennial obsession of the Turkish nationalists in the military and the security establishment regarding the emergence of a Kurdish entity across Turkey's southern borders in Syria with access to the Mediterranean. With such an outlook, the Blue Homeland Doctrine of Gürdeniz does not confine itself to being a legitimate Turkish response to the excessive Greek claims in the Eastern Mediterranean. It also serves as an ultra-nationalist anti-Kurdish blueprint that

---

[132] Cailleaud interview with Cem Gürdeniz , *op. cit.*

concerns itself even with the developments in the Levant.

The association of the Blue Homeland Doctrine with the Eurasianist anti-West shift in Turkey's foreign policy orientation is apparent. The creator of the Blue Homeland Doctrine is an avowed Eurasianist. With his usual candour, he explained the existence of NATO with the arguable aim of *"containing Russia and China from the South"* and to prevent the Chinese Belt and Road Initiative. He enunciated his clear preference for Russia, Iran, and China, in contrast to Turkey's NATO bonds which he sees as harmful and against national interests:

> *For me, NATO's role ended in November 1989 when the Berlin Wall fell. That's all. Why does NATO still exist? To contain Russia from the south, China and its new silk routes from the southeast, and Iran from the south again... When you look at Turkey's relations with these three countries now, China, Russia, and Iran, they are excellent. After the coup attempt on July 15, our relations with these three countries improved. Why? Because NATO supported the Gülenists... At the moment, who supports the PKK, the PYD, the YPG? Most of the NATO countries. Who gives arms to these organizations, who lifts the arms embargo against the Greek Cypriots? Our NATO allies. Not Russia, not China, not Iran.[133]*

The unconcealed hostility of its creator against NATO, the US, the EU, and the Kurds defines the spirit of the Blue Homeland Doctrine. With all its ultranationalist connotations, it is a Eurasianist sequel to Turkey's belligerent foreign policy. Its more problematic aspect is the sacrosanctity attributed to it. Just as any inch of the land territory is sacred to defend, one cubic centimetre of the waters under maritime jurisdiction is equally sacred. It is an integral part of the homeland. Espousing such tenets, the Blue Homeland Doctrine sets an opprobrious measure of patriotism. In the absence of a public debate and in the autocratic country that Turkey is, any criticism of *Mavi Vatan* as a doctrine is liable to the accusation of high treason, or, to say the least, disregard for the national interest.

---

[133] Ibid.

IN RUSSIA'S BACKYARD:
TURKEY IN THE SOUTH CAUCASUS

TURKEY'S ENTRY INTO RUSSIA'S "NEAR ABROAD"

The balance of power in the Libyan civil war shifted in summer 2020 with Turkey's effective military intervention on behalf of its ally, the Tripoli government. Although at different levels, Turkey stood against a bizarre array of countries ranging from France to Russia, and from Egypt to the United Arab Emirates. In August and September, the East Mediterranean waters witnessed a dangerous escalation that could lead to war between Turkey and Greece. While the tensions in North Africa and the Eastern Mediterranean were not defused completely, Turkey entered into the fray between Armenia and Azerbaijan at the other end of its geopolitics, the South Caucasus.

The South Caucasus, widely regarded as a de facto sphere of influence of Russia, fits into what former Russian foreign minister Andrei Kozyrev described as the country's *near abroad*. What marks the South Caucasus power politics revolving around Nagorno-Karabagh is the conflict between the two countries that form the South Caucasus alongside Georgia: Armenia and Azerbaijan.

The Nagorno-Karabagh issue broke out as a political dispute in the Soviet Union in 1988, accelerated the ultimate downfall of the Union in 1991, and turned into an inter-state war between Armenia and Azerbaijan, two former Soviet republics. They became independent in 1991 and fought for Nagorno-Karabagh until 1994. When the war stopped, the Nagorno-Karabagh conflict was already perceived as inherently intractable and became frozen.

When the bloody war ended in 1994, seven Azerbaijani districts (*rayons*) surrounding the Nagorno-Karabagh region had fallen under Armenian military control. One million Azerbaijani refugees were forced to leave their lands and properties. The land-locked region of Nagorno-Karabagh, which military occupation of the Azerbaijani territories had separated from Armenia proper, was physically integrated into the Republic of Armenia. The Republic of Nagorno-Karabagh was declared with 3,170 square-kilometres of territory, covering the area that had been an autonomous *oblast* under the sovereignty of the Azerbaijan Soviet Republic. In 2006 the breakaway republic adopted the name Republic of Artsakh, the name (according to Armenian allegations) used in the 10th century when it was an Armenian principality. Although it was a self-styled independent state to reunify with Armenia, the Republic of Nagorno-Karabagh or Artsakh was not formally recognized even by Yerevan.

From 1994, the year the war stopped with a fragile ceasefire. The OSCE (Organization for Security and Cooperation in Europe) was entrusted with settling the Nagorno-Karabagh conflict. The mechanism of the OSCE for the purpose was co-chaired by Russia, France, and the United States with a membership of Sweden, Finland, Belarus, Germany, Italy, and Turkey, along with the belligerents, Armenia and Azerbaijan. It was called the Minsk Group, referring to the venue of its foundation.

From 1994 on, various initiatives either by the Minsk Group or direct talks between the presidents and high-level officials of Armenia and Azerbaijan, or second-track mechanisms to resolve the conflict, did not bear fruit.

Nonetheless, after more than a quarter century of frozen conflict in the South Caucasus, the possibility of outbreak of war to completely alter the balance of power in the region looked as slim as ever.

Yet it happened, and Azerbaijan emerged as the winner with Armenia the traumatized loser. Turkey, determined to project its power to Russia's near abroad, enabled the outcome with steadfast active political and military support to Azerbaijan. What has been seen in North Africa in June 2020 was repeated in the South Caucasus in November of the same year. Neo-Ottomanist Turkey became the lowest common denominator connecting the two regions separated by almost 3,000 kilometres.

TIMID TURKEY 1992: ASSERTIVE TURKEY 2020–2021

Turkey's intervention in the South Caucasus providing decisive military assistance to Azerbaijan to unleash war against Armenia on September 27, 2020, was in stark contrast to its posture in the earlier phase of the Nagorno-Karabagh conflict.

As a new regional power, an assertive Turkey emerged in the South Caucasus in 2020, a geopolitical zone considered perennially to be a Russian sphere of influence. The phenomenon inspired comparisons with the 1990s.

In 1992, Armenia and Azerbaijan were four years into their first war for the control of the mountainous Nagorno-Karabakh region when Armenian troops raided and seized Shusha, a strategic town that controls access to the region's capital, Stepanakert. In Turkey, pressure rose on then Prime Minister Suleyman Demirel to back Azerbaijan, but he quickly shelved plans for a military expedition after Russian military leader Yevgeny Shaposhnikov warned that any intervention could drive the planet "to the brink of a third world war."[134]

---

[134] David Gauthier-Villars, "An Assertive Turkey Muscles into Russia's Backyard", *The Wall Street Journal*,

I remember vividly that period, as I was a special advisor to President Turgut Özal. President Özal tried to push the Turkish military to conduct exercises on the Armenian border to deter Yerevan in its war against Baku for Nagorno-Karabagh. Turkey's borders intersected with Armenia as well as with Nakhchivan, the autonomous exclave belonging to Azerbaijan. For Özal, the Popular Front's pro-Turkey regime, which was established in Azerbaijan under Abulfez Elchibey following an uprising that removed President Ayaz Mutalibov regarded as "Moscow's man", was an asset to connect Turkey with the newly independent Turkic republics of Central Asia. Özal was an advocate of an assertive-revisionist Turkish foreign policy replacing the hands-off approach attributed to the Kemalist dictum "Peace at Home, Peace Abroad" since the foundation of modern Turkey in the 1920s.

In Özal's mind, the end of the Cold War opened up promising prospects for Turkey to assert itself as one of the leading ten countries in the new unipolar world where the United States remained the sole superpower. His prime minister Süleyman Demirel – who succeeded him in the Presidency from 1993 to 2000 – had an opposite opinion. He was careful not to antagonize Russia. Veteran politician Demirel, who belonged to the conservative school of politics, saw Russia as the inheritor of the mighty Soviet Union. He took seriously the warning of the last defense minister of the Soviet Union, the Russian military leader Yevgeny Shaposhnikov.

Turkey's inaction vis-à-vis the developments in the South Caucasus and the prevailing political chaos in Azerbaijan had laid the groundwork for the balance of power established in the First Karabagh War (1988–1994) and surviving until the Second Karabagh War (September 27 to November 9, 2020).

Erupting in a very different historical period and under equally very different circumstances, the Second Karabagh War yielded almost opposite results compared to the first war. The new political landscape that originated at the end of the Second Karabagh War, in a nutshell, can be defined as:

The Second Karabakh War (September 27–November 9, 2020) has resulted in an Azerbaijani national triumph, a self-inflicted Armenian trauma, geopolitical gains for Russia, another debacle of Western diplomacy, and Turkey's reassertion as a regional power in the South Caucasus.[135]

December 11, 2020. https://www.wsj.com/articles/an-assertive-turkey-muscles-into-russias-backyard-11607696623
[135] Vladimir Socor, "The South Caucasus: New Realities After the Armenia-Azerbaijan War", *Eurasia Daily*

A leading specialist on South Caucasus, Thomas De Waal (best known for his magnum opus *Black Garden: Armenia and Azerbaijan Through Peace and War*) evaluated the end of the Second Karabagh War by acknowledging the changed geopolitical configuration of the region that gave a central role to Russia:

> On November 10, 2020, a Russia-brokered ceasefire agreement halted a forty-four-day-long Armenia-Azerbaijan war over the disputed territory of Nagorny Karabakh, confirming a decisive Azerbaijani military victory…

> The end of fighting reversed roles of victor and defeated, as Armenians were forced to give up the land they had won in the conflict of 1991–1994. Azerbaijan regained the seven districts around Nagorny Karabakh that it had lost in the first war… also captured around one-third of Nagorny Karabakh itself, including the town of Shusha.

> The November trilateral agreement radically changes the geopolitical configuration of the region, giving Moscow a central role it last held in the Soviet era three decades ago… In 2021 all actors in the dispute must make a number of crucial decisions on next steps. Yet so far there is little evidence of strategic planning from anyone, with the possible exception of Russia.[136]

DUAL CORRIDOR OR THE ROAD TO CENTRAL ASIA AND CHINA

Inserting the word *Turkey* would make De Waal's assessment more accurate. Without Turkey's acquiescence and cooperation, Russia's brokering of the nine-point agreement between Armenia and Azerbaijan would likely not have been possible.

The last and ninth point of the trilateral agreement dispelled any doubt I might have had on whether Turkey had achieved a new status in the South Caucasus power game when the war for Nagorno-Karabagh stopped in the early minutes of November 10, 2020. The ninth point signalled far-reaching strategic prospects for Turkey going beyond the scope of the South Caucasus.

Quoted verbatim, it said:

> *All economic and transport links in the region shall be unblocked. The Republic of Armenia shall guarantee the safety of transport links between western regions of the Republic*

Monitor, Vol. 17, No. 179 (December 16, 2020). https://jamestown.org/program/the-south-caucasus-new-realities-after-the-armenia-azerbaijan-war-part-one/

[136] Thomas de Waal, "Unfinished Business in the Armenia-Azerbaijan Conflict", *Carnegie Europe*, February 11, 2021. https://carnegieeurope.eu/2021/02/11/unfinished-business-in-armenia-azerbaijan-conflict-pub-8384

of Azerbaijan and the Nakhcivan Autonomous Republic with a view to organizing the unimpeded movement of citizens, vehicles and cargo in both directions. The Border Service of the FSB (Federal Security Service) of Russia shall exercise control over the transport communication. Subject to agreement by the Parties, the construction of new infrastructure linking the Nakhchivan Autonomous Republic with regions of Azerbaijan shall be carried out.[137]

In February 1992, President Turgut Özal of Turkey dispatched me to Baku to meet Ayaz Mutalibov, first president of the independent, post-Soviet Azerbaijan. As Özal's special envoy, I would convey his confidential message to Mutalibov and try to win his consent to the "Dual Corridor" deal, as the Turkish president formulated it. The deal envisaged a swap of territory, giving the Azerbaijani region of Lachin to the west of Nagorno-Karabagh to connect and integrate a big chunk of it with Armenia. In return Armenia would concede part of its southern territory called Zangezur, which separated Nakhchivan, the Azerbaijani exclave, from the Azerbaijani mainland to its east.

Turkey had a common border with Nakhchivan. If the deal worked, then as Özal dreamed, it would establish an uninterrupted territorial link to connect Turkey across the Caspian Sea with the newly-independent Turkic republics of Central Asia (Turkmenistan, Uzbekistan, Kazakhstan, Kyrgyzstan, and Tajikistan). Özal was sure of American support for the "Dual Corridor" deal, given the strong rapport of trustworthiness established between President George Bush and himself during the Gulf War in 1991. Özal had a project in his mind to introduce a free-market economy to the newly-emerging Turkic world and to lead it into the globalizing unipolar world now centred around the United States. Connecting Turkey to Azerbaijan over Nakhchivan without any territorial interruption would be an essential element in that endeavour.

Mutalibov was disinterested in Özal's proposal. He rejected it. Not only did he not want to relinquish Lachin, an Azerbaijani territory, but he also claimed Zangezur. He told me Zangezur is historically an Azerbaijani land that one day has to be reinstituted back to Azerbaijan.

Three months after my encounter with Mutalibov in Baku, Lachin fell to Armenian forces, and Mutalibov lost his power and left Baku, taking refuge in Moscow.

---

[137]   http://en.kremlin.ru/events/president/news/64384;   https://en.president.az/articles/45923; https://www
.primeminister.am/en/press-release/item/2020/11/10/Announcement/

Coincidentally, during the same period an American State Department official, Paul Goble, prepared a background paper on the Karabagh conflict for former Secretary of State Cyrus Vance, who was planning to visit the South Caucasus, in which he offered some thoughts that interested Vance:

The various participants need to begin to consider the possibility of a territorial swap including the following concessions: sending part of the NKAO (Nagorno-Karabagh Autonomous Oblast) to Armenia, with the area controlling the headwaters of the river flowing to Baku and areas of Azerbaijani population remaining in Azerbaijani hands; and transferring the Armenian-controlled landbridge between Azerbaijan and Nakhichevan to Azerbaijani control.[138]

Unlike Özal's "Dual Corridor" initiative which was never publicized, the American blueprint – very similar in its general framework – came to be known as "The Goble Plan". It occupied the most crucial part in the direct talks between Armenian and Azerbaijani presidents Robert Kocharian and Heydar Aliyev in 1999 and 2001. Although seeming eager to make radical concessions, the presidents could not ultimately agree on the controversial swap of territories.[139]

It took almost three decades for the "Dual Corridor" principle to materialize with new content and in a different format in the aftermath of the Second Karabagh War in 2020.

Besides the ninth point, the seventh point of the Trilateral Agreement stipulated:

The Lachin corridor (5 km (3.1 mi) wide), which will provide access from Nagorno-Karabakh to Armenia and bypass the town of Shusha, shall remain under the control of the peacekeeping contingent of the Russian Federation. Subject to agreement by the Parties, a construction plan will be determined in the next three years for a new route of movement along the Lachin corridor, providing a link between Nagorno-Karabakh and Armenia with the subsequent redeployment of the Russian peacekeeping contingent to guard this route. The Republic of Azerbaijan shall guarantee the safety of traffic of citizens, vehicles, and goods along the Lachin corridor in both directions.[140]

With its seventh point as detailed above and the ninth point spelled out

[138] https://reliefweb.int/report/armenia/how-goble-plan-was-born-and-how-it-remains-political-factor
[139] Thomas de Waal, *Black Garden, Armenia and Azerbaijan Through Peace and War,* New York University Press, 2013, 274-278.
[140] http://en.kremlin.ru/events/president/news/64384; https://en.president.az/articles/45923; https://www.primeminister.am/en/press-release/item/2020/11/10/Announcement/

earlier, the trilateral agreement was nothing but a reactivation of the "Dual Corridor" deal with the new balance of power in the South Caucasus.

The Ceasefire Agreement between Armenia and Azerbaijan, as it is officially titled, was signed by the presidents of Russia and Azerbaijan, Vladimir Putin and İlham Aliyev, and the prime minister of Armenia, Nikol Pashinyan. It was in fact more than a ceasefire text. Although falling short of a peace plan as it left the final status of Nagorno-Karabagh in ambiguity, it nevertheless portended important strategic prospects for Turkey among the other protagonists. *The Economist* grasped this point:

Though not mentioned in the trilateral agreement signed between the two belligerents and Russia, Turkey is a big beneficiary of it. It is to get access to a transport corridor through Armenian territory from the Azerbaijani enclave of Nakhchivan, which borders Turkey, to the main bit of Azerbaijan and the Caspian Sea, thus linking Turkey to Central Asia and China's Belt and Road Initiative. Russia will control the road itself, but Turkish and Chinese goods will travel along it, and all parties stand to benefit economically. "This trade route could transform the entire region and become the main staple of a peace settlement," says Mikayil Jabbarov, Azerbaijan's American-educated economy minister.[141]

According to the Trilateral Ceasefire Agreement, the transport corridor from Nakhchivan (in blue) will cross Armenia's territory Zangezur (in green) and link to Zengilan in the Azerbaijan mainland (in blue). The designed corridor is approximately 45 km long and north of Iran, separated from Armenia and Azerbaijan by the Aras river that forms the frontier with both countries.

The political implications of the accord signed on November 10, 2020 will be colossal, not to mention the substantial economic potential it carries. If implemented, the ninth point of the Agreement will prove to be the most critical element because it will propel Turkey toward a tentative Eurasian alignment. While the appeal of the Western security alliance, namely NATO, diminishes according to Turkey's perceived national interest, which is increasingly interpreted in a neo-Ottomanist outlook, the magnetism of the alignment and partnership with Russia and China increases. Turkey's power projection in the South Caucasus through its strong commitment to Azerbaijan and aid in achieving a military victory in the Nagorno-Karabagh war became a watershed development in its new orientation.

---

[141] *The Economist*, "Peace for Now: A Peace Deal Ends a Bloody War over Nagorno-Karabagh", November 12, 2020. https://www.economist.com/europe/2020/11/12/a-peace-deal-ends-a-bloody-war-over-nagorno-karabakh

Nagorno-Karabakh Conflict — www.polgeonow.com

Approximate Territorial Control
As known Dec. 1, 2020
- ● Armenia govt. forces
- ● Artsakh/Armenia forces
- ● Azerbaijan govt. forces
- ▲ Russian peacekeepers

Historical Status
Former NKAO

Sources: News reports, ISWNews, Suriyak, others

Some Armenian circles promoted the argument that loss of Nagorno-Karabagh would open the way to the loss of Zangezur (the region in Armenia's south, called Syunik in Armenian), forming a corridor to connect Nakhchivan and the Azerbaijani mainland, and uninterruptedly, all the way from Turkey to Central Asia. The allegation that if Nagorno-Karabagh falls, then Zangezur (Syunik) would follow, was originally put forward by Monte Melkonian. Melkonian, an Armenian-American who was killed in 1993 in Nagorno-Karabagh and venerated as a "martyr" by Armenians, is a notorious figure for Turkey. He was a leader of ASALA (Armenian Secret Army for the Liberation of Armenia), a terrorist organization responsible for the assassination of scores of Turkish diplomats and bomb attacks in the 1970s and 1980s. His name is associated with the possibility of a new conflict on Zangezur, following the Second Nagorno-Karabagh War:

It appears that a new conflict is about to breakout. After a humiliating loss... a direct land route was supposedly granted to Azerbaijan so it can access its Nakhchivan exclave via a corridor through Armenia's Syunik province, which Azerbaijani's call Zangezur. This was supposedly agreed upon with the signing of the November 10 trilateral (Armenia-Azerbaijan-Russia) ceasefire agreement. Monte Melkonian, a Lieutenant Colonel from the first Nagorno-Karabakh War (1988-1994), said in the early 1990's that if Armenians lost Nagorno-Karabakh to Azerbaijan, they would next lose Syunik Province, the thin strip of land separating Azerbaijan-proper from Nakhchivan. He stated that "If we lose [Karabakh], we turn the final page of our people's history." He believed that if Azerbaijani forces succeeded in deporting Armenians from Karabakh, they would then advance on Syunik and other regions of Armenia. If Azerbaijan were to capture Syunik province, this would not only connect Azerbaijan-proper to Nakhchivan, but it would also give Turkey direct access to the oil and gas rich Caspian Sea and onwards to Central Asia.[142]

Referring to Monte Melkonian's allegations in the early nineties and the speech delivered by Azerbaijani President İlham Aliyev on March 5, 2021, at the 14th Summit of Economic Cooperation Organization (ECO), the conclusion was: *"It appears that Azerbaijan is preparing for a new war to capture Syunik from Armenia".*[143]

In his speech at the virtual summit of the ECO (members include Afghanistan, Azerbaijan, Iran, Kazakhstan, Kyrgyzstan, Pakistan, Tajikistan, Turkey, Turkmenistan, and Uzbekistan), İlham Aliyev addressed the participating presidents, Recep Tayyip Erdoğan of Turkey, Imran Khan of Pakistan, and Ashraf Ghani of Afghanistan. He began with lavish praise of Erdoğan:

I would like to inform all our colleagues that President Erdogan's constant support for Azerbaijan not only during the war, but throughout the time he is President and leader of Turkey played very important role in the liberation of Azerbaijani territories. Turkey is our brother. Turkey is our great ally. And people of Azerbaijan are happy to have such an ally. People of Azerbaijan and of Turkey and I am sure many people around the world clearly know the historic role of President Erdogan in not only transforming Turkey into one of the strongest centers of power in the world but also in providing security to the region.

Turkey plays an outstanding role in providing security and stability in a broader region. And as I many times said and want to say once again that the stronger Turkey is, the stronger is Azerbaijan and all its partners.[144]

He emphasized the future prospects regarding the Zangezur corridor, calling it the *"historic Azerbaijani land Zangezur"* which stirred the fears of Armenians about a new war in the South Caucasus:

The Nagorno-Karabakh conflict ended after the glorious victory of Azerbaijan over Armenia. The Nagorno-Karabakh conflict was left in the past. Now we are looking into the

[142] Paul Antonopoulos, "Is Azerbaijan Preparing a New War against Armenia?", *Greek City Times*, March 11, 2021. https://greekcitytimes.com/2021/03/11/azerbaijan-new-war-armenia/?amp

[143] Ibid.

[144] https://menafn.com/1101703022/President-Aliyev-gives-speech-at-virtual-Summit-of-Economic-Cooperation-Organization-

future. With the aim of providing the peace and stability in the region, we have started discussing transportation projects connecting a number of states. Azerbaijan, Turkey and Iran share the same vision for the implementation of the regional transportation projects. Armenia can also benefit from the process if behaves in normal way.

In this context, the new connectivity corridor which will pass through historic Azerbaijani land of Zangezur and link mainland Azerbaijan with its inseparable part Nakhchivan Autonomous Republic and Turkey will create new opportunities in the transportation sector in the region. We invite ECO member states to benefit from the 'Zangezur corridor.[145]

İlham Aliyev – who four months after the signing of the deal that ended the Second Karabagh War had remarked that the Zangezur corridor was a historic achievement thanks to the particular provision in the Trilateral Statement which should be seen as Azerbaijan's landmark political victory – reiterated its geopolitical significance. On March 31, 2021, at the Informal Summit of Cooperation Council of Turkic-Speaking States held in video conference format, he said:

The war is over and the conflict has been consigned to history. New opportunities have emerged. I think the most important opportunity among these is transport. We are already working very hard on the Zangazur corridor. I said at the summit in Nakhchivan that the decision to separate Zangazur from Azerbaijan and annex it to Armenia led to a geographical divide of the Turkic world. If we look at the map, it looks as if a dagger was stuck in our body and the Turkic world was divided. Zangazur, the land of ancient Azerbaijan, will now play the role of uniting the Turkic world because the transport, communication and infrastructure projects passing through Zangazur will unite the whole Turkic world and create additional opportunities for other countries, including Armenia. Armenia currently has no railway links with its ally Russia. This railway link can be established from the territory of Azerbaijan. Armenia has no railway connection with its neighbor Iran. This railway can be provided through Nakhchivan. Azerbaijan will be connected with Turkey through the Nakhchivan Autonomous Republic, Central Asia will be connected with Europe. So a new transport corridor is being created. Azerbaijan has already started this work. I am confident that our partner countries will also take advantage of these opportunities.[146]

Thanks to my own involvement with the "Dual Corridor" initiative of

---

[145] Ibid.

[146] *Azertac* (Azerbaijan State News Agency), "Informal Summit of Cooperation Council of Turkic-Speaking States Was Held in Video Conference Format, Azerbaijani President İlham Aliyev Made a Speech at the Summit", March 31, 2021. https://azertag.az/en/xeber/Informal_Summit_of_Cooperation_Council_of_Turkic_Speaking_States_was_held_in_video_conference_format_Azerbaijani_President_Ilham_Aliyev_made_a_speech_at_the_Summit

Turkey's President Turgut Özal in 1992, I had immediately grasped the unique significance of the provision regarding the "Zangezur Corridor" when I read the Trilateral Agreement on November 10, 2020. İlham Aliyev's statement on the matter in March 2021 validated my assessment.

The following noteworthy assessment on the geopolitical significance of the Zangezur Corridor further confirmed my perception on the matter:

The unblocking of the Zangezur corridor will have wide-ranging geopolitical reverberations for both the directly concerned states, Armenia and Azerbaijan, and surrounding countries. For Azerbaijan, the reopening of the corridor has geostrategic significance in multiple domains. This route was the most direct land passage between mainland Azerbaijan and its Nakhchivan exclave soon after World War I, when the historical Zangezur (now Syunik) province was granted to Armenia and the autonomous Nakhchivan territory came under Azerbaijani protection under the Treaty of Kars (1921). The termination of the Zangezur land route connection with Nakhchivan following the breakout of the First Karabakh War of the early 1990s, however, seriously isolated the Azerbaijani exclave. Since then, Baku could physically reach Nakhchivan only by air or by circumventing Armenia to the south, via Iranian territory. The latter route came with myriads of security and geopolitical challenges to Azerbaijan, in addition to notable economic consequences...

The direct land route with Nakhchivan will additionally shorten transit between Azerbaijan and Turkey. Although the two countries are already linked via the Baku–Tbilisi–Kars Railroad and roads across Georgia, the shorter route through Zangezur has the potential to boost economic and human ties between the two sides. This could also play an important role in the regional integration of the Turkic states, which have been developing an ambitious agenda toward this goal over the last few years.[147]

Under the circumstances of the third decade of the 21st century, the Agreement signalled the new political orientation of Turkey entraining economic and commercial aspects with Eurasian magnitude. That new orientation propels Turkey towards Russia and China, but it is a two-way avenue. While the tentative alignment to Russia and China provides an area to manoeuvre for Erdoğan vis-à-vis the United States and the European Union from political and economic perspectives, China's appetite for expansion into Western Asia and Europe through its Belt and Road Initiative (BRI) offers Erdoğan another lifeline.

---

[147] Vasif Huseynov, "Azerbaijan Embarks on Construction of Nakhchivan Railway (Part Two)", *Eurasian Daily Monitor*, Vol. 18, No. 59 (April 13, 2021). https://jamestown.org/program/azerbaijan-embarks-on-construction-of-nakhchivan-railway-part-two/

Zangezur Corridor

Source: Media reports

...... Railroads
...... Planned railroad
—— Transport corridor that would connect Armenia with Russia and Iran
—— Transport corridor that would connect Azerbaijan with Turkey

BAKU-TBILISI-KARS RAILWAY

The cooperation between Turkey and China has expanded exponentially, especially since 2016, the turning point year for Erdoğan's increasingly autocratic power.

China is now Turkey's second-largest import partner after Russia. China has invested $3 billion in Turkey between 2016 and 2019 and intended to double that by the end of 2020... When the lira's value dropped by more than 40 percent in 2018, the state-owned Industrial and Commercial Bank of China provided the Turkish government $3.6 billion in loans for ongoing energy and transportation projects. In June 2019, in the wake of Istanbul municipal *elections that indicated crumbling support for Erdogan, China's central bank transferred $1 billion – the largest cash inflow under a swap agreement between the two countries' central banks.[148]*

Cash flowing from China has become a bank account for Erdoğan's regime and helped him enormously at desperate moments. The financial cooperation allowed Turkish companies to use the Chinese yuan to make trade payments, thereby stretching a helping hand to Erdoğan who was facing a severe currency shortage aggravated by the coronavirus crisis in 2020.

The ambitious Chinese BRI project offers Turkey a fresh cash source – and Beijing a strategic foothold on the Mediterranean Sea. As part of the infrastructure-building initiative, Turkey completed a railroad reaching Baku, Azerbaijan, on the Caspian Sea, where it links to transportation networks to China.

Hence, Turkey's new foothold in the South Caucasus enabling it to project its power from Transcaucasia (South Caucasus) to Transcaspian (Turkic Central Asian) in China's proximity has crucial geopolitical importance.

Besides the broadening and deepening partnership with Russia, Turkey's ties to China on strategic sectors like energy under the BRI umbrella, as well as military and security, have paramount value. Ankara plans to sign a deal with China to build Turkey's third nuclear power plant.

Beyond infrastructure, Sino-Turkish cooperation involves deepening bilateral military and security ties, including in intelligence and cyberwarfare... China has found a highly strategic foothold in Turkey – a NATO member with a large market for energy, infrastructure, defense technology, and telecommunications at the crossroads of Europe, Asia, and Africa. For Turkey and Erdoğan, China provides desperately needed resources to fund high-profile megaprojects... and... Chinese cash helps Erdogan avoid seeking help from Western-dominated institutions such as the International Monetary Fund, which would require him to commit to reforms and other measures that could undermine his unfettered control over the country's economy.[149]

While this book was in print, the world's largest financial newspaper *Nikkei Asia* published a story on June 28, 2021, concerning Erdoğan's allegedly "crazy"

---

[148] Ayca Alemdaroglu, "Sultan Tepe, Erdogan Is Turning Turkey into a Chinese Client State", *Foreign Policy*, September 16, 2020. https://foreignpolicy.com/2020/09/16/erdogan-is-turning-turkey-into-a-chinese-client-state/; Didier Chaudet, "Analyse, Vers un Rapprochement entre la Chine et la Turquie?", *Asialyst*, November 28, 2020. https://asialyst.com/fr/2020/11/28/chine-turquie-rapprochement/
[149] Alemdaroglu, "Sultan Tepe", *op. cit.*

Canal Istanbul project connecting the Black Sea to the Sea of Marmara, a massive endeavor. The Canal would have a length of 45 kilometers if ever to be achieved. *Nikkei Asia's* report wrote, *"Canal Istanbul is widely regarded as Erdogan's greatest infrastructure challenge, coming as it does in the midst of an ailing economy waylaid by the coronavirus, a plunging Turkish lira, and cratering public support approaching record lows, according to multiple polls."* According to *Nikkei Asia*, the over-ambitious project of Erdoğan is related to China's Belt and Road Initiative, and Turkey's President is eyeing Chinese investment, implicitly, further confirming Turkey's Eurasianist trajectory. Nikkei Asia provided the following interesting information on the deepening Turkey-China ties:

"It remains to be seen whether Erdogan is serious about advancing the project or China will ultimately get involved after supplying Turkey more than 34 million doses of coronavirus vaccines so far as well as much-needed foreign exchange infusion for the country's depleted central bank reserves. Erdogan on June 13 announced a new deal between the two countries' central banks just before his departure for the recent NATO summit and his meeting with U.S. President Joe Biden. Under the deal, the existing currency swap arrangement increases the limit to $6 billion from $2.4 billion…

[On June 26 (2021)] *Turkish President Recep Tayyip Erdogan attended the groundbreaking ceremony of a bridge that marks the first move to build his pet that he hopes will win foreign support, including China's… Politically, Erdogan hopes the mega project breathes new momentum into the economy, creates jobs and boosts his popularity ahead of the 2023 presidential elections.* [In his speech at the ceremony] *'Certainly we should add other strategic elements such that our country plays a more effective role in global trade and gain a greater share of transportation and logistics corridors,'* Erdogan added.

Ahead of the ceremony, transportation minister… implicitly drew parallels to China's Belt and Road initiative and said the canal project would significantly boost Turkey's share of global trade.

Turkey has been a strong supporter of the ambitious Beijing-led initiative and signed a memorandum of understanding with China in 2015 to align its own "Middle Corridor Initiative" linking Turkey and Europe with China via a Trans-Caspian, east-west route. In 2017, President Erdogan attended a forum in China on the Belt and Road, and in 2019, on the sidelines of his visit to Beijing, he told China's Xinhua News Agency that the two initiatives were in "natural harmony…

China's economic presence in Turkey has grown as the latter's relations have frayed with the EU and U.S. In 2020, China was Turkey's largest import partner, bringing in $23 billion for the year, up 20% from the previous year.

In 2015, a consortium of state-owned Chinese companies acquired a major container terminal in Istanbul for almost $1 billion.

Bloomberg reported in March that China Merchants Group and other partners were closing in on a deal to acquire an initially agreed majority stake in the third bridge spanning the Bosporus and its connecting roads for $688 million. However, the deal was said to have been interrupted by the pandemic at the end of 2019. According to the report, the deal has been revived this time including refinancing for $1.6 billion of the original loan to the bridge operator by banks including Industrial and Commercial Bank of China, Bank of China, and China Merchants Bank.

The high-profile deals illustrate that Chinese investors are not indifferent to the infrastructure developments of Istanbul, Turkey's largest city, home to more than 15 million people and geographically linking the Asian and European continents."

Nikkei Asia in its report quoted Selçuk Çolakoğlu, director of the Turkish Center of Asia Pacific Studies, who said, a project of this magnitude could only be financed by either G-7 members or China, and added, "*It will also come with political and diplomatic strings attached, where the financier will seek a maximum degree of foreign-policy strategy coordination.*"

The linkage between Erdoğan's Canal Istanbul project and China's Belt and Road Initiative, and Turkey's increasing financial dependency on Beijing illustrates Turkey's potential strategic Eurasianist prospects. It is highly symbolic that Erdoğan announced a new Turkey-China deal a day before his encounter at the sidelines of the NATO Summit in Brussels with U.S. President Joe Biden, who was widely regarded as the initiator of a new Cold War against China.

Turkey's projection of its power to the South Caucasus would pave the way to aggrandizing its political, economic, and commercial relations with Russia and China. It would also grant Turkey an exclusive status in its dealings with the Turkic world of Central Asia.

Beyond changing the map of the southern Caucasus, the 2020 Nagorno-Karabakh war has cemented Turkey's presence in Azerbaijan and enhanced Ankara's ability to project its influence in Central Asia. By changing the rules of the game in the South Caucasus, Turkey has also upended the geopolitics of connectivity in Central Asia, elevating itself from a transit state to one of the principal agenda-setters of Eurasian connectivity.

Ankara is likely to capitalize on its new position and prestige by rededicating more of its efforts to deepening its level of economic and security cooperation with the Turkic states of Central Asia. As it does so, Turkey could increasingly hold the balance of power between

Russia and China in the Eurasian architecture… The manner and extent to which Turkey succeeds in parlaying its soft and hard power gains from the Nagorno-Karabakh War to deepen its strategic partnerships in Central Asia will determine the scope of its power as a Eurasian actor. The outlook is promising.[150]

During the last decade, Turkey had steadily increased its relations with Turkic-Central Asia on multiple fronts. The pan-Turkic solidarity espoused by Turkey's nationalist leadership focused mainly on the sphere of defence cooperation as Turkish foreign policy increasingly took on attributes of militarized diplomacy, thereby enhancing the Eurasianist orientation:

Ankara also appears set on revitalizing the idea of pan-Turkic solidarity to build an alliance across Central Asia and the Caucasus. Turkey was a founding member of the Cooperation Council of Turkic-Speaking States that was formed in 2009 with the primary goal of deepening cooperation between Ankara and the Turkic-speaking states of the former Soviet Union. This group was seen as 'tailor-made to extend Turkish influence in Central Asia'. While it got off to a slow start, it appears to have gained relevance and momentum since late 2019 when Uzbekistan formally joined.

Significantly, Turkey is also pursuing a program of defense cooperation with the two largest Central Asian states, Kazakhstan and Uzbekistan... Kazakhstan has entered into a military cooperation agreement with Turkey that encompasses defense industry, intelligence-sharing, joint exercises, information systems and cyber defense, as well as military training and military scientific and technical research. Uzbekistan signed a similar agreement with Turkey in late October [2020], during a visit by the Turkish defense minister. This visit also gave rise to an intriguing albeit largely fanciful debate about the creation of an 'Army of Turan' and a NATO-style military bloc of all six Turkic-speaking states led by Ankara.[151]

With its relentless and persistent stand against the ceasefire initiatives until the balance of power in the South Caucasus was radically changed by the uncontested military victory of Azerbaijan, Turkey once again defied the Western world. France had stood behind Greece in the Eastern Mediterranean standoff during summer 2020, had rivalled Turkey in Libya and finally in the South Caucasus, where as one of the Minsk Group co-chairs it was supportive of Armenia. The end result of the Nagorno-Karabagh war could thus also be

---

[150] Michaël Tanchum, "Has Turkey Outfoxed China to Become a Rising Eurasian Power", *The Turkey Analyst*, January 19, 2021. https://www.turkeyanalyst.org/publications/turkey-analyst-articles/item/659-turkey-outfoxed-china-in-azerbaijan-to-become-a-rising-eurasian-power?.html

[151] Connor Dilleen, "Turkey Forges a Strategic Future Independent of Russia and the West", *The Strategist*, Australian Strategic Policy Institute, December 21, 2020. https://www.aspistrategist.org.au/turkey-forges-a-strategic-future-independent-of-russia-and-the-west/

interpreted as Turkey's win over France and its further distancing from the West.

Turkey asserted its role as a top player in the South Caucasus. It overtook the West with US and France, members of the so-called Minsk Group managing Karabakh on behalf of the Organization for Security and Co-operation in Europe, appearing irrelevant.[152]

As seen on several occasions since 2016, Turkey's drift further from the West moved it closer to Russia and China. That rapprochement came at the expense of the Turkic people of China, the Uyghurs, who are being subjected to ethnic cleansing and cultural genocide. Turkey's endeavours projecting its power to Turkic Central Asia stop at the realpolitik wall of China's western frontier region of Xinjiang (Eastern Turkistan) inhabited by the Uyghur people. The disappointment and resentment over Erdoğan's disregard for the Uyghur plight, associated with Turkey's growing economic dependence on China, found its expression in the following words:

Erdogan's authoritarian efforts to keep power in Turkey by muzzling the free press and locking up dissidents have made him an uneasy ally for liberal democracies. All the more reason for him to look to Russian President Vladimir Putin and Chinese President Xi Jinping while grappling with a floundering economy. Unfortunately, this often translates into changing Ankara's policy toward Turkey's 35,000 Uyghurs, from offering a safe haven to imposing downright repression… This is happening as Turkey shifts away from its NATO allies and toward Russia and China. China just ratified an extradition agreement with Turkey in what it calls a counterterrorism partnership. Erdogan has plenty of allies in this new status quo.[153]

As much as it was feeble vis-à-vis China in Xinjiang, Turkey was robust in the South Caucasus with regard to Russia.

COMPETITIVE COOPERATION OR ADVERSERIAL COLLABORATION WITH RUSSIA

With the Second Karabagh War that lasted 44 days from September 27 to November 10, 2020, the assumption that Russia would not allow Turkey in its sphere of influence, the South Caucasus proved wrong.

---

[152] Dimitar Bechev, "What Does the Nagorno-Karabagh Deal Mean for Turkey and Russia?", *Aljazeera*, November 18, 2020. https://www.aljazeera.com/opinions/2020/11/18/the-nagorno-karabakh-settlement-and-turkish-russian-relations

[153] Kuzzat Altay, "Why Erdogan Has Abandoned the Uyghurs", *Foreign Policy*, March 2, 2021. https://foreignpolicy.com/2021/03/02/why-erdogan-has-abandoned-the uyghurs/?utm_source=PostUp& utm_medium=email&utm_campaign=30788&utm_term=Editors%20Picks%20OC&?tpcc=30788

A striking analysis which in the first instance looked fairly reasonable was as follows:

Ankara probably presents more significant strategic challenges for Moscow than for the West. While Turkey is currently at odds with Greece and other NATO partners in the eastern Mediterranean, it is also pursuing a deliberate and nuanced strategy of engagement with countries across the Black Sea littoral region, the Caucasus and Central Asia. This strategy will provide it with a new sphere of influence and strategic partnerships independent of its traditional NATO 'allies', while also increasing the prospect of a confrontation with Russia by encroaching on Moscow's traditional zones of influence and control...

Turkey is arguably applying a similar calculus to its growing engagement with Ukraine. A mid-October presidential summit between the two countries advanced a defense cooperation partnership, bringing about a 'new geopolitical reality in the Black Sea region'. The cooperation agreement signed by Ankara and Kyiv encompasses advanced defense industrial collaboration on aerospace engines and unmanned aerial systems, including the co-production of an unmanned fighter jet. In a direct challenge to Moscow, Turkey also agreed to sell its well-regarded Bayraktar armed drone to Ukraine and has purchased the Ukrainian-modernized S-125 (Goa-3) surface-to-air-missile system...

These initiatives, [including the ones directed towards Turkic republics in Central Asia] all of which appear to be conducted in stark defiance of Russian interests given they are directed at countries historically within Moscow's orbit, suggest that Ankara is heading on a collision course with Moscow rather than towards a detente. And while Russia may have tolerated confrontations with Turkey in Syria and Libya, where their proxy armies have been in direct conflict, it's likely to be less tolerant of Ankara's maneuverings in its own backyard.[154]

What is necessary to remember is that although the presidential summit between Turkey and Ukraine that culminated in the defence agreement between the countries, which presumably changed the power equation in the Black Sea region, was held in October 2020. Turkey's initiatives with the former Soviet republics of Central Asia, primarily on military cooperation, were made mainly in 2019 and 2020. Expert opinion regarded these as an encroachment on Russia's traditional zone of influence, even its backyard. Therefore, it concluded that Moscow would not be tolerant of Ankara, as it had been elsewhere. That assumption did not materialize when Russia and Turkey cooperated in the South Caucasus in November 2020.

First of all, there was not much Russia could do to prevent Turkey from

---

[154] Dilleen, "Turkey Forges a Strategic Future", op cit.

projecting power into its backyard. More importantly, Russia was keen to cooperate with Turkey in multiple areas where their ambitions seemingly brought them into conflict.

The two countries have the necessary experience to strike a bargain based on compromises and compensation. Their acceptance of the principle of spheres of influence, the EU's sluggishness on strategic issues in the Mediterranean, and the US's reluctance to embark on new military adventures give them extra room to manoeuvre and arrive at a solution that accommodates their respective interests. After all, both are keen to avoid a direct confrontation.[155]

Turkey and Russia have already built a geo-economic partnership based on energy, namely natural gas and nuclear energy projects. The Blue Stream pipeline that crosses the Black Sea has supplied natural gas to Turkey since 2003, and Turk Stream began operation in January 2020 to supply natural gas to southern and southeastern Europe via Turkey. The Russian pipelines carrying natural gas enhance Turkey's ambition to become an energy hub and provide a significant geopolitical advantage. Russia is also building Turkey's first nuclear power station at the cost of $25 billion. In 2020, Turkey became the second-largest importer of Russian agro-industrial products in the world. Turkey's purchase of Russian S-400 anti-missile defence systems at a cost of $2.5 billion not only put in jeopardy Turkey's ties with the United States and its status as an ally in NATO, but augurs a strategic relationship with Russia, going beyond the partnership. It poised Turkey on the verge of crossing the line with the West.

Alternating between economic partnership and reaching even to the sphere of military-industrial cooperation, the Turkey-Russia relationship is very unusual for a NATO member and Moscow. And, they been proxy warring to see which has dominance from North Africa to the Caspian Sea. However, according to some Russian strategy minds, the ambiguity in the relationship is beneficial for Russian policy. Turkey's drift from the Western security mechanisms helps Russia, which is interested in undermining them. In this regard, Turkey's intervention in the Nagorno-Karabagh conflict rendered the OSCE Minsk Group irrelevant and thereby strengthened Russia's pivotal position in its near abroad such as the South Caucasus.

---

[155] Igor Delanoë, "Bras de fer dans russo-turc dans le Caucase", *Le Monde diplomatique*, December 8, 2020. https://www.monde-diplomatique.fr/2020/12/DELANOE/62586; Igor Delanoë, "Russia and Turkey, Friends or Enemies?", *Le Monde diplomatique English Edition*, December 8, 2020. https://mondediplo.com/7 search?s=Igor+Delanoë

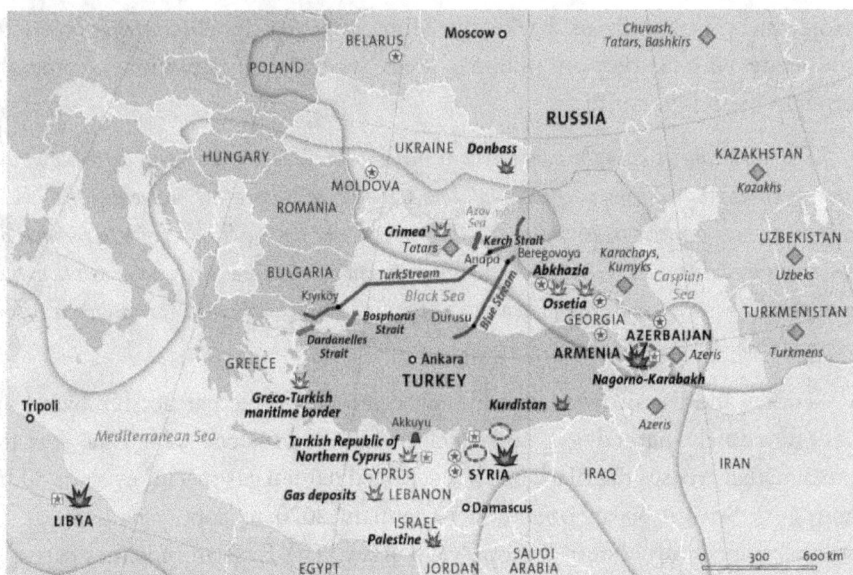

Originally printed in Cécile Marin's article "Russia and Turkey: Partners and Rivals" in Le Monde Diplomatique, December 2020.

Despite the active anti-Turkish media campaign in Russia and fears of Ankara's growing influence in Transcaucasia, it turned out that it was Turkey's support for Azerbaijan that disabled the amorphous OSCE Minsk Group, ensuring Russia's dominance in the Karabakh peace process.[156]

Nicholas Danforth observed how Turkey's policies in the Levant and North Africa undercut the Western influence and led to a particular perception of convergence of interests between Ankara and Moscow. Added to the simultaneous Turco-Russian rivalry and partnership, the new dynamics set in motion in the South Caucasus created a *sui generis* character in their relationship that can be described as competitive cooperation.

So even when Ankara's gains have undercut Russia's allies, Moscow has accepted, even welcomed, Turkish intervention in order to weaken American and European influence in

---

[156] Anton Mardasov and Kirill Semyonov, "Best Frenemies: Russia and Turkey", *Riddle*, November 26, 2020. https://www.ridl.io/en/best-frenemies-russia-and-turkey/

Syria and Libya. These interventions, in turn, created the dynamic of cooperative competition that currently characterizes Turkish-Russian relations. By backing opposing sides in proxy conflicts, then working together to negotiate their resolutions, Moscow and Ankara have both gained influence at the expense of Western actors…

All this is in keeping with Turkey's broader foreign policy shift, which has increasingly prioritized the use of hard power, often in conjunction with local proxies, to alter regional dynamics in its favor. Convinced that the world is becoming more chaotic and more multipolar, Ankara has emphasized its willingness to act independently of, or even in direct opposition to, its former Western allies while building a relationship with Russia that is simultaneously cooperative and competitive.[157]

ERDOĞAN AND PUTIN: OBSERVING REALPOLITIK

Yet, the decisive role the leaders played should not be missed in evaluating the main characteristics of Turkish-Russian relations. It is Recep Tayyip Erdoğan and Vladimir Putin who have put their strong mark on shaping bilateral relations. Even in 2014, striking similarities between the two men were observed by the careful eye of Natalie Nougayrède. She provided a startling account that goes far towards explaining the mode of relationship accomplished years later in the post-2016 period. Under the firm grip of Erdoğan and Putin, Ankara and Moscow, with a spirit of partnership on multiple fields of broad geopolitics, sailed away from the West.

Two angry men. They govern large countries that border Europe. They rail against the west, which is at great pains to find the right way to deal with them… Erdogan and Putin have much in common. Both in their early 60s, they have been in power for a long time (since 1999 for Putin, since 2002 for Erdogan), holding either the position of prime minister or president. They aspire to be fathers of the nation. Their political narrative mixes nationalism and anti-liberal traditionalism.

Their vision of society, as well as their methods of governance, run counter to the values Europe promotes. They concentrate power, repress opposition, restrict media freedom, control the internet, and have cowed the judiciary. Both play religious cards. Erdogan's ideology is that of the Muslim Brotherhood: he sees himself as the defender of Sunni Muslims in the Middle East. Putin uses the Orthodox church to boost patriotism, and strengthen Russian influence

---

[157] Nicholas Danforth, "What did Turkey gain from the Armenia-Azerbaijan War?", *Eurasianet*, December 11, 2020. https://eurasianet.org/perspectives-what-did-turkey-gain-from-the-armenia-azerbaijan-war; Güney Yıldız, "Turkish-Russian Adversarial Collaboration in Syria, Libya, and Nagorno-Karabakh", *SWP Comment*, March 2021.

in the Slavic world. Restoring national pride is central… Both claim they were deceived by the west. European countries rapidly gave Erdogan and Turkey the cold shoulder treatment. Putin says Russia's strategic interests were never taken into account by NATO or the EU. An important common feature between Erdogan and Putin is their obsession with conspiracy theories. All political opposition is ascribed to western-led plots.[158]

Both leaders harboured similar imperial ambitions. Both had no interest in conforming to liberal democratic norms. Such similarities, ostensibly, further facilitated the rapport between Erdoğan and Putin.

Both autocrats share a nostalgia for empire. Mr Putin portrays himself as a patriot who is rebuilding parts of the Soviet empire, and has waged wars against Georgia and Ukraine. He strives to keep what he sees as client states, most recently Belarus and Armenia, on a tight leash. Mr Erdogan has placed his country's Ottoman past in the service of a more aggressive foreign policy, making noises about restoring Turkish rule over Greek islands close to its Aegean shores, and confronting Greece, Cyprus and France in the gas-rich eastern Mediterranean. He fancies himself the voice of the Muslim world.[159]

There is also a strong element of personal communications between Erdoğan and Putin in managing the relations between the two countries. Both Vladimir Putin and Recep Tayyip Erdoğan took office in the early 2000s, and the two nationalist autocrats in their own right have identical governance styles. Over time, they learned to compartmentalize issues between the two countries, in line with their realpolitik.

A brilliant observation in this respect is presented by Andrey Kortunov, Director General of Russian International Affairs Council. In responding to a question on the current state of relations between Turkey and Russia, he identified similar traits between Erdoğan and Putin. He explained the characteristics of the Turkey-Russia relationship.

There are a number of obvious parallels between the two. Recep Tayyip Erdogan, like Vladimir Putin, is not exactly enamored with Western liberal principles. Both have become disillusioned with their countries' experience of cooperation with Europe. Both preach "traditional values", rely on the so-called "Deep People" and call for a "religious revival". Both staunchly defend their positions on the international stage and have no qualms about

---

[158] Natalie Nougayrède, "The Two Angry Men on Europe's Borders: Loud, Proud, and Impossible to Ignore", *The Guardian*, October 29, 2014. https://www.theguardian.com/commentisfree/2014/29/europe-two-angry-men-west-vladimir-putin-recep-tayyip-erdogan-russias-turkey.
[159] *The Economist*, "The Odd Couple", *op. cit.*

challenging their many external critics and, where necessary, going against the dominant global attitudes and trends.

The fact that the two have almost identical ideologies, carry themselves in a similar fashion and quite obviously share the same view of the modern world and where it is heading, should in itself contribute to a rapprochement between Moscow and Ankara. What is more, Russia and Turkey objectively have many converging interests. The two countries complement each other quite successfully in a variety of areas – from energy, to tourism, from transport and logistics, to military-technical advancements, etc.

That said, bilateral relations remain fragile and inconsistent. Russia and Turkey are at the same time companions and competitors.[160]

Being reconciled to Turkey's broader role in the South Caucasus, within the perceived sphere of influence of Russia, is related to how Putin sees, in terms of realpolitik, the post–Cold War world. For him, Turkey in the South Caucasus is an inevitable fallout from the downfall of the Soviet Union which he sees as the greatest geopolitical catastrophe of the 20th century.

A week after the cessation of the war in the South Caucasus, responding to the Russian press voicing irritation over Turkey's projection of its power in alliance with Azerbaijan in the region, Putin gave an impressive realpolitik lecture.

Regarding Turkey and its role, it is well known, as Azerbaijan has explained on numerous occasions. Turkey has never made any secret that Azerbaijan has its unilateral support.

What can I tell you? These are the geopolitical ramifications of the breakdown of the Soviet Union. So far we have been discussing this topic in broad terms, but the developments we are currently witnessing are the specific manifestations of these consequences. What am I talking about here? Well, Azerbaijan is an independent sovereign state, and has every right to choose allies as it deems fit. Who can deny it this right?[161]

Not only did he acquiesce to Turkey's entry to the South Caucasus as Azerbaijan's main military ally and legitimizer, Putin also went further to envisage a Turkey-Russia partnership in the future. It was reminiscent of the post–WW II unity forged between Germany and France, which eventually led

[160] Institut Montaigne, "Shaky Bridges between Russia, Turkey and the EU: Three Questions to Andrey Kortunov", November 2, 2020. https://www.institutmontaigne.org/en/blog/shaky-bridges-between-russia-turkey-and-eu

[161] Kremlin, "Interview with Vladimir Putin: Replies to Media Questions on Developments in Nagorno-Karabakh", November 17, 2020. http://en.kremlin.ru/events/president/news/64431

to the EU.

We know the history, often dramatic history of relations between Turkey and Russia over the centuries.

But do you know what I would like to focus on? The fact that many European nations had, let us say, an equally difficult and tragic history of relations with each other. France and Germany are a case in point. How many wars did they have with each other? Today they are jointly performing their NATO defence and security duties the way they think fit and are cooperating within the European Economic Community. They have overcome all this and stepped over it, and they are moving forward in the interests of their nations' future. Why cannot we do the same here, in the Black Sea region?

Certainly, our positions and points of view are not always the same, nor are they the same in all respects. Occasionally, they are diametrically opposite. But this is what the art of diplomacy is all about: finding compromises. And any compromise is based on respect for one's partner.[162]

As a faithful disciple of realpolitik and a flexible pragmatist disguised under hardliner outfits, Putin never forgot his priority: to weaken NATO at any cost and cultivate the cracks that appear in the adversarial security alliance. Recep Tayyip Erdoğan, also a pragmatist observing realpolitik, presented himself as such a perfect partner that the Russian leader could well afford to disregard the differences with his Turkish counterpart as being of secondary importance.

To reach the primary objectives he envisages, Putin is able to absorb the damage that Turkey may inflict on Russia from time to time – as also happened during the war in the South Caucasus. The pragmatism that guided the relationship between Vladimir Lenin and Kemal Atatürk, both of whom resented the West in the wake of the Great War, inspired Putin in establishing a comparable relationship with Erdoğan in a new multipolar world – as he views it – in the aftermath of the Cold War.

There is one NATO country, and candidate EU member, that Mr Putin is happy with: Turkey. Recep Tayyip Erdogan, Turkey's president, has said nothing about the mistreatment of Mr Navalny or the arrests of thousands of Russians who protested against it.

His silence is testimony to a remarkable entente that has developed between the two authoritarian leaders. It is an improbable relationship. Deep historical rivalries divide Russia and Turkey, and their interests collide, sometimes violently, in many areas. Yet the two men

---

[162] Ibid.

share a bond in hard power that is reshaping regional politics and posing awkward problems for Turkey's Western allies.

Yet even as Turkey's drones pummelled the Russian tanks used by the Armenian side, Mr Putin praised Mr Erdogan as someone he could do business with. "Working with such a partner is not only pleasant but also safe," he told an audience of foreign experts at the Valdai Discussion Club in October. Mr Erdogan, in turn, saluted Mr Putin by testing the s-400 missile system that Turkey had bought from Russia. In November they ended the fighting by striking a bargain that gives Russia a military presence in Nagorno-Karabakh and Turkey an economic stronghold in the South Caucasus.

That deal represents one of the biggest geopolitical shake-ups since the end of the cold war, when Russia and Turkey were on opposite sides. It also carries a message about the use of hard power and the reality of a multipolar world.

And after nearly 30 years of fruitless talks over Nagorno-Karabakh, it was Turkey's military backing and Russia's acquiescence that helped Azerbaijan regain territory and shake up one of the least soluble conflicts in the Caucasus.

To Mr Putin, this was a demonstration of a new multipolar order, something he had been advocating since 2007, when, at the Munich Security Conference, he first took issue with the post-cold-war order with its "one centre of authority, one centre of force, one centre of decision-making". Russia's mission was to constrain America's new hegemony.

Nagorno-Karabakh was not the first time Russia had collaborated with Turkey to minimise the influence of Western powers. In the aftermath of the Bolshevik revolution and the collapse of the Ottoman empire, Kemal Ataturk briefly saw Lenin as an ally against the imperial West and the Bolsheviks saw Turkey as an accomplice in their quest for world dominance. They supplied Turkey with arms to fight the Greeks and the British, and the Turks allowed the Bolsheviks to take control of the oilfields of Azerbaijan and establish their rule in the South Caucasus. The deal between Ataturk and Lenin in 1921 that fixed Turkey's north-eastern border and limited its presence in the South Caucasus has held ever since.

Last year's war over Nagorno-Karabakh was a mirror image of that deal. It is now Mr Putin who is wooing Turkey in his confrontation with the West, hoping to use it as a wedge in NATO, while Mr Erdogan is projecting Turkey into its former spheres of influence. The warmth is all the more remarkable given that Turkey is the only NATO country to have collided with Russia militarily in recent years. In 2015 Turkey shot down a Russian warplane that had violated its airspace after flying over Syria.[163]

In 2005, Putin said that the collapse of the Soviet Union had been the greatest geopolitical catastrophe of the century. Thus, for him, since 2016, seeing Recep Tayyip Erdoğan's Turkey shaking the foundations of the Western collective security system and steadily moving away from the West represents the most valuable geopolitical prize Russia could acquire following that catastrophe. That outlook endeared Erdoğan to the Russian leader more than his Syrian protégé, Bashar al-Assad, and Turkey more than Armenia in the South Caucasus that relied on Russia for its defense.

As much as NATO-member Turkey moving away from the West could be considered a geopolitical prize for Russia, for Turkey itself, being rewarded in the South Caucasus – thanks to its partnership with Russia – was a real boost politically and entailed promising economic prospects.

As far as Mr Putin is concerned, using Turkey to undermine NATO from within is even more important than helping Mr Assad in Syria. The same motive partly explains Russia's acquiescence in Azerbaijan's war over Nagorno-Karabakh, when Turkey helped the Azeris. Mr Putin has managed to convert Russia's role as a mediator there into getting military boots on the ground, in the shape of peacekeepers, to supervise the new deal. Turkey has won both prestige in the region and a promise of a transport corridor through Armenia to Baku, which could join up with China's Belt and Road Initiative. The West got nothing.[164]

FIRST TURKISH MILITARY PRESENCE IN CAUCASUS IN OVER A CENTURY

One of the most significant consequences of the 44-day war in the last quarter of 2020 has been the return of Turkey, establishing its political and, albeit symbolically, military presence in the South Caucasus for the first time in more than a century. A very brief period in the turbulent years in the aftermath of World War I aside, Turkey has never had a solid presence in the South Caucasus except for relatively short periods at the end of the 16th century and in the 17th century. Therefore, enjoying a degree of partnership and cooperation with Russia in the region might have far-reaching strategic ramifications.

It is remarkable that years ago in 2006, Fiona Hill (a Russia specialist who served in the U.S. National Security Council and clashed with Donald Trump)

[163] *The Economist*, "The Odd Couple", *op. cit.*
[164] Ibid.

and Ömer Taşpınar could foresee the potential for a new bilateral relationship for Turkey and Russia. They also comprehended the frustration of both with the U.S. regional policies and European attitudes:

Since 2003, Turkey and Russia have drawn together in a new bilateral relationship. Mutual frustration with US regional policies and European attitudes has been the main driver of this rapprochement, along with expanding trade and increasing common ground on foreign-policy issues. Turkish-Russian relations have not yet blossomed into a strategic partnership, and suspicions linger after centuries of geopolitical competition, but the United States can no longer rely on Turkey as an automatic counterweight to Russia in regions like the Black Sea and the Caucasus. Together, Turkey and Russia also have the potential to obstruct American policy initiatives in the Middle East.[165]

What Hill and Taşpınar foresaw in 2006, as Brookings Institution fellows in Washington, was realized in 2020–2021 and culminated in the South Caucasus. Azerbaijan sought a counterweight to a newly strengthened Russian influence in the Caucasus and found it in Turkey. Russia acquiesced to Turkey's role, and the unprecedented cooperation between Russia and Turkey was realized as the immediate outcome of a mutual understanding of realpolitik. That unprecedented cooperation had been Turkey's and Russia's opening a joint military facility in Azerbaijan to help monitor the ceasefire agreement that came into force on November 10, 2020, a stark indicator of shifting geopolitics in the region.

Staffed by an equal number of Russian and Turkish troops, the centre formally opened on January 30, 2021 in Azerbaijan, very close to Nagorno-Karabagh. The principle of equality was observed to the extent that the formal name of the centre avoided favouring one side over the other. In Turkish, it is called the "Turkish-Russian Joint Centre," while in Russian, the "Joint Russian-Turkish Centre."

The former Russian president who is currently the deputy chairman of the national security council, Dmitriy Medvedev, viewed the joint military centre as a "*stabilizing factor*" in the region. He underlined the importance of cooperation with Turkey. Medvedev stated: "*We* [the Russians] *need to recognize the reality in our region, that today we need to discuss this issue with our partners in Turkey*".[166]

---

[165] Fiona Hill and Omer Taspinar, "Turkey and Russia: Axis of the Excluded?", *Survival*, Vol. 48, No. 1 (March 2006), 81-92

[166] *The Moscow Times*, "Russia, Turkey Open Joint Military Center in Azerbaijan", February 3, 2021. https://www.themoscowtimes.com/2021/02/03/russia-turkey-open-joint-military-center-in-azerbaijan-a72818

The establishment of the joint military centre with Turkey, *"a rare case of direct military cooperation between the two historical foes who have lately become custodians of a shaky security condominium in their shared neighborhood"*,[167] was also important for Russia because it represented the first Russian military presence on Azerbaijani-controlled territory in the South Caucasus since Baku terminated it in 2013.

For Turkey, it was much more important. It represented the first formal Turkish military presence in the Caucasus in more than a century. In 1918, Enver Pasha, the Minister of War of the Ottoman Empire during the Great War and the leader of the Committee of Union and Progress (CUP), the nationalist party that led Ottoman Turkey into World War I, ordered the establishment of the Islamic Army of the Caucasus in July 1918. Enver looked for victory in the void Russia had left the Caucasus in the wake of the Bolshevik Revolution of 1917. The Islamic Army of Caucasus aimed to mobilize Muslims in the Caucasus and Transcaspian regions.

Under the command of his half-brother Nuri Pasha, the Islamic Army of Caucasus, with its 20 thousand soldiers comprising Turks, Azerbaijanis, Daghestanis, and Chechens, fought mainly against the Armenians and captured Baku in September 1918. It withdrew from Baku and Azerbaijan following the collapse of the Syrian front and when Istanbul's defence was endangered. Those battlefield developments led to the Armistice at the end of November 1918.

Turkish and Azerbaijani soldiers near Baku, during the battle for the city, 1918. Unknown photographer.

President Recep Tayyip Erdoğan turned the spotlight on this very little-

[167] Ibid.

known and rarely referenced episode of modern Turkish history in his speech during the victory parade in Baku, on December 10, 2020, where troops from Turkey participated along with the Azerbaijani soldiers who fought in the 44-day war for Nagorno-Karabagh. Erdoğan, for the first time, eulogized the controversial figure of Turkish history, Enver Pasha, identified with pan-Turkism during the end of his political career and regarded as the main culprit who deposed Sultan Abdulhamid, the historical icon for Turkey's Islamists.

Speaking next to Ilham Aliyev, the President of Azerbaijan, in front of Turkish and Azerbaijani troops on the victory parade ground decorated with the crescent and starred flags of Turkey and Azerbaijan, Erdoğan in nationalistic glorification exclaimed:

Today is the day the souls of Nuri Pasha, Enver Pasha, and the heroic soldiers of the Islamic Army of Caucasus are blessed.

After more than a century, Turkish boots were back in the South Caucasus. The flag of Turkey was hoisted on the shores of the Caspian Sea, looking towards the Turkic sphere of Transcaspian, Central Asian geopolitics.

Erdoğan's neo-Ottomanism had attained its full Eurasianist magnitude, more concretely than at any time previously, by establishing Turkey's politico-military presence, alongside economic and commercial prospects, in the South Caucasus.

The incontestable victory achieved by Azerbaijan thanks to Turkey's military support in the last quarter of the year 2020 crowned the military achievements of the first half of the year and glorified Erdoğan's nationalist autocratic regime.

Turkey's militarized foreign policy and belligerence had paid off.

NEO-OTTOMANIST TURKEY: FOR HOW LONG?

WARS COST MONEY

Erdoğan's militarized foreign policy within the context of neo-Ottomanist ambitions provided political capital for his autocratic regime, but also gave rise to questions concerning to what extent and for how long such a policy could be sustainable given the frailty of the Turkish economy.

Comparing Hitler with Mussolini and both with Erdoğan in terms of competence to accomplish imperial glory, an Israeli pundit offered a salient analysis:

The difference between Hitler and Mussolini wasn't ambition or a willingness to dispatch troops in the name of imperial glory. The key difference was that Hitler had the economic and technological resources of Germany to conquer nearly all of Europe. Without comparable industrial might, Mussolini could invade Ethiopia and Albania but by the time his armies reached Greece, they had met their match.

In the East Mediterranean and much of the Middle East and North Africa, Erdogan seems to be going down the same route as the two dictators, employing angry, aggressive rhetoric with boots on the ground. Turkey right now has troops in no fewer than 13 countries, is routinely sending drill ships and naval vessels into economic waters claimed by its neighbors and is meddling diplomatically everywhere from Palestine to Azerbaijan.

Erdogan doesn't conceal his great power ambitions, which makes Turkey appear even more threatening to the countries it regards as part of its ambit, namely those that were once part of the Ottoman Empire.

But the threat is illusory. In the first half of the Erdogan era, Turkey looked like it was on its way to becoming an Asian (Minor) Tiger. Its economy was growing 7% annually, and Turkish industry was emerging as a global player and export powerhouse. In the second half of the Erdogan era, GDP continued to grow but fueled mainly by the short-term fix of showering cheap credit on the construction industry.[168]

The statistical data on economy and finance indisputably illustrates that Turkey is far from being a rising economic power. A country in serious enough trouble that it should be seeking a bailout from the International Monetary Fund is in stark contradiction to its aspiring great power image. The discrepancy between being a rising revisionist power on the international stage of power politics and being far from a rising economic power poses an insoluble problem

---

[168] David Rosenberg, "Turkey Doesn't Have the Economic Bite to Back Up Erdogan's Bark", *Haaretz*, October 28, 2020. https://www.haaretz.com/middle-east-news/turkey-erdogan-doesn-t-have-the-economic-bite-to-back-up-erdogan-s-bark-1.9263259

for Erdoğan's mid-term or long-term objectives.

David Rosenberg pointed out a simple fact:

The economy is important because armies and even more so, wars, cost money. The pressure arising from Erdogan's foreign adventures is already straining the country's budget as the military by one estimate is eating up a quarter of government spending… A lot of that spending is going to Turkey's defense industry, which Erdogan correctly sees it as the linchpin of Turkey's rise to great power status. No country can seriously aspire to push around its neighbors and issue threats if it doesn't have the tanks and planes to back it up. And, it's no good to rely on imported tanks and planes both for reasons of prestige and to protect itself from an arms embargo.[169]

Due to Erdoğan's prioritizing it, Turkey now (as of 2020–2021) has the 14th largest military industry in the world.

Turkey had one company on the list of Top 100 Global Defense Companies. Presently it has seven more companies than Israel, Russia, Sweden and Japan combined. Turkey's share of arms imports from 2015 to 2019 decreased by 48 percent compared to the preceding five-year period. The country has transitioned from importing 70 percent of its military hardware to 30 percent… Turkey is one of only twenty-two states manufacturing armed drones, adding another dimension to its regional military might.[170]

Although Turkey's growing military industry provided the essential ingredients for Erdoğan to implement his militarized foreign policy driven by neo-Ottomanist impulses, it could not overcome a major problem: technological depth. As long as Turkey relies on imported components, like the engines needed to power its biggest platforms, it cannot be militarily independent. That means Turkey is not exempt from sanctions imposed as a foreign policy tool when its interests and foreign policies may contradict those of military technology suppliers.

For tanks, tank engines, drones, submarines, fighter planes, and missile defense systems, Turkey depends on countries that vary from Germany to Ukraine and Canada to the United States. As a Carnegie Endowment report documented, showcase projects such as a major battle tank, an amphibious assault ship, an armed drone, and a jet fighter project have all run into problems completing development or filling export orders because the other countries

---

[169] Ibid.
[170] Ferhat Gurini, "Turkey's Unpromising Defense Industry", Carnegie Endowment for Peace, October 09, 2020.

involved won't give permission to Turkey to use their technology.[171]

Therefore, because in the 21st century a truly great military power has to be a great technology power, and Turkey is far from being this, it will hardly be able to sustain its ambitious foreign policy. *"Turkey if anything is heading backwards. Never a great tech power to begin with – it ranks 35th among 60 countries in the Bloomberg Innovation Index, behind Portugal, Greece, and Romania".[172]*

Turkey's domestic political and cultural climate is not conducive to advancing technologically, given that Erdoğan's regime is tainted by repressive policies and cronyism that have sparked a brain-drain, which has only accelerated since the crackdown in 2016 following the botched coup. Rosenberg explained the discernible phenomenon of Turkey today in the following terms:

Erdoğan's vision of Turkish greatness, which is inseparable from a society that distrusts and discourages independent thinking, is antithetical to the kind of tech culture that might make Turkey at least a contender for great power-dom.[173]

The conclusion reached is remarkable: that likening Erdoğan to Putin rather than Mussolini would be more contemporary and telling.

A more contemporary analogy than Mussolini might be Vladimir Putin's Russia. Russia may be a second-rater industrially and is only a few notches higher in innovative prowess than Turkey (No. 26 in the world, according to Bloomberg), but at it does have a real defense industry and vast natural resources. Even so, Putin can't begin to compete with the U.S. or China. He fights his wars on the cheap. And, Turkey isn't even in Putin's league.[174]

Given that Erdoğan's Turkey is far from being a technological power – and not even in the same league with Putin's Russia, an industrial second-rater – then the future does not bode well for its militarized foreign policy. Technological capability can thus well be regarded as an insurmountable barrier to the successful outcome of Erdoğanist neo-Ottomanism.

TURKEY: A "SICK MAN" THAT NEVER WAS

Resentment of Recep Tayyip Erdoğan's neo-Ottomanism, Turkey's diplomatic isolation in the international arena, and the never-ending cycles of economic and financial crises Turkey is subjected to under his crony-capitalism

---

[171] Ibid.
[172] Ibid.
[173] Rosenberg, "Turkey Doesn't Have the Economic Bite to Back Up Erdogan's Bark", op. cit.
[174] Ibid.

and corruption have inspired the "sick man" analogy. It is a way of expressing autocratic Turkey under Erdoğan; pursuing a militarized foreign policy is unsustainable because it would probably succumb under pressure to Turkey's ailing economy.

In its review of the year 2020, *Foreign Policy* ascertained that "*Turkey took its expansionist vision to new heights*". However, it repeatedly referred to Turkey as a country "*with a battered economy*", casting doubt on the sustainability of Turkish foreign policy activism as it was manifested in 2020. It remarked:

> *Despite the strongman facade, there are signs that Erdogan's foundation is cracking… and his foreign policy has proved onerous and costly… The Turkish economy, once a poster child of GDP growth is wheezing.*[175]

The apparent asymmetry between the ostensible robustness of Turkish foreign policy and the frailty of the economy gave rise to Turkey's prognostication as a "sick man", a metaphor extensively used for its predecessor, the Ottoman Empire in the 19th century.

Krzysztof Strachota, Head of the Department of Turkey, Caucasus, Central Asia of Centre for Eastern Studies (the Polish acronym is OSW), was among the very rare European experts on Turkey to notice the triviality or truism of this recurring "Sick Man of Europe" theme. He summarized the overall European outlook to the assertive Turkish foreign policy in these words:

> *This country [Turkey] is irritating and tiring… Much to the annoyance [of the West], Turkey delivers power – with high frequency and regularity, and calibrated to almost any level of sensitivity in Western audiences. The most recent is the support that the Turkish authorities give to Azerbaijan in its offensive against the Armenians in Nagorno-Karabakh… The vision of such a new aggressive Turkey, almost a "caliphate", is dominated by an autocrat, pursuing an adventurous policy that does not bring results and serves only to strengthen the nationalist mandate of the government.*[176]

According to Strachota, the Europeans generally associated Turkey's economic woes with the execution of a militarized foreign policy, thereby foreseeing its eventual doom. Turkey in other words is, rather than a robust newly-born power, again a "sick man".

[175] Allison Meakem, "The Year in Review: Turkey's Year of Living Dangerously", *Foreign Policy*, December 25, 2020. https://foreignpolicy.com/2020/12/25/turkeys-year-of-living-dangerously/
[176] Krzysztof Strachota, "Dwie Turcje" [Two Turkeys], *Tygodnik Powszechny* [Weekly Standard], October 5, 2020. https://www.tygodnikpowszechny.pl/dwie-turcje-165079

In this perspective, Turkey is bankrupt, with foreign debts amounting to USD 460 billion (including short-term debts of USD 123 billion), with a weakening currency, a flight of investors and the threat of further sanctions. This Turkey – as is commonly believed in the West – has exhausted itself.[177]

Published in the respected Polish weekly *Tygodnik Powszechny* (which can boast Karol Wojtyla, later Pope Jean-Paul II, and the great poet and Nobel laureate Czesław Miłosz among its writers), Krzysztof Strachota's piece "Two Turkeys" cautioned Europeans about any superfluous predictions that economic and financial crises would mean the end of a coercive Turkey. The flaw in the Western assessment of Turkey is highlighted:

As for the economy – strangely enough, its collapse (and consequently the collapse of the government), predicted for many years, is not happening... The problem with Turkey is that it has developed an alternative to the Western paradigm of thinking and acting, becoming a binding point of reference for itself... The West can also be wrong, because it does not notice how much the world is changing, how much such a new Turkey has to look for new paths.[178]

In actuality, Europe was never right in conceiving of Turkey as a "sick man" even in the 19th century or in the last days of the Ottoman Empire. I am inspired by the Polish weekly to challenge the "Sick Man of Europe" metaphor of European historiography. It was after all nothing but a cliché, generally conceived as an established fact for decades by the Western elites.

The metaphor was coined in early 1853 by Tsar Nicholas I of Russia. While discussing his plans for Ottoman Turkey's partition with the British ambassador, he referred to it as the *"Sick Man of Europe"*. Tsar Nicholas was hoping to gain the Danubian Principalities that largely correspond to today's Romania and Moldova, as well as Bulgaria and Serbia. For his envisaged gains from Ottoman Turkey, he offered Egypt and Crete to Britain. They were under Ottoman suzerainty. The Ottoman capital Istanbul would become a free port as a result of the Russo-British deal. Nicholas I described the Ottoman Empire as *"sick man – a very sick man"*, a *"man who has fallen into a state of decrepitude"*, and a *"sick man... gravely ill"*.[179]

The irony of the history is that this same very sick man, gravely ill and fallen into a state of decrepitude, remained alive for almost 70 more years. Tsarist

---

[177] Ibid.
[178] Ibid.
[179] Caroline Finkel, Osman's Dream: The Story of the Ottoman Empire 1300-1923, Great Britain: John Murray Publishers, 2005.

Russia predeceased it. A few months after Nicholas I's depiction of Ottoman Turkey as "the Sick Man of Europe", whose territories he envisaged to partition between Russia and Britain, the Crimean War broke out. Britain and France allied with Ottoman Turkey against Russia in the war, which ended in 1856. Russia lost the Crimean War and was considerably weakened at its end. At the Congress of Paris, which served as a peace conference following the Crimean War, Ottoman Turkey was accepted as a European power in the Concert of Europe.

The promulgation of the Ottoman Edict of Reform following the Crimean War became another ground-breaking development of paramount historical importance in 1856. For most historians on modern Turkey, the Ottoman Reform of 1856 is a milestone in Turkey's perennial Western vocation.

In the three years from 1853 to 1856, the Ottoman Empire depicted by the Russian Tsar as the sick man of Europe rejuvenated, while Russia itself subsided under an ironic twist of events.

OVERTURNING CONVENTIONAL HISTORY

Both empires vanished around the same period, at the end of World War I. The outbreak of the Great War had terminated the Concert of Europe as such. Nonetheless Tsarist Russia's life came to an end, and not because it was on the Great War's losing side. On the contrary, Russia's allies, Britain and France, emerged as the World War I victors. The Bolshevik Revolution in 1917, an upheaval from within, terminated the Tsardom, and the Russian Empire transformed into a socialist republic.

Paradoxically, Ottoman Turkey was on the losing side of the Great War alongside its allies, Germany and Austria-Hungary, yet despite traumatic territorial losses, the Empire was left to survive. Christopher de Bellaigue, in his *Turkey's Hidden Past*, explained the peculiar situation in which the Ottoman Empire found itself:

Allied with Germany during the war, the Ottomans hoped to check Russian expansionism, win back territory in the Balkans, and, eventually, as the war progressed, to create a new Turkic empire in Central Asia. Instead, the Ottoman officials watched their subjects collude with the enemy in expelling them from Arab lands. Allied troops occupied Istanbul, eastern Thrace, the Aegean port city of Izmir, and parts of southern Anatolia. By

1918 the "sick man" was dead, and the Great Powers were about to decide how to dispose of his remains, even though the Ottoman government still formally held power.[180]

Whether by 1918 the sick man was dead or not is a disputable issue. The death of the Ottoman Empire needs to be sought elsewhere. It did meet its inevitable end, but not because it was a sick man already on the deathbed of history. In a sense similar to Russia, the Ottoman Empire ended from within, with the foundation of the Republic of Turkey. The republic founded in 1923 was formed in the Turkish nation-state format that replaced and succeeded it. Its birth resulted from a successful national struggle led by Ottoman generals. They succeeded in liberating certain Ottoman territories from the invading Greek armies supported by Britain in Asia Minor and those French forces attempting to invade the Cilicia and parts of the Southern Anatolia bordering Syria. They were the same Ottoman military leaders who fought on multiple fronts to defend the Empire's territories – in other words, the "Fatherland" – from Libya in 1911 or the Balkan wars in 1912, and from 1914 to 1918 in the Great War.

In hindsight, depiction of the Ottoman Empire as "the Sick Man of Europe" in the mid-19th century has proved to be inaccurate. The demise of the Empire in the aftermath of World War I should also not be viewed as an inevitability. The Ottoman Empire could have remained outside the Great War. The partitioning of its territories at the war's end was not preordained. Şükrü Hanioğlu, prominent historian at Princeton and professor of late Ottoman history, provided convincing arguments on this matter relying on archival data.

According to Prof. Hanioğlu, until August 1914, the date it signed an alliance with Germany, Turkey, seeking great power protection, knocked on the doors of every power in Europe, from Britain to France and even Russia. While Britain, France, and Russia were trying to obtain Ottoman Turkey's neutrality, the military top brass in Germany thought of an alliance with Turkey as more of a liability than an asset.[181]

Overriding his military's objections, Emperor Wilhelm II was determined to ally Turkey with Germany, thereby meeting the aspirations of the Turkish nationalist leadership of the CUP. The CUP was the ruling party of the Empire and had established autocratic rule in 1913, a year before the war. The CUP

---

[180] Christopher de Bellaigue, "Turkey's Hidden Past", *The New York Review of Books*, March 8, 2001.
[181] M. Şükrü Hanioğlu, "Dünya 'Biz''i Parçalamak için mi Savaştı?", *Sabah*, November 25, 2018; *Sabah Daily*, "Has the World Fought to Partition 'Us'?", November 25, 2018. https://www.sabah.com.tr/yazarlar/hanioglu/2018/11/25/dunya-bizi-parcalamak-icin-mi-savasti

government carried Ottoman Turkey into the Great War, perpetrated the Armenian Genocide in 1915, and stayed in power until 1918.

Hanioğlu maintains that to enter the war on the side of Germany was not a foregone conclusion. It was more the result of a miscalculation regarding the fortunes that the war would bring, and mismanagement of the asymmetric alliance on the part of the Ottoman Turkish government.

To confirm Prof. Hanioğlu's argument, from my viewpoint, it was the Sublime Porte under the grip of the CUP that was enthusiastic about the war. Like the other belligerents, the Young Turks' government also thought the war would be short-lived, at the most from August 2014 to Christmas. The Ottoman Turkish leadership, craving the territories lost by the Empire in the preceding decade, calculated it would sit among the winners at the peace conference table by the end of 1914.

Therefore, the Great War in the Ottoman Turkish leadership's eyes and minds was a war of choice, an opportunity to get back the recently lost territories. Losing the Empire entirely was never in their minds.

In that respect, the Turkish leadership's psyche following World War I was entirely different from that of its erstwhile wartime allies, namely the Germans and Austrians. In Germany, the trauma of losing its Reich led to the ascent of Hitler in pursuance of the Third Reich that initiated World War II. The traumatized Austrians reconciled to ending up in a small landlocked country in Central Europe.

The Turks, on their part, erected a new, vibrant state over the Ottoman imperial debris. The founders of the Turkish republic were former CUP members who had governed the Ottoman Empire during the Great War. With their pre-war and post-war experiences galvanized in the victorious national liberation struggle waged against the Great War winners, they succeeded in regaining territory where they embarked on establishing a modern state.

Thus, the continuity of power from the Ottoman Empire to Republican Turkey relieved the sense of loss and the trauma that could otherwise have resulted from the fall of the empire. Moreover, the momentous achievement of the liberation of Asia Minor and Eastern Thrace followed by modern statecraft was a source of national pride.

More importantly, the successful transition from decrepit state to the new, ambitious one paradoxically supplied the urge to regain imperial grandeur. The invisible foundations of neo-Ottomanism were laid during the birth of modern Turkey, almost a century ago. Those foundations were however long overshadowed by the determination of Kemalist Turkey with a conspicuous pro-Europe, Western vocation.

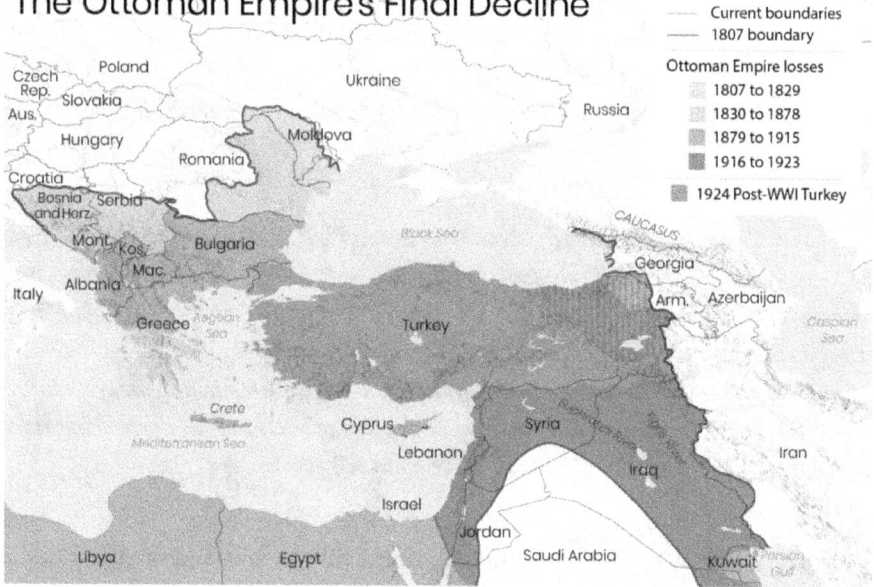

The Ottoman Empire's Final Decline

Current boundaries
1807 boundary

Ottoman Empire losses
1807 to 1829
1830 to 1878
1879 to 1915
1916 to 1923

1924 Post-WWI Turkey

Source: britannica.com

THE RECKONING

In the centennial of the Turkish Republic's foundation, neo-Ottomanism emerged as its new orientation and shaped its future ambitions. The new Turkey has a Eurasianist trajectory in contrast to the pro-Europe perspectives of the Republic's founders. Following World War II, Turkey – a mainstay of the Truman Doctrine, a bulwark against the Soviet Union and ultimately a Transatlantic Alliance (NATO) member – was firmly anchored in the Western system. In 1959, it applied for associate membership of the European Economic Community (EEC), the EU's precursor, and signed the Ankara Agreement in 1963, which initiated a three-step process towards creating a customs union to help secure Turkey's full membership in the EEC. The EU-Turkey Customs Union eventually came into effect at the end of 1995. In 1999, Turkey was declared a candidate member of the European Union. Negotiations for full membership were started in October 2005. Since 2016, accession negotiations have stalled. Turkey arrived at the crossroads of history to make an impelling strategic choice. The dramatic moment reached in recent Turkish history inspired the riveting analysis:

> *In 1945, having survived the war without having to fight and avoiding invasion by the German army, Turkey found itself pretty lonely after D-Day. The Soviet Union asked for two Turkish provinces and joint control over the straits. At that point in 1945, alone in standing against the Soviet threat for nearly a year and a half, Ankara made the strategic decision to become an integral part of the American side of the Cold War division. The Truman Doctrine was announced to protect Greece and Turkey and eventually these two countries both joined NATO in 1952.*

> *Today Turkey may be facing another "1945 moment". It is geopolitically stronger, capable of projecting military power in its neighborhood, as was demonstrated in the Caucasus most recently, but also very alone. Its relations with allies are conflictual, there is in both the Middle East and the Eastern Mediterranean a bloc of countries that treat it as a rival. 2021 is likely to be a year when consequential decisions will have to be made regarding Turkey's strategic identity. How much autonomy can Turkish foreign policy afford to enjoy while remaining either in the Atlantic Alliance or getting closer to the Russian Federation?[182]*

Despite the compelling historical moment at which Turkey had arrived, its track record throughout the second half of the 20th century and the first decade of the 21st century meant that quitting the Euro-Atlantic system was almost impossible to envision. For numerous Western politicians and Turkey experts, Turkish secularists, and pro-Western Turks alike, such a prospect sounded unthinkable. Notwithstanding occasional deviations due to its illiberal political culture and peculiar geopolitical aspect, Turkey, anchored in the Euro-Atlantic system, was a given. Following the botched coup in July 2016, Turkey's Eurasianist odyssey, under Erdoğan's leadership and the nationalist coalition, was watched with disbelief by many of them. Pro-Western secularist Turks and their American and European peers could not come to terms with the reality of Turkey's changing course.

---

[182] Özel, "2021: Year of Decisions", *op. cit.*

SEARCHING FOR NEW GEOPOLITICAL AXES IN A MULTIPOLAR WORLD

Many pundits took pains to prove why Turkey would not turn its back on its Euro-Atlantic ties. In vain. With Erdoğan at the helm, Turkey began to navigate Eurasianist geopolitics, dragging its anchor out of the Euro-Atlantic system. The widespread disbelief about Turkey's change of strategic course, and the futile efforts to assert the unlikeliness of such change, stemmed either from short memory or from carelessness. There were already strong signals that illustrated Turkey's deviation from its affiliation from the West and the Euro-Atlantic system more than a decade ago.

This testimony is what I had written in 2009 in a policy brief whose cover carried a photo of the Turkish and Syrian presidents, Recep Tayyip Erdoğan and Bashar al-Assad, who had developed a fraternal bond at the time:

Since the beginning of Fall 2009, not a single day goes by without reading titles and headings like "How the West Lost Turkey," "What Happens If Turkey Leaves the West," "Turkey: An Ally No More," "Turks' Eastern Turn," "The Turkish Temptation," "Turkey's Worrisome Approach to Iran and Israel," "The New Turkish Lexicon," "A NATO Without Turkey," "Is Turkey Iran's Friend?" "An Islamist Pivot to the East," "Disillusioned with Europe, Turkey Looks East," "Turkey and the Middle East - Looking East and South.

These are a few examples of titles of think-tank reports and the headings of op-ed pieces and articles appearing in periodicals and dailies in the West ranging from the United States to the United Kingdom, France, and Germany. They underscore the prevailing sentiment on both sides of the Atlantic on Turkey's current foreign policy direction. Implicit in all these analyses is a foregone conclusion that Turkey has reoriented itself and is making a historically significant detour away from the West towards its South and East, primarily the Muslim world. With it comes the perception – mainly among the Europeans – that "Neo-Ottomanism" is replacing some of the basic tenets of Republican Turkey. The Western-oriented secular Republican Turkey, which has remained loyal for decades to the principles laid out by its founder Kemal Atatürk, is seen to markedly contrast with the Ottoman Empire that reigned over the Middle East and parts of Eastern Europe for 400 years. Turkey's current foreign policy initiatives are considered to be a revival of the Ottoman vision.[183]

Moreover, my subsequent lines attest to the fact that the heated discussion on Turkey's strategic trajectory and changing the camps was also underway in

---

[183] Cengiz Çandar, "Turkey's 'Soft Power' Strategy: A New Vision for a Multipolar World", *Seta Policy Brief*, No. 38, December 2009.

2009, even before the Arab Spring and when Turkey's relations with the West had not yet gone awry:

There is a lively debate centered on whether Turkey is undergoing an axis shift, meaning Turkey is drifting away from the Transatlantic system and heading towards the Middle East in the most acclaimed dailies and journals of the Western world. One may witness a flurry of commentaries, appraisals and op-ed articles published in these media outlets. Taking notice of the vibrant debate on Turkey's orientation in the international sphere, Turkey's leaders underlined Turkey's position with varying degrees of emphasis. Despite the statements of Turkey's policymakers, which argue against the idea of shift of axis, the debates over Turkey's identity and foreign policy orientation have not lost steam. The shift should not be attributed to Turkey's departure from its Western ties to be replaced by those with the East but rather, a shift of power as the inevitable outcome of the end of the Cold War and a fact of the new millennium.[184]

My conclusion concerning the debate on Turkey's orientation prevalent at the end of the first decade of the 21st century was summarized in the title of my essay *"Turkey's 'Soft Power' Strategy: A New Vision for a Multipolar World"*. Rather than Turkey shifting its axis from the West to the East or the Middle East, it was navigating in a multipolar world. This would have to be seen as the inevitable outcome and underlying feature of the post–Cold War era. In hindsight, it may be considered a legitimate assessment of Turkey's posture, but not anymore.

Interestingly, more than a decade later, I encountered some reverberations of my account on Turkish foreign policy in two essays written by scholars from very different corners of the world. One from Australia at the end of 2020, the other from Georgia during the first quarter of 2021, they both argued that Turkey's forging a new geopolitical axis should be seen as a future independent of the West and of Russia. For the Georgian, it is the balancing act for Turkish foreign policy. In essence, their arguments were close to what I had envisaged for Turkey in 2009, in the emerging multipolar world.

In his clairvoyant piece, the Australian scholar Connor Dilleen wrote:

Turkey under Erdogan is increasingly pursuing an activist foreign policy designed to achieve two objectives: challenge the status quo and forge a global leadership role and enhance the regime's domestic legitimacy and ensure its survival. Erdogan's strategic disposition has also been categorized as both pan-Islamist and neo-Ottomanist, designed

---

[184] Ibid.

to leverage Islamic identity and renew a 'classical, civilizational model of the Ottoman Empire's legacy anchored by economic, military, and political power'…

Turkey's continued membership of NATO remains an important objective for both Brussels and Washington, despite Ankara's increasingly antagonistic attitude towards its NATO partners and its destabilizing military adventurism in Syria, Iraq, Libya, the eastern Mediterranean and Nagorno-Karabakh… Brussels' and Washington's willingness to make concessions to preserve Ankara's participation in NATO was evident… But, unlike the US and the EU, Turkey doesn't necessarily view its future as a binary choice between the West and Russia. For Ankara, this likely represents a false choice between two options that would likely constrain rather than enable its ambitions.[185]

The Georgian scholar Emil Avdalani evaluated Turkish foreign policy's activism as a quest for autonomy in the West. In his formulation, that is the pursuance of *a multi-vector approach to foreign affairs*. Apparently well-versed on Russian history and with a keen interest in geopolitics, Avdalani, to advance his argument, made a comparative analysis of Russian and Turkish perceptions and highlighted similarities. In his assessment, Turkey's distancing itself from the West to eventually break with it is a myth.

A revealing element in Ankara's foreign policy is that geography still commands the country's perception of itself and its place in the world, perhaps more so than for any other large country. Rather than being attached solely to the Western axis, over the past two decades Turkey has pursued a multi-vector approach to foreign affairs.

The country is on the European periphery. Its experience is similar to Russia's in that both have absorbed extensive western influence, whether in institutions, foreign policy, or culture. Both have been anchored for centuries on the geopolitics of the European continent. Because a multi-vector foreign policy model provides more room for maneuver, economic gains, and growth of geopolitical power, both countries wanted to break free of their single-axis approach to foreign policy…

Over the past two decades Turkey has been actively searching for new geopolitical axes. For Ankara, close relations with Russia – lamented by Western observers – is a means to balance its historical dependence on European geopolitics. The same foreign policy model can explain Moscow's geopolitical thinking since the late 2000s, when its ties with Asian states developed quickly as an alternative to a dependence on, and attachment to, Western geopolitics.

Thus, we come to the first myth of Turkish foreign policy: that Ankara is distancing itself from the West with the aim of eventually breaking those ties entirely. Breaking off relations

---

[185] Dilleen, "Turkey Forges a Strategic Future Independent of Russia", *op. cit.*

with NATO is not an option for Turkey. Its goal is to balance its deep ties with the West, which were not producing the benefits it was hoping for, with a more active policy in other regions. Hence Turkey's resurgence in the Middle East.[186]

The disbelief that Turkey would ever turn its back on the West, whatever the contrary signals are, is understandable in light of the historical record. Eric Rouleau's observation in 1993 when new horizons opened to Turkey with the end of the Cold War is a stark example of the perception that Turkey's European vocation and pro-Western trajectory is irreversible. The wording and the dominant spirit of Rouleau's seminal piece titled "The Challenges to Turkey" vividly reflected such perception:

But even when Turkish enthusiasm over prospects in Central Asia and the Middle East was at its height, Ankara never deviated from its long-standing and deep conviction that Turkey's future lies with Europe. While analysts were still overestimating regional potential, the authorities steadfastly maintained that there was no substitute for the European Community, and that Turkey's integration would be accelerated the day Europeans understood that Turkey alone could serve as a bridge, or even a buffer, between East and West.

Turkey's determination to become an integral part of Europe is the fruit of a national consensus that could seem strange in a Muslim country with nothing more than a geographical toehold in Europe. In fact, this aspiration is not recent. The Ottoman Empire was itself a European power by virtue of vast possessions in the continent, and as early as the beginning of the nineteenth century, the reformist sultans sought to modernize the empire by adopting the structures, behaviors and customs of its more developed Western neighbors (and especially, paradoxically, of Republican France). The Young Turk Revolution at the beginning of this century, and especially Atatürk's revolution two decades later transformed what had been an orientation into a deliberate policy, if not a dogma: Turkey's rebirth, modernization and democratization could be achieved only through full integration in the advanced industrial world, Western and more precisely European.[187]

Along the rosy global horizon in the aftermath of the Cold War, Turkey's relatively belle epoque ushered in by Turgut Özal's reforms had left no space to imagine Turkey's future on the rails of Eurasianism, steaming away from the West.

---

[186] Emil Avdaliani, "Turkey's Foreign Policy Balancing Act", *Besa Center Perspective Paper*, No. 1972, March 21, 2021. https://besacenter.org/perspectives-papers/turkey-foreign-policy-balancing/
[187] Rouleau, "The Challenges to Turkey", op. cit.

TURKEY'S HOSTILE DANCE WITH THE WEST

Until the mid-2010s, analyses emphasized that Turkey did not view its future as a binary choice between the West and Russia, or that what it has ultimately been trying to achieve was balancing its ties with the Euro-Atlantic world. These kinds of inherently conservative Turkish foreign policy analyses contradicted the revisionist aims and the nationalist/neo-Ottomanist ideological motivations that set Turkey on a new path. The main flaw of the realpolitik school is that it consistently either disregards or underestimates the ideological element underlying specific historical circumstances, which nonetheless becomes the main driver for nations.

Another point usually missed in the analyses of Turkish foreign policy is not paying deserved attention to the internal political scene and the nature of the regime. Turkey's foreign policy performance in the aftermath of 2016, the year the consolidation of autocracy took a dramatic turn, presents a mirror image of the internal political scene. The ultra-nationalist repressive regime that stifled dissent by curtailing fundamental freedoms was trying to resurrect the glory of the past. That vision, resurrecting the past imperial glory, the reflection of nationalist authoritarianism, drove Turkey's foreign policy. Such dynamics would unavoidably push Turkey to distance itself from the West and proceed along the Eurasianist trajectory.

Within a decade, in the most crucial geopolitics, Turkey had abandoned its soft power strategy and instead adopted hard power as a tool to advance its foreign policy objectives – but more importantly, especially after 2016, to set out on a Eurasianist track. What has not changed is Turkey's formal status in specific Euro-Atlantic organizations.

The dramatic evolution in Turkey's strategic choices did not formally affect its membership in Western institutions. Neither did Turkey wish to leave them, nor was there any drive on the part of Turkey's erstwhile Western allies to terminate its affiliation with those institutions: they were unwilling to let Turkey join Russia and China by breaking its formal ties to the Euro-Atlantic institutions. On the side of Turkey, there was no urge to make an institutional break, as long as these affiliations do not serve as insurmountable barriers on Turkey's Eurasianist route. On the other side, the Western world felt no urge to push Turkey out totally.

It is evident that Turkey is forging a new geopolitical axis that may see it increasingly diverge from the core objectives of NATO. But, importantly, this axis will also act as a counterbalance to Russia across the Middle East and Eurasia. Policymakers in Washington and Brussels ruminating on how to manage Ankara should remain mindful of this. They should continue to leverage the transactional nature of Turkish foreign policy under Erdogan to encourage Ankara to work with the West, rather than against it, regardless of whether Turkey remains a functional member of the NATO alliance.[188]

The US Secretary of State Antony Blinken, who never had spared critical remarks on Turkey's Russia connection, revealed the Atlanticist thinking on Turkey at the NATO meeting in March 2021. In his first public conversation with NATO Secretary-General Jens Stoltenberg, he said: *"It is no secret that we have problems with Turkey, but it is also no secret that it is in our interest to keep Turkey anchored to the Alliance...NATO should be used as a platform to resolve problems"*.[189] Only two months before, he had accused Turkey of not acting like an ally over its acquisition of S-400 Russian missile defense systems.

Parallel to Blinken, his EU equivalent Josep Borrell, the High Commissioner of the European Union for Foreign Affairs and Security Policy – in other words, the EU "foreign minister" – revealed in his blog the footing of the EU-Turkey relationship in 2020–2021. The EU position vis-à-vis Turkey was interpreted by experts like former EU ambassador in Turkey, Marc Pierini, as *"reversible and conditional"* as expressed in Borrell's blog, albeit hidden in carefully selected diplomatic wording. The blog entry highlighted the seemingly insurmountable obstacles on the road for the EU and Turkey's joint journey, if such would ever be possible. It also reflected the transactional nature of the relationship acquired in the second half of the second decade of the 2000s, and that replaced the main aspiration of Turkish foreign policy since the1950s: European accession:

Turkey is an important regional power and its historical destiny could well be to join the rest of Europe in the unique peace project that we are building under the banner of the European Union. At a moment when strategic polarisation seems to be resurfacing around the world, the strengthening of a European democratic pillar that includes Turkey could be a key balancing element. This is not a given, but the European Council has offered a possible bridge.

We now have to build this bridge and I believe we can do this. With political clear choices and commitment from all sides. On our side, the EU is ready to invest the required efforts. If

---

[188] Dilleen, "Turkey Forges a Strategic Future Independent of Russia", *op. cit.*
[189] https://www.state.gov/secretary-antony-j-blinken-and-nato-secretary-general-jens-stoltenberg-at-a-moderated-conversation-with-rosa-balfour/

Turkey is equally willing to do so, and underlines its more positive rhetoric with respective actions, we can continue to move from de-escalation to building a mutually beneficial agenda.

The situation remains fragile... Indeed, the EU has a strategic interest in the development of a cooperative and mutually beneficial relationship with Turkey. And this is equally true for Turkey. The EU is by far Turkey's number one import and export partner, as well as source of investment. Looking at the latest pre-pandemic figures, we see €69.8 billion of Turkey's exports directed towards the EU, and €58.5 billion of its foreign direct investment (FDI) coming from the EU. More than 5.5 million Turkish citizens are living in EU member states, and according to Eurobarometer 61% of Turkish citizens look at the EU as an actor that counts in the world. And with its security and defence anchored within NATO, it seems difficult to believe that Turkey could realistically envisage better options than pursuing a European path.

It would of course be naive to consider that problems are over. The report on EU-Turkey relations that I have presented jointly with the European Commission to the European Council has a double-track approach and identifies four main elements of tension in the relationship: maritime disputes in the Eastern Mediterranean; the Cyprus settlement question; divergent objectives in regional conflicts, notably in Libya and Syria; and the deterioration of democratic standards in Turkey.[190]

Marc Pierini had noted already in 2018 that Turkey's feelings toward Europe are not credible for two reasons, and he cited those:

First, for years President Erdoğan has based his electoral strategy on sharp criticisms of Europe. In 2017, he even pelted EU leaders with offensive remarks, including references to "Nazis" and "gas chambers," a total anathema in European politics. No politician in Berlin, Paris, The Hague, or Vienna will easily be convinced of that these were passing, innocuous campaign words. They are seen as part of a carefully crafted nationalist narrative, and they have lasting effects.

Second, a return to the rule of law in Turkey is conceivable in principle but will not happen... Looking at the European side of the story, a striking sea change on Turkey's accession has taken place... Now, not only France has ruled out accession, but the Austrian, Dutch, and German governments have made "no accession" one of the pillars of their coalition agreements. Add to this EU's rule of unanimity for all enlargement issues, and it becomes obvious that accession will not happen- not even preparatory work for accession...

---

[190] Josep Borrell, European Union External Action Service (EEAS), "EU-Turkey Relations: The Need to Build Bridges", *From the Blog*, March 30, 2021. https://eeas.europa.eu/headquarters/headquarters-homepage/9593 0/eu-turkey-relations-need-build-bridges_en

European governments consider Turkey a strategic partner for a host of reasons and want to maintain strong ties with the country, particularly in the commercial, economic, military, counterterrorism, and humanitarian fields. Therefore, even if a political alliance – once embodied in the accession ambitions of Turkey- is now out of question due to Ankara's going down the autocratic path…

It seems likely that the atmosphere of EU-Turkey relations will remain tense, for reasons mostly related to Turkey's domestic politics. President Erdoğan's political fortunes are now linked to the goodwill of the nationalist party, the MHP, which itself is not pro-European and backs the ultra-presidential system now in place. This means that Turkish politics will uphold the one-man rule system and will not steer the country toward the European democratic standards.[191]

Arguably the most prolific American Turkey expert in the second decade of the 2000s, Nicholas Danforth penned the captivating title *Turkey and the West: A Hostile Dance*, where he referred to different scenarios regarding Turkey's future. Danforth had stepped out in 2020 as the proponent of a necessary respite in American-Turkish relations. In December 2020, in an unconventional manner not typical of Washington's political environment, he suggested to then U.S. President-elect Joseph Biden that letting Turkey go might be the best way to repair the ties in the long run. Nicholas Danforth boldly made the following main point in his treatise:

The United States long been condemned for cooperating with authoritarian regimes in the Middle East. Trump added a twist to this, accommodating Erdogan's authoritarianism and not even getting cooperation in return. Biden may have inherited a train wreck in the making, but at least he has no room for moral compromise. You can't cooperate with an authoritarian regime that is dead set against cooperating with you.[192]

Three months later, in his depiction of Turkey's hostile dance with the West, although not ruling out a hard break – as he termed it – Danforth was more prudent. He predicted that both sides, namely Turkey and the West, will avoid an irrevocable rupture, at least for the near future.

As Turkey's relations with the United States and European Union have grown ever more strained over the past five years, analysts have struggled to anticipate how this trend will develop, and where it will ultimately lead. To aid in this inevitably speculative act of

[191] Marc Pierini, "Turkey Needs the EU", *Euronews*, September 3, 2018. https://www.euronews.com/2018/09/03/turkey-needs-the-eu-the-question-is-how-much-its-relationship-will-cost-
[192] Nicholas Danforth, "It Is Time to Let Turkey Go", *Foreign Policy*, December 15, 2020. https://foreignpolicy.com/2020/12/15/it-is-time-to-let-turkey-go/

prognostication, they have suggested a number of scenarios, running from the likely to the unlikely and the optimistic to the pessimistic... A number of predictions begin from the assumption that, when relations eventually reach a breaking point, Erdoğan will be forced to back down, enabling Ankara and its estranged allies to muddle through. Others start from the opposite position but reach a similar conclusion, assuming that the West will continue to back down and thereby preserve some semblance of the current status quo...

A plausible scenario that could play out in the coming years involves both Ankara and its Western partners offering just enough concessions at key moments to avoid an irrevocable rupture, even as the relationship steadily becomes more hostile. In this adversarial dance, Ankara would continue many of its provocative activities, while the US and EU would slowly shift toward a policy of containment. Yet Erdoğan, eager to avoid a complete economic collapse or unwinnable military conflict, would always step back from provoking too forceful of a backlash. America and Europe, meanwhile, would continue to ratchet up the pressure, but, equally wary of an economic crisis or military conflict, recoil from anything that might push Erdoğan over the brink.

The question remains, of course, whether a misstep by either side could throw off this constantly recalibrated arrangement, or whether at a certain point it will simply become untenable. So far Turkey and the West have already muddled through longer than many pessimists thought possible. They will probably continue to for the near future, but a hard break should not be ruled out.[193]

It is not an easy fix to disentangle transnational security mechanisms without a history-making paradigm shift. The dissolution of the Warsaw Pact, NATO's weaker adversary, required the end of the Cold War and the breakup of the Soviet Union.

Significant strategic shifts of big or middle-sized powers like Turkey cannot happen overnight. Therefore, preserving its place in the Euro-Atlantic organizations and institutions was not mutually exclusive of Turkey's Eurasianist new strategic orientation. With time, Turkey's new trajectory became more discernible, and it carried the potential of being one of the most crucial strategic changes in the post–Cold War period.

---

[193] Nicholas Danforth, "Turkey and the West: A Hostile Dance", *Eliamep,* March 19, 2021. https://www.eliamep.gr/wp-content/uploads/2021/03/Policy-paper-60-Nick-Danforth-final.pdf

DIFFERING VIEWS ON CHINA & RUSSIA

Moreover, Turkey's turnaround should be conceived within the context of the structural changes at a global scale. In the second and third decades of the 21st century, the replacement of unipolarity in the international system with multipolarity is practically an indisputable fact. The centre of gravity is moving from Euro-Atlantic geopolitics to the Asian-Pacific. The United States, starting during the Obama presidency, gaining pace during Trump's and continuing with Joseph Biden, has increasingly deprioritized the Middle East. All this serves as ingredients for Turkey's neo-Ottomanism, which has seemed, albeit in different forms, to outlive Erdoğan. The prevailing international climate has been particularly conducive for illiberal and/or authoritarian projects.

Where do things stand now? Liberals are on the defensive. They argued that globalization would build on itself and increasingly tie the world together, but instead it provoked a massive backlash, and states are weaponizing interdependence. They saw democracy as improving at its core and marching forward on the periphery, but it is now regressing and retreating. They saw Chinese authoritarianism as doomed to fail, but it has succeeded beyond all expectations. They preached cosmopolitanism, but it turns out that everybody's a little bit nationalist (and gets more so under stress). They claimed that norms constrained behavior, but the reality is that shameless people can break them without consequence. These setbacks may be temporary, and the world may get back on the upward track it seemed to be traveling. But maybe not.[194]

The "maybe not" option would prolong the life of Turkey, an autocracy, a neo-Ottomanist ambitious player on the international stage. The renowned American foreign policy theorist and historian Walter Russell Mead hypothetically analysed the reasons underlying what he described as the failure of the liberal international order which he interchangeably termed as the Wilsonian order. He argued that *"Beyond Europe, the prospects for the Wilsonian order are bleak… The Wilsonian project requires a high degree of convergence to succeed; the member states of a Wilsonian order must be democratic, and they must be willing and able to conduct their international relations within liberal multilateral institution"* and presented the unique proposition:

At least for the medium term, the belief in convergence can no longer be sustained. Today, China, India, Russia, and Turkey all seem less likely to converge on liberal democracy than they did in 1990. These countries and many others have developed economically and technologically not in order to become more like the West but rather to achieve a deeper

---

[194] Gideon Rose, "Foreign Policy for Pragmatists", *Foreign Affairs*, March/April 2021. https://www.foreignaffairs.com/articles/united-states/2021-02-16/foreign-policy-pragmatists

independence from the West and to pursue civilizational and political goals of their own. In truth, Wilsonianism is a particularly European solution to a particularly European set of problems.[195]

The natural conclusion to be reached is that at least for medium term Turkey – along with Russia, China, and India – will not converge on liberal democracy. Hence, a neo-Ottomanist Turkey on a Eurasianist trajectory will be alive on the international stage for the foreseeable future, in the strategic sense, with a mid-term existence.

Mid-term, obviously, is an ambiguous time frame. Nonetheless, the neo-Ottomanist Turkey will not be eternal. It will come to an end. *"But if the end of every order is inevitable, the timing and the manner of its ending are not. Nor is what comes in its wake. Orders tend to expire in a prolonged deterioration rather than a sudden collapse".*[196]

If there is such a rule, it spells a tortuous future for neo-Ottomanist Turkey, even if it preserves its formal institutional ties to the Western system. Turkey's political departure from the Euro-Atlantic system, its pursuit of civilizational and political goals independent of the West, may not bring the glory and well-being it seeks. Its efforts to forge a new geopolitical axis with Russia and ultimately with China may arrive at a dead end. Its allegedly revisionist and stronger peers, Russia and China, probably will never have the power the United States possessed. They might not provide Turkey with suitable substitutes for America, if the analysis of G. John Ikenberry is proven correct.

Ikenberry, a respected American political thinker identified as a "liberal internationalist", engaged in polemics with Walter Russell Mead. In 2014, he developed the argument that Russia and China are spoilers rather than emerging revisionist powers. He pronounced that even if the United States no longer enjoys the hegemony it had during the unipolar era, Russia and China would not match its power. Ikenberry believed the United States would preserve its technological advantages and a degree of wealth that would be out of reach for Russia and China:

Walter Russell Mead paints a disturbing portrait of the United States geopolitical predicament. As he sees it, an increasingly formidable coalition of illiberal powers – China,

---

[195] Walter Russell Mead, "The End of the Wilsonian Era, Why Liberal Internationalism Failed", *Foreign Affairs*, January/February 2021. https://www.foreignaffairs.com/articles/united-states/2020-12-08/end-wilsonian-era

[196] Richard N. Haass, "How a World Order Ends", *Foreign Affairs*, January/February 2019. https://www.foreignaffairs.com/articles/2018-12-11/how-world-order-ends

Iran, and Russia – is determined to undo the post–Cold War settlement and the U.S.-led global order that stands behind it. Across Eurasia, he argues, these aggrieved states are bent on building spheres of influence to threaten the foundations of U.S. leadership and the global order.

But Mead's alarmism is based on a colossal misreading of modern power realities. It is a misreading of the logic and character of the existing world order, which is more stable and expansive than Mead depicts, leading him to overestimate the ability of the "axis of weevils" to undermine it. And it is a misreading of China and Russia, which are not full-scale revisionist powers but part-time spoilers at best, as suspicious of each other as they are of the outside world. True, they look for opportunities to resist the United States' global leadership, and recently, as in the past, they have pushed back against it, particularly when confronted in their own neighborhoods. But even these conflicts are fueled more by weakness – their leaders' and regimes' – than by strength. They have no appealing brand…

For Mead, Eurasia has returned as the great prize of geopolitics. Across the far reaches of this supercontinent, he argues, China, Iran, and Russia are seeking to establish their spheres of influence and challenge U.S. interests, slowly but relentlessly attempting to dominate Eurasia and thereby threaten the United States and the rest of the world.

This vision misses a deeper reality. In matters of geopolitics (not to mention demographics, politics, and ideas), the United States has a decisive advantage over China, Iran, and Russia. Although the United States will no doubt come down from the peak of hegemony that it occupied during the unipolar era, its power is still unrivaled. Its wealth and technological advantages remain far out of the reach of China and Russia.[197]

THE OLD OVERLORD IN THE NEW MIDDLE EAST

Besides its indefinite future tilting towards Russia and China, the Euro-Atlantic geopolitics will inevitably involve Turkey more deeply in the Middle East imbroglio. With an increasingly Hobbesian outlook on international politics, Turkey will most probably be obliged to engage in power politics. Belligerence will be its defining posture.

Vali Nasr astutely predicted the competition likely to shape the Middle East. The competition he referred to is no longer between Arab states and Israel or the sectarian struggle between Sunni and Shiites, but among the three non-Arab rivals – Turkey, Iran, and Israel – as the United States reduces its commitment

---

[197] G. John Ikenberry, "The Illusion of Geopolitics", *Foreign Affairs*, May/June 2014. https://www.foreignaffairs.com/articles/china/2014-04-17/illusion-geopolitics

to the region. Nasr caught the defining feature of the new epoch in the Middle East. *"The Arab moment has passed"*, he wrote. The Arab moment has passed, and with the arrival of the neo-Ottomanist moment, Turkey has re-emerged in the region. However, Turkey's neo-Ottomanist emergence is different from what it was during the Ottoman period when centuries-long stability – if not lethargy – prevailed in the region.

What is new is Turkey's emergence as an unpredictable disrupter of stability across a much larger region. No longer envisioning a future in the West, Turkey is now more decidedly embracing its Islamic past, looking past lines and borders drawn a century ago. Its claim to the influence it had in the onetime domains of the Ottoman Empire can no longer be dismissed as rhetoric. Turkish ambition is now a force to be reckoned with.[198]

Where the new Turkey stepped in, is the new Middle East. The new Middle East of the post–Cold War era was mainly shaped by the war on Iraq launched by the United States in 2003 and its aftermath.

Richard Haass prognosticated in 2006 the main characteristic of the new Middle East where neo-Ottomanist Turkey would tacitly compete against Iran and Israel almost a decade later:

Just over two centuries since Napoleon's arrival in Egypt heralded the advent of the modern Middle East – some 80 years after the demise of the Ottoman Empire, 50 years after the end of colonialism, and less than 20 years after the end of the Cold War – the American era in the Middle East, the fourth in the region's modern history, has ended. Visions of a new, Europe-like region – peaceful, prosperous, democratic – will not be realized. Much more likely is the emergence of a new Middle East that will cause great harm to itself, the United States, and the world.[199]

Almost a decade after Richard Haass's prognosis about the "New Middle East", arguably one of the most impressive strategic minds of the 20th century, Henry Kissinger, presented his brilliant description of the Middle East, old and new:

The Middle East has been the chrysalis of the world's greatest religions. From its stern landscape have issued conquerors and prophets holding aloft banners of universal aspirations. Across its seemingly limitless horizons, empires have been established and fallen; absolute

---

[198] Vali Nasr, "The Middle East's Next Conflicts Won't Be Between Arab States and Iran", *Foreign Policy*, March 2, 2021. https://foreignpolicy.com/2021/03/02/the-middle-easts-next-conflicts-wont-be-between-arab-states-and-iran/

[199] Richard N. Haass, "The New Middle East", *Foreign Affairs*, November/December 2006. https://www.foreignaffairs.com/articles/middle-east/2006-11-01/new-middle-east

rulers have proclaimed themselves the embodiment of all power, only to disappear as if they had been mirages. Here every form of domestic and international order existed, and been rejected, at one time or another.

The world has become accustomed to calls from the Middle East urging the overthrow of regional and world order in the service of universal vision. A profusion of prophetic absolutisms has been the hallmark of a region suspended between a dream of its former glory and its contemporary inability to unify around common principles of domestic and international legitimacy. Nowhere is the challenge of international order more complex – in terms of both organizing regional order and ensuring the compatibility of that order with peace and stability in the rest of the world.

In our time, the Middle East seems destined to experiment with all of its historical experiences simultaneously – empire, holy war, foreign domination, a sectarian war of all against all –before it arrives (if it ever does) at a settled concept of international order. Until it does so, the region will remain pulled alternately toward joining the world community and struggling against it.[200]

That is where Erdoğan's neo-Ottomanist Turkey craved to shape the future and simultaneously let Turkey's future be shaped. Departure from the Euro-Atlantic geopolitics may come to Turkey with a price tag: by sharing the Middle East's destiny and navigating through Eurasianist geopolitics, the last decades of the Ottoman Empire could reanimate.

Forging a Eurasianist new axis would necessitate – even if gradually – untying Turkey's Western knots, which would be fatal in the economic sense. The economy is considered one of the most critical determinants for the life span of neo-Ottomanist Turkey because its complete collapse was never out of the question. It was widely believed that the European Union, wary of the devastating consequences of Turkey's economic collapse for Europe, would do all it could not to let such a collapse happen. However, it could be unpreventable and of Turkish making. Around the end of the year 2020, the sick man metaphor employed for the 19th century of the Ottoman Empire was resumed in a different context in discussing the worrying prospects of Turkey's economy:

Three hundred years ago, Montesquieu described the Ottoman Empire as "a sick body not supported by a mild and regular diet, but by a powerful treatment which continually exhausted it." True economic change will only come about when this exhaustion has peaked. This realization will hopefully set in before the Turkish economy completely collapses. If history

[200] Henry Kissinger, World Order: Reflections on the Character of Nations and the Course of History, New York: Penguin Group, 2014, 96-97.

teaches us anything it is that inefficient rule by despots can only persevere for so long. For the time being though, it appears that Erdogan is content to try.[201]

At the time of that writing, the sarcastic reference to what Recep Tayyip Erdoğan was attempting was the main concern of all the savvy Turkey experts and observers. In addition to its *Eurasian Odyssey*, Turkey's economic performance was being watched by them in angst.

Turkey's neo-Ottomanist moment, the new historical moment that has arrived, in fact recalls the final era of the Ottoman Empire. Revival of imperial glory carries the potential of paying a heavy toll for Erdoğan's neo-Ottomanism or Turkey's neo-Ottomanist moment.

I was careful not to miss closely knit ties between the vested interests and ideological commitments of the nationalist power structure that was ruling the country with a tacit coalition, especially since 2016 and the Eurasianist spell in the foreign policy. In my outlook, they could not be disassociated, and thus whatever the mutual pragmatic concerns are, Turkey's relations with the West structurally looked very problematic and pregnant for a break. Nicholas Danforth, in a sophisticated way, also reflected my views:

There are also a number of observers who believe that Turkey and the West are moving steadily, even inexorably, toward a more formal, definitive and acrimonious break. Like Tolstoy's unhappy families, these scenarios are all disastrous in their own unique way. Some imagine Turkey formally leaving NATO, launching a nuclear program or going to war with one of its neighbors. Some picture Turkey going rogue like Iran, becoming indebted to China or entering into an alliance with Russia. In many cases these scenarios are accompanied by a more nakedly authoritarian turn in Turkey's domestic politics, with Erdoğan forcibly overturning elections and violently crushing protests.

Interestingly, pessimistic predictions vary in the degree to which they see this geopolitical break as the fulfillment of Erdoğan's own ideological agenda or the result of circumstances escalating beyond his control. Erdoğan has made it clear how committed he is to a more "independent" Turkish foreign policy, one that would make his country a civilizational and geopolitical center in its own right, rather than a part of any other great power's sphere of influence. He has also made it clear that he expects to have to achieve this in the face of sustained Western resistance. Yet, as laid out in the previous scenario, Erdoğan seems convinced that Turkey's success in this venture will eventually bring Western powers around. Thus, while there is good reason to think Erdoğan's worldview or domestic political needs

---

[201] Shlomo Roiter Jesner, "Erdogan's Economic Hail Mary Won't Work", *Foreign Policy*, November 30, 2020. https://foreignpolicy.com/2020/11/30/turkey-economic-problem-erdogan-mismanagement/

might lead him to take provocative measures that could trigger a break, it seems unlikely that he would see the break as a goal in itself.

There remain, however, plenty of ways Turkey and the West could find themselves caught in a dynamic that neither side could fully control.[202]

The chaotic, even anarchic transition from the unipolar world to multipolarity adds to the uncertainty of the future awaiting Turkey and the West. Turkey is centred in the geopolitical nexus among the United States which along with the European Union constitutes the West; Russia, the Eurasian power; and China, the emergent global power that compelled the transition from unipolarity to multipolarity. Those tectonic shifts in the international system further impacted the abyss developing between Turkey and the West.

In *Surrogate Warfare (2017),* co-authored by Andreas Krieg and Jean-Marc Rickli, the prominent British and Swiss security policy experts determined that "the world looks more anarchical in the early twenty-first century than it has ever been in modern times" and has entered an era of "everywhere conflicts". Their description of surrogate warfare in 2019 – like a patron's outsourcing of the strategic, operational, or tactical burdens of warfare, in whole or in part, to human and/or technological substitutes in order to minimize the costs of war, ranging from arming proxies to the use of armed drones – is precisely what Turkey performed in 2020.[203]

Referring to the arguments developed in *Surrogate Warfare*, Aris Roussinos described the Middle East as a giant arena of experimentation in the disastrous 21ˢᵗ century warfare, with Turkey as one of the decisive external actors.

The catastrophic civil war in Syria, the parallel conflict in Yemen and the widening destabilisation of Iraq, Lebanon and Libya exemplify these trends, where external actors like the United States, Russia, Turkey, Iran and the Gulf kingdoms manipulate their local proxy militias like chess pieces while their drones, ballistic missiles and jets lay waste to the ground on which they fight. Instead of democratising the Middle East as pundits first hoped, the unintended intersection of the Arab Spring, globalisation and new technologies have seen the entire region spiralling into a giant arena of experimentation in 21st century warfare, almost wholly disastrous to its people, as a result of global trends they had no part in making.[204]

---

[202] Danforth, "Turkey and the West: A Hostile Dance", *op. cit.*
[203] Andreas Krieg and Jean-Marc Rickli, Surrogate Warfare, The Transformation of War in the Twenty-First Century, Georgetown, 2019.
[204] Aris Roussinos, "Anarchy Is Coming", *UnHerd*, March 22, 2021. https://unherd.com/2021/03/anarchy-is-coming/

The concept of *Surrogate Warfare* in the 21st century was exemplified nowhere more strikingly than in Turkey in 2019–2020. Perhaps only Russia could be a parallel case. Turkey trained, armed, provided military support, and practically sent its Syrian proxies to fight the Kurds in northeastern Syria in October 2019. It transported its Syrian proxies to the Libyan battlefield in May/June 2020 and to a lesser extent to the Nagorno-Karabagh War in the South Caucasus in September 2020. Turkey's drones in Libya in June 2020 and in the South Caucasus from September to November 2020 brought military victory to its allies and partners.

Turkey was exempted from the unsustainable burden of costly wars that it had been involved in, thanks to the human substitutes like Syrian mercenaries or technological substitutes like its drones sold to Libya, Azerbaijan, and Ukraine. This approach brought military and financial dividends. Proxies and drones became the mainstay of Turkey's assertive foreign policy. The fatal consequences of its foreign policy choices lay elsewhere, beyond its control.

As the chasm with the West to a large extent due to Erdoğan's nationalist-autocratic posture was almost unavoidable, the exacerbating great power rivalries between the United States and Russia or the US and China carried a potential that might prove fatal for Turkey, a nationalist autocracy.

GREAT POWER RIVALRIES OF THE "SECOND COLD WAR"

With Donald Trump's departure from the White House on January 20, 2021, and Joseph Biden's inauguration as the United States president, a new era of great powers competition was also inaugurated. That new era was characterized as perhaps the worst relationship the US has had with Russia since the fall of the Berlin Wall (1989) and China since it opened diplomatic relations in 1972. A perceptive *New York Times* op-ed asserted that the new epoch's superpower rivalries bear little resemblance to the past. It argued that the Cold War in its familiar form *"has not resumed — there is little of the nuclear menace of that era, and the current competition is over technology, cyberconflict and influence operations"*.[205]

Gideon Rachman of the *Financial Times*, in reference to the *New York Times* op-ed, while conceding that the superpower realities of the epoch bear

---

[205] David E. Sagner, "That Was Fast: Blowups with China and Russia in Biden's First 60 Days", *New York Times*, (updated) March 25, 2021. https://www.nytimes.com/2021/03/20/us/politics/china-russia-biden.html

little resemblance to the past, expressed the opinion that *"those differences exist, of course. But to me, the parallels between today's events and the early years of the cold war look increasingly convincing, even eerie. Once again you have a Russia-China axis arrayed against a western alliance, led from Washington... The tensions between two sides are heightening".*[206] In contrast to David Sagner of the *New York Times*, he characterized the situation as *"this second cold war"* or *"a new cold war".* He brought to the fore a phenomenon that would push Turkey into an awkward position, much different than the position it had held during the long decades of the "First" Cold War when it was firmly anchored in the collective security system of the Western alliance.

In this second cold war — as in the first — there are regional flashpoints where the conflict could heat up. In Asia, some of these are actually unresolved issues left over from the first cold war, namely the status of the Korean peninsula and of Taiwan. In Europe, the front lines have moved east. It is now Ukraine, rather than Berlin, that is the focus of tensions between Moscow and the west.[207]

With Ukraine replacing Berlin of the Cold War era as the focus of tensions between the West and Moscow, due to the ensuing conflict between Ukraine and Russia after the Russian occupation and annexation of Crimea, the Black Sea emerged as a geopolitical hotbed between the two sides. For some analysts, developments with the potential of confronting or at least containing Moscow in the conflictual Black Sea region could terminate the adversarial collaboration Turkey has enjoyed with Russia in Syria, Libya, and the South Caucasus.

THE BLACK SEA DILEMMA

Turkey did not recognize the annexation of Crimea by Russia and stood by Ukraine, which conflicted with Moscow. It provided its much-praised drones to Ukraine to be used against Russia. Ukrainian president Volodymyr Zelenskyy, in his official visit to Ankara at a time of military showdown with Russia, was heartened by his supportive reception in the Turkish capital. He praised the relationship between the two Black Sea countries in his account on social media: *"Ukraine is glad to have a reliable neighbor, even if our border is the sea".*

The official readout of the Ukrainian Presidency issued on April 10, 2021

---

[206] Gideon Rachman, "A Second Cold War Is Tracking the First, US-Led Western Alliance Is Once Again Squaring Up to Russia and China", *Financial Times*, Opinion Geopolitics, March 29, 2021. https://www.ft.com/content/b724fbb0-6c62-4175-85c9-b17ac98dde7d
[207] Ibid.

revealed how Turkey had committed itself to the position of Kyiv against Moscow:

President of Ukraine Volodymyr Zelenskyy and President of the Republic of Turkey Recep Tayyip Erdoğan thoroughly discussed the issues of security and joint counteraction to the challenges in the Black Sea region.

"It is worth noting that the vision of Kyiv and Ankara coincide - both in terms of the threats themselves and in terms of ways to properly respond to these threats"... "Turkey supports the independence, sovereignty and territorial integrity of Ukraine. We have reaffirmed our basic principle of non-recognition of the illegal annexation of Crimea. We have also announced our support for the Crimean Platform, which is aimed to unite the lands of Ukraine," said Recep Tayyip Erdoğan.[208]

A few days before visiting Erdoğan in Ankara, Zelenskyy had called for a permanent presence of NATO in the Black Sea region to maintain a powerful deterrent to Russia, hence indicating how volatile the Black Sea geopolitics could turn out to be. The Ukrainian official readout was as follows:

He [Ukrainian President Vlodymyr Zelenskyy] briefed [NATO Secretary General] Jens Stoltenberg on Russia's continued accumulation of troops near Ukraine's borders and on their increased readiness for offensive action.

The President thanked the Secretary General for the Alliance's attention to the security situation around Ukraine and called on NATO members to pay more attention to security issues in the Black Sea and to strengthen their military presence in the Black Sea region.

"Such a permanent presence should be a powerful deterrent to Russia, which continues the large-scale militarization of the region and hinders merchant shipping," said Volodymyr Zelenskyy.

The President of Ukraine stressed that the most urgent issue in relations with NATO for Ukraine was the possibility of obtaining the NATO Membership Action Plan.

"We are committed to reforming our army and defense sector, but reforms alone will not stop Russia. NATO is the only way to end the war in Donbas. Ukraine's Membership Action Plan [for NATO] will be a real signal for Russia," the President said.[209]

---

[208] President of Ukraine Volodymyr Zelenskyy Official Website, "Ukraine and Turkey Share a Common Vision of Security Threats in the Black Sea Region and Ways to Respond to Them", April 10, 2021. https://www.president.gov.ua/en/news/ukrayina-j-turechchina-mayut-spilne-bachennya-bezpekovih-zag-67917

[209] President of Ukraine Volodymyr Zelenskyy Official Website, President Of Ukraine Had a Phone Conversation with the Secretary General of NATO, April 6, 2021. https://www.president.gov.ua/en/news/prezident-ukrayini-proviv-telefonnu-rozmovu-z-generalnim-sek-67813

The Ukraine-Russia conflict pulled NATO into the Black Sea. The Transatlantic Alliance has three littoral countries as its members, Turkey, Bulgaria, and Romania. To align with NATO the remaining two, Ukraine and Georgia, were anxious already to push into the Black Sea to contain Moscow. The intensification of the great power rivalries encompassing the Black Sea region, where Ukraine and Russia are locked in a seemingly intractable conflict, caught Turkey on the wrong foot. Turkey, a NATO-member country, aligned with Ukraine regarding the Crimea issue.

Notwithstanding the substantial nature of Turkey's relationship with Ukraine, which also provided opportunities to Ankara for collaboration with the United States and the West, a prudent outlook did not see Erdoğan go so far as to collide with Russia. Dimitar Bechev emphasized that Turkey cannot extend the same support to Ukraine in the Black Sea as it has given Azerbaijan in the South Caucasus.

There is substance to the Ukraine-Turkey relationship, not just grand rhetoric. In 2019, Kyiv purchased 12 Bayraktar TB2 Unmanned Aerial Vehicles (UAVs), the very weapon system that gave Turkish allies advantage on the battlefields of Syria, Libya, and Nagorno-Karabakh. General Ruslan Khomchak, the commander-in-chief of Ukraine's armed forces, has confirmed plans to acquire five more.

The two countries have long been discussing joint defence production, with Turkey benefitting from Ukrainian industries that had been cut off from the Russian market and Ukraine obtaining access to drone technology.

The Turkish government is furthermore leveraging its links to Ukraine in order to engage the US. While the reset Erdogan is probing with the West is bearing fruits regarding the EU, Biden's team has thus far been ignoring Ankara's overtures. Washington is not taking at face value arguments that Turkey is the only power ready and willing to curb Moscow's expansionism, whether in Libya, Syria, or the Southern Caucasus. Erdogan's double act with Putin has left a lasting negative impression across the Atlantic.

Biden's team opted for imposing a new round of sanctions on Russia, linked to interference in American politics rather than Ukraine, instead of ramping up American military presence in the region.

Turkey is therefore unlikely to take a gamble risking a head-on collision with Russia over Ukraine. At the joint press conference with Zelensky, Erdogan called for de-escalation in the Black Sea. There is no indication that Turkey is prepared to up the ante, sending direct military assistance to the frontlines, as it did in Nagorno-Karabakh or in Libya last year.

It is in no position to tip the balance of power in Kyiv's favour and, in addition, might have to face harsh consequences.[210]

Having more irreconcilable differences with the West than those it has with Russia, Turkey collaborated with the latter in multiple conflict zones, above all in the crucial South Caucasus.

Turkey's irreconcilable differences, especially with the U.S. administration, emanated from its authoritarian nature. Its authoritarianism has more parallelism and overlap with Russia and China. In terms of timing, the years when Turkey under Recep Tayyip Erdoğan's nationalist-autocratic rule drifted from the West and set on the Eurasian trajectory coincided with *"President Vladimir V. Putin of Russia and President Xi Jinping of China* [taking] *sharp turns toward authoritarianism"*.[211]

In a period when the United States has had the worst relationship with Russia and China in decades, further aggravated because of Putin's and Xi's sharp turns toward authoritarianism, Erdoğan's Turkey has had a similar orientation. Therefore, it would be unthinkable that a certain level of Turkish collaboration and rapprochement with these powers could rely on American tolerance.

Rachman recalled the stark differences between the United States under Trump and his successor Biden. The former courted authoritarian leaders worldwide, starting with North Korea's Kim Jong-un and including Russia's Putin and Turkey's Erdoğan, and even China's Xi Jinping.

During the Trump administration, the emerging rivalry between the US and China often lacked the ideological dimension of the first cold war. Donald Trump was a transactional president who was focused above all on the US trade deficit with China. According to John Bolton, his former national security adviser, Trump even privately encouraged Xi Jinping to pursue his policy of mass internment in Xinjiang. With the advent of the Biden administration, however, ideological competition is back. Biden has said that he wants to convene a summit of democracy and is clearly intent on reasserting the US claim to be the "leader of the free world".[212]

Turkey, although proceeding gradually, is bound to find itself at the crossroads at some point in history: either a member of the free world or in the

---

[210] Dimitar Bechev, "Ukraine-Turkey Cooperation Has Its Limits", *AlJazeera*, April 18, 2021. https://www.aljazeera.com/opinions/2021/4/18/ukraine-turkey-cooperation-has-its-benefits-but-also-limits

[211] Sagner, "That Was Fast", *op. cit.*

[212] Rachman, "Second Cold War Is Tracking the First", *op. cit.*

congregation of the authoritarian regimes led by China and Russia.

In the post-2016 period it has had much more common features with Russia and common interests with China than with its traditional Western allies. Moreover, to sustain itself the authoritarian-nationalist regime will require Chinese technological power and assistance more than its American-European friends and partners preaching respect for human rights, fundamental freedoms, and the rule of law.

David E. Sagner illustrated vividly the instruments China utilized to project itself to a global power position and its appeal that might transcend to the future:

Its pathway to power is building new networks rather than disrupting old ones. Economists debate when the Chinese will have the world's largest gross domestic product – perhaps toward the end of this decade – and whether they can meet their other two big national goals: building the world's most powerful military and dominating the race for key technologies by 2049, the 100th anniversary of Mao's revolution.

Instead, it arises from their expanding economic might and how they use their government-subsidized technology to wire nations be it Latin America or the Middle East, Africa or Eastern Europe, with 5G wireless networks intended to tie them ever closer to Beijing. It comes from the undersea cables they are spooling around the world so that those networks run on Chinese-owned circuits.

Ultimately, it will come from how they use those networks to make other nations dependent on Chinese technology. Once that happens, the Chinese could export some of their authoritarianism by, for example, selling other nations facial recognition software that has enabled them to clamp down on dissent at home.[213]

In all likelihood, the future for Turkey's authoritarianism lies in China more than the United States and the European Union which stick to liberal democratic values and the rule of law – and even they could experience hypocritical moments when they sacrifice such principles for the imperatives of realpolitik.

THE UYGHUR CASE: MORAL BANKRUPTCY OF TURKISH NATIONALISM AND EURASIANISM

Turkey's neediness vis-à-vis China was revealed during the COVID-19 pandemic recovery period in 2021. To vaccinate its population, Turkey became

---

[213] Sagner, "That Was Fast", *op. cit.*

one of the principal recipients of the Chinese vaccine Sinovac which had been cleared by neither the World Health Organization (WHO) nor by the EMA (European Medicines Agency) of the European Union. In return, Turkey's ultranationalist regime turned its back on the repression of its Uyghur kin in Xinjiang by China.

In 2009, the then prime minister Erdoğan had called Chinese repression a "genocide" thereby drawing Beijing's wrath but at the same time making a reputation for himself as a dignified leader unafraid to challenge a totalitarian power. In 2021, Turkey itself turned into a quasi-totalitarian country under Erdoğan, depicted as a "dictator" by some Western leaders including the prime minister of Italy, Mario Draghi. It signed an extradition agreement with China in 2017. China ratified it in 2021 and interpreted it as a counterterrorism partnership. The irony is the U.S. State Department labelled China's actions in Xinjiang against Turkey's Uyghur kin in its annual human rights report; during the same time, Turkey developed close relations with Beijing turning a deaf ear to the plight of the Uyghurs.

In 2021 the ultranationalist-Muslim regime in Turkey was enjoying close relations with Beijing and maintaining a shameful silence about the Chinese atrocities against Uyghurs. In contrast, the U.S. Secretary of State Anthony J. Blinken went on record pronouncing the word "genocide" for what China committed against the Turkic-Muslim Uyghur people:

> *Too many people continued to suffer under brutal conditions in 2020. In China, government authorities committed genocide against Uyghurs, who are predominantly Muslim, and crimes against humanity including imprisonment, torture, enforced sterilization, and persecution against Uyghurs and members of other religious and ethnic minority groups.*[214]

Turkey's bowing to China in 2021 despite Beijing's genocidal campaign against the Uyghurs exposed the limitations of its foreign policy at its neo-Ottomanist moment. The ambition of reviving its imperial greatness in its dealings with China laid bare Turkey's weakness. More importantly, it was emblematic in illustrating the moral bankruptcy of a nationalist-authoritarian regime, hiding behind the dictates of realpolitik. China bought Turkey's silence on its repression of the Turkic-Muslim Uyghurs and possessed the capacity to export some of its authoritarianism to be purchased by Turkey – like the

---

[214] *Foreign Policy*, "Blinken Accuses China of Uyghur Genocide in Xinjiang", March 31, 2021. https://foreignpolicy.com/2021/03/31/blinken-uyghur-china-human-rights-report/; U.S. Department of State, "2020 Country Reports on Human Right Practices", Bureau of Democracy, Human Rights and Labor, March 30, 2021. https://www.state.gov/reports/2020-country-reports-on-human-rights-practices/

controversial anti-COVID-19 vaccine Sinovac – to enable it to clamp down on dissent at home.

Erdoğan's pseudo-nationalist and autocratic Turkey's convergence of interests with China simultaneously coincided with an increasing divergence of interests with the United States. U.S. President Joe Biden, unlike his predecessors, recognized the annihilation of Ottoman Armenians as genocide in its 106th anniversary on April 24, 2021. In a psychological sense, this had been the most sensitive issue for Turkey, with the symbolism to reflect the durability of the American-Turkish alliance. With his dramatic move, Biden illustrated his disregard of the sensitivity of the Turkish leadership on the issue, signalling that the American commitment to human rights outweighed the risk of further fraying the American-Turkish alliance. The statement indicated that, in the eyes of its strongest traditional ally, Turkey had lost strategic significance.

There always had been a somewhat self-assuring assertion on the indispensable, unique nature of Turkey's geopolitical importance. As a foregone conclusion it has provided powerful leverage to policymakers. However, drifting away from the West while the US was changing its geostrategic priorities stripped Turkey of its supposedly everlasting most potent leverage. Thus, the following lines could never have been envisaged before:

[Turkey-US] ties have been increasingly strained by Turkey's arms deliveries to Islamist-held areas, imprisonment of journalists, purchase of S-400 anti-aircraft missiles from Russia, use of proxies in various conflicts, and growing authoritarianism under Erdogan. The U.S.-Turkish divide was most obvious in Syria, where Washington backed the Kurdish-dominated Syrian Democratic Forces to defeat the Islamic State while Turkey attacked them.

If further proof of the United States and Turkey's divergent interests was needed, look no further than Erdogan's sympathies for his fellow strongman, Russian President Vladimir Putin. Despite contrary interests in Syria, Libya, and the South Caucasus, Russia and Turkey have maintained a pragmatic relationship… Perhaps above all, the Putin-Erdogan liaison is possible because their relationship weakens NATO – an alliance both Erdogan and Putin likely regard as a long-term nemesis…

The pundits debate endlessly whether Erdogan's strategic posture today is best described as neo-Ottoman, pan-Islamist, or ethno-supremacist, but this is not really relevant. What matters is Turkey is an increasingly malign state that shares few interests or values with the West. The partnership's benefits are quite simply outweighed by the costs… The United States is in the process of ending its overextension in the Middle East, Turkey included. Today, Turkey is a regional power in a part of the world that no longer has the geostrategic significance to the United States it did 20 years ago.[215]

Turkey's arrival at its neo-Ottomanist moment and the Eurasian odyssey it has embarked on are firmly embedded in its passage from a flawed democracy to a repressive autocracy. It seems likely to endure until a paradigm shift happens on a global scale.

The duration of its Eurasian odyssey is impossible to know. When and how it will end is hard to predict. Where it will end is chilling to imagine.

---

[215] Andrew Doran, "Stop Giving Erdogan a Veto Over U.S. Recognition of the Armenian Genocide", *Foreign Policy*, April 23, 2021. https://foreignpolicy.com/2021/04/23/armenian-genocide-turkey-erdogan-biden-recognition-allies-nato-syria-russia/

Sources

[1] S. Frederick Starr, *Lost Enlightenment, Central Asia's Golden Age from the Arab Conquest to Tamerlane*, Princeton University Press, 2013

[2] Cengiz Çandar, Turkey's Mission Impossible, War and Peace with the Kurds, Lexington Books, 2020

[3] Cengiz Çandar, "Turkey in the 21st Century", *United States Institute of Peace* (Unpublished Paper), Washington, D.C., presented on May 18, 2000.

[4] *Presidential Documents* [weekly compilation], Monday November 15, 1999, Vol. 35, No. 45, pp. 2267-2372, at p. 2290. https://www.govinfo.gov/content/pkg/WCPD-1999-11-15/pdf/WCPD-1999-11-15.pdf

[5] Cengiz Çandar, "Turkey in the 21st Century", *op cit.*

[6] Ibid.

[7] G. John Ikenberry, "The Next Liberal Order", *Foreign Affairs*, July/August 2020. https://www.foreignaffairs.com/articles/united-states/2020-06-09/next-liberal-order

[8] Richard Haass, "The Pandemic Will Accelerate History Rather Than Reshape It, Not Every Crisis Is a Turning Point", *Foreign Affairs*, April 7, 2020. https://www.foreignaffairs.com/articles/united-states/2020-04-07/pandemic-will-accelerate-history-rather-reshape-it

[9] Ibid.

[10] Francis Fukuyama, "The Pandemic and World Order", *Foreign Affairs*, July/August 2020. https://www.foreignaffairs.com/articles/world/2020-06-09/pandemic-and-political-order

[11] *Ibid*

[12] Francis Fukuyama, "Droning On in the Middle East", *American Purpose*, April 5, 2021. https://www.americanpurpose.com/blog/fukuyama/droning-on/

[13] Paul Taylor, "Turkey's Year of Belligerence", *Politico*, December 10, 2020. https://www.politico.eu/article/turkey-erdogan-year-of-belligerence/

[14] Allison Meakem, "The Year in Review: Turkey's Year of Living Dangerously", *Foreign Policy*, December 25, 2020. https://foreignpolicy.com/2020/12/25/turkeys-year-of-living-dangerously/

[15] Zvi Bar'el, "Analysis, Erdogan Is Planning a New World Order in Which Turkey Is the Rising Star", *Haaretz*, October 26, 2020. https://www.haaretz.com/world-news/.premium.HIGHLIGHT-erdogan-is-planning-a-new-world-order-in-which-turkey-is-the-star-1.9257381

[16] Ibid.

[17] Gerard Araud, twitter.com > gerardaraud > status, August 30, 2020.

[18] Yaroslav Trofimov, "The Dangers in a New Era of Territorial Grabs", The Wall Street Journal, September 17, 2020.

[19] Jacques Attali, September 7, 2020. https://twitter.com/jattali/status/1302874004097847296

[20] David Rosenberg, "Turkey Doesn't Have the Economic Bite to Back Up Erdogan's Bark", *Haaretz*, October 28, 2020.

[21] https://www.tccb.gov.tr/en/news/542/120571/-turkey-has-become-a-powerful-regional-actor-; https://podcast.ausha.co/hold-your-fire/episode-7-turkey-flexes-its-foreign-policy-muscles

[22] https://www.crisisgroup.org/europe-central-asia/western-europemediterranean/turkey/turkey-flexes-its-foreign-policy-muscles

[23] Robert Malley, "10 Conflicts to Watch in 2021", *Foreign Policy*, December 29, 2020. https://foreignpolicy.com/2020/12/29/10-conflicts-to-watch-in-2021-ethiopia-iran-yemen-somalia-venezuela/

[24] https://www.eurasiagroup.net/issues/top-risks-2021, January 4, 2021.

[25] Henri Barkey, "Turkey's Strategy to Build Influence Focuses on Africa", Asia Times, January 25, 2020. https://asiatimes.com/author/henri-j-barkey/-

[26] https://www.lemonde.fr/blog/filiu/2020/12/27/la-menace-en-2021-dune-offensive-majeure-de-la-turquie-en-irak/

[27] Soli Özel, "2021: Year of Decisions", *Observatoire de la Vie Politique Turque*, January 7, 2021. https://ovipot.hypotheses.org/15684

[28] *Javanonline.ir*, December 12, 2020.

[29] Ibid.

[30] https://etemadonline.com/content/460318, January 23, 2021.

[31] Sadeq Maleki (interview), "The Old Ottomanism Was Looking to Expand to the Gates of Vienna and to the West, Neo-Ottomanism Has Its View Toward the East", *Shargh*, December 15, 2020.

[32] Yaakov Lappin, "As Turkey's Lira Tumbles, Erdoğan Pursues Neo-Ottoman Visions", *BESA Center Perspectives*, No. 1, 796, November 2, 2020.

[33] Ibid.

[34] https://www.thenationalnews.com/world/europe/armenian-pm-accuses-turkey-of-continuing-the-genocide-in-nagorno-karabakh-1.1089761

[35] https://armenian.usc.edu/voices-on-karabakh/#avedis-hadjian

[36] Darko Tanasković, *Neo-Ottomanism: Turkey's Return to the Balkans* [in Serbian], Belgrade: J. P. Službeni Glasnik, 2010, 19-20.

[37] M. Hakan Yavuz, *Nostalgia for the Empire, The Politics of Neo-Ottomanism*, Oxford University Press, 2020, Kindle Edition, 220.

[38] Ibid.

[39] Dimitar Bechev, "Erdogan in the Balkans: A neo-Ottoman Quest?", Aljazeera, October 11, 2017. https://www.aljazeera.com/opinions/2017/10/11/erdogan-in-the-balkans-a-neo-ottoman-quest

[40] Vassilis Nedos, "Comment: Dendias: Turkey Not the Same as in 2000 or 2016", *Kathimerini*, January 12, 2021. https://www.ekathimerini.com/261135/article/ekathimerini/comment/dendias-turkey-not-the-same-as-in-2000-or-2016

[41] Nicholas Danforth, "Forget 2020, This May Be My Favorite Professional Accomplishment of All Time", December 28, 2020.

[42] *Nicholas Danforth, "The Non-Sense of Neo-Ottomanism", War on the Rocks, March 29, 2020.*

[43] *Ibid.*

[44] Yavuz, Nostalgia for the Empire, op. cit., 181.

[45] Ibid., 8.

[46] Ibid., 5.

[47] Ahmet Erdi Öztürk, *Religion, Identity and Power: Turkey and Balkans in the Twenty-first Century*, Edinburgh: Edinburgh University Press, 2021, 51-52.

[48] I must also recognize and pay tribute to the late David Barchard (1947–2020), a British journalist and an acquaintance, as the first to coin neo-Ottomanism back in 1985. I learned this a few days before his tragic death on Christmas eve of 2020, a result of an accident. Nostalgia for the Empire–The Politics of Neo-Ottomanism referred to him as follows: "In 1985, David Barchard, a British journalist, coined the term neo-Ottomanism as one of several options for Turkey's possible future orientation. He offered the aptest definition of the term as "a consciousness of the imperial Ottoman past," which is "a more potent force in Turkey than Islam, [and] as Turkey regains economic strength, it will be increasingly tempted to assert itself." Yet, while David should be commended for his clairvoyance, that does not alter the fact that his premonition has gone largely unnoticed, because the neo-Ottomanism paradigm regarding Turkish foreign policy was related to post–Cold War circumstances that emerged with the fall of the Berlin Wall and the dissolution of the Soviet Union. All these events were beyond the scope of David Barchard's prediction.

[49] David Barchard, *Turkey and the West*, Routledge, Chatham House Papers, 1985.

[50] Nicholas Danforth, "Ideology and Pragmatism in Turkish Foreign Policy: From Atatürk to the AKP", *Turkish Policy Quarterly*, Vol. 7, No. 3 (Fall 2008).

[51] *Robert Cenzon, "Geopolitics in a Post-Historical World: A Comparative Analysis of the Foreign Policies of Germany and Turkey",* Cosmopolite, Vol. 4 No. 1 (Fall 2010), 85, 86; Lerna K. Yanik, "Constructing 'Turkish Exceptionalism': Discourses in Liminality and Hybridity in Post-Cold War Turkish Foreign Policy, Political Geography, No. 30 (2011).

[52] Zoltán Egeresi, Neo-Ottomanist Hegemonic Order and Its Implications on Ankara's Foreign Policy in the Balkans, PhD thesis submitted to Corvinus University of Budapest, 2018.

[53] Yılmaz Çolak, "Ottomanism vs. Kemalism: Collective Memory and Cultural Pluralism of 1990s Turkey", Middle Eastern Studies, Vol. 42, No. 4 (July 2006), 587-602.

[54] *Türkiye Günlüğü* [Turkey Chronicle], No. 19 (1992).

[55] Igor Torbakov, *"Neo-Ottomanism versus Neo-Eurasianism? Nationalism and Symbolic Geography in Postimperial Turkey and Russia",* Mediterranean Quarterly, Vol. 28, No. 2 (June 2017).

[56] Eric Rouleau, "The Challenges to Turkey", *Foreign Affairs*, November/December 1993. https://www.foreignaffairs.com/articles/europe/1993-12-01/challenges-turkey

[57] Cengiz Candar and Graham E. Fuller, "Grand Geopolitics for a New Turkey", *Mediterranean Quarterly*, Vol. 12, No. 1 (Winter 2001), 22-38.

[58] Igor Torbakov, Neo-Ottomanism versus Neo-Eurasianism, op. cit.

[59] Göktürk Tüysüzoğlu, "Strategic Depth: A Neo-Ottomanist Interpretation of Turkish Eurasianism", *Mediterranean Quarterly*, Vol. 25, No. 2 (April 2014), 85-104.

[60] Yavuz, Nostalgia for the Empire, op. cit., 182-185.

[61] Soner Cagaptay, "Turkey's Imperial Foreign Policy: Vision vs. Reality", *Washington Institute*, March 6, 2020. *https://www.washingtoninstitute.org/policy-analysis/turkeys-imperial-foreign-policy-vision-vs-reality*

[62] Turkish Ministry of Foreign Affairs, "Büyük Restorasyon: Kadim'den Küresellesmeye Yeni Siyaset Anlayisimiz", 15 March 2013. http://www.mfa.gov.tr/disisleri-bakani-ahmet-davutoglu_nun-diyarbakir-dicle-universitesinde-verdigi-_buyuk-restorasyon_-kadim_den-kuresellesmeye-yeni.tr.mfa

[63] Yavuz, Nostalgia for the Empire, op. cit.,186, 187.

[64] In Ottoman times, its territory that lies in today's Libya was called Trablusgarp, which means Tripoli of the West, to distinguish it from the city of Tripoli in today's Lebanon, which was hailed as Trablusşam, meaning Tripoli of Sham, in other words Tripoli of Syria. The North African port city of Tripoli (Trablusgarp) was

conquered by the Ottomans in 1551 and remained in the Empire until 1911. The Syrian-Lebanese port of Tripoli (Trablusşam) was an Ottoman city from 1516 to 1918.

[65] Ahmet Davutoğlu, "Turkey's New Foreign Policy Vision", *Insight Turkey*, Vol. 10, No. 1 (2008), 78. http://www.mfa.gov.tr/disisleri-bakani-sayin-ahmet-Davutoğlu_nun-turk-ocaklari_nin-kurulusunun-100_-yilini-kutlama-etkinlikleri-kapsaminda-duzenlenen.tr.mfa

[66] Yavuz, Nostalgia for the Empire, op. cit.,187.

[67] https://www.al-monitor.com/pulse/originals/2014/08/zaman-davutoglu-ideologue-behlul-ozkan-academic-akp-islamic.html#ixxzz6jmuVh5

[68] Davutoğlu'nun Özal eleştirisi Ahmet Davutoglu, "Yakın Tarihimizin Ana Akımları ve Seçim Sonuçları", *Yeni Şafak,* 23 April 1999.

[69] Behlül Özkan, "Turkey, Davutoğlu and the Idea of Pan-Islamism", *Survival,* published online July 23, 2014.

[70] Yavuz, Nostalgia for the Empire, op. cit., 118.

[71] Özkan, "Turkey, Davutoğlu and the Idea of Pan-Islamism", *op. cit.*

[72] *Tanzimat* in the old Ottoman-Turkish language meant reorganization. In the Turkish historiography, the Ottoman modernization and Westernization process inaugurated in 1839 is called *Tanzimat*. Several Ottoman statesmen carrying the honorary title of "Pasha" were identified with the history-making undertaking of *Tanzimat*, which, according to some historians, is seen as the precursor of modern Turkey. However, in the Turkish Islamist lexicon, *Tanzimat* is synonymous with a spiritual and cultural betrayal to the Muslim nation and the state. Therefore, Davutoğlu's likening Özal to Tanzimat pashas can be interpreted as an irreverent metaphor.

[73] Ibid.

[74] Ibid.

[75] Özel, "2021: Year of Decisions", *op. cit.*

[76] Yaakov Lappin, **"As Turkey's Lira Tumbles, Erdoğan Pursues Neo-Ottoman Visions"**, *BESA Center Perspectives*, No. 1, 796, November 2, 2020.

[77] Çandar, Turkey's Mission Impossible, War and Peace with the Kurds, op. cit., 187.

[78] *Ibid.,* 187, 188.

[79] *Ibid.,* 194.

[80] *Ibid.,* 193.

[81] Gallia Lindenstrauss and Remi Daniel, "The Erdoganian Amalgam: The Ottoman Past, the Ataturk Heritage, and the Arab Upheaval", *Strategic Assessment*, Vol. 24, No. 1 (January 2021). https://strategic assessment.inss.org.il/en/articles/the-erdoganian-amalgam-the-ottoman-past-the-ataturk-heritage-and-the-arab-upheaval/

[82] Memri, an Israeli press monitoring organization believed to be close to Israeli military intelligence, published excerpts from an article of the Iranian daily *Entekhab* from March 1, 2020 that, according to Memri, came out against the expansionist ambitions of Turkish President Recep Tayyip Erdogan, who, it said, wishes to restore the political and territorial glory of the Ottoman Empire. Titled "When Sultan Recep [Tayyip Erdogan] Fantasizes that He Is the Equal of the Ottoman Sultans and Can Tell the Word What to Do: How Erdogan Thinks and Analyzes the World".

[83] Memri (Middle East Media Research Institute), Iran, *Turkey Special Dispatch* No. 9078, December 9, 2020.

[84] Lindenstrauss and Daniel, *op. cit.*

[85] *Financial Times,* "Erdogan's Great Game: Soldiers, Spies and Turkey's Quest for Power", January 12, 2021.

[86] *The Economist,* "The odd couple: Putin and Erdogan have formed a brotherhood of hard power", February 27, 2021. https://www.economist.com/europe/2021/02/23/putin-and-erdogan-have-formed-a-brother hood-of-hard-power?itm_source=parsely-api

[87] Sinem Adar, "Understanding Turkey's Increasingly Militaristic Foreign Policy", Centre for Applied Turkey Studies at the German Institute for International and Security Affairs (CATS-SWP), *MENA Politics Newsletter*, Vol. 3, No. 1 (Spring 2020). https://apsamena.org/wp-content/uploads/2020/06/apsa-mena-politics-newsletter-spring-2020-final.pdf

[88] Çandar, Turkey's Mission Impossible, op. cit., 247.

[89] Ryan Gingeras, "How Deep State Came to America: A History," *War on the Rocks*, February 4, 2019. https://warontherocks.com/2019/how-the-deep-state-come-to-america

[90] Edhem Eldem, "Sultan Abdulhamid II: Founding Father of the Turkish State," *Journal of the Ottoman and Turkish Studies Association*, Vol. 5, No. 2 (Fall 2018), 44.

[91] Cengiz Çandar, "New Turkey: Neo-Nationalist or the Reincarnation of the Old?", *Turkey Analyst,* December 20, 2017. http://www.turkeyanalyst.org/publications/turkey-analyst-articles/item/592-new-turkey-neo-nationalist-or-the-reincarnation-of-the-old?.html

[92] *Ibid.,* 276, 277.

[93] Omer Taspinar, "Foreign Policy after the Failed Coup: The Rise of Turkish Gaullism", September 2, 2016. https://lobelog.com/foreign-policy-after-the-failed-coup-the-rise-of-turkish-gaullism/

[94] Hercules Millas, "Rediscovering and Re-evaluating the New Turkey", *Ahval*, December 5,

2020. https://ahvalnews.com/turkish-politics/rediscovering-and-re-evaluating-new-turkey

[95] Hay Eytan Yanarocak and Jonathan Spyer, *Turkish Militias and Proxies*, Jerusalem Institute for Strategy and Security, TRENDS Research & Advisory of Abu Dhabi, UAE, January 27, 2021. https://trendsresearch.org/research/turkish-militias-and-proxies; Hay Eytan Yanarocak and Jonathan Spyer, "Erdoğan's Private Armies", *Middle East Forum*, January 27, 2021. https://www.meforum.org/61963/turkish-militias-and-proxies

[96] "Turkey's Increasingly Assertive Foreign Policy", *IISS*, Vol. 26, No. 6, Comment 24, 30 September 2020.

[97] Brett McGurk, "Hard Truths in Syria", *Foreign Affairs*, Vol. 98, No. 3 (May/June 2019). https://www.foreignaffairs.com/articles/syria/2019-04-16/hard-truths-syria

[98] Sinem Adar, "Turkey's Gains in Syria, Turkish Intervention in Syria Heightens Authoritarianism in Turkey and Fragmentation in Syria", *MERIP*, July 14, 2020. https://merip.org/2020/07/turkish-intervention-in-syria-heightens-authoritarianism-in-turkey-and-fragmentation-in-syria/

[99] https://etemadonline.com/content/460318, January 23, 2021.

[100] Adar, "Turkey's Gains in Syria", *op. cit.*

[101] Ibid.

[102] David Axe, "Guess Who's a Drone Power Now. Turkey", *The National Interest*, February 6, 2021. https://nationalinterest.org/blog/reboot/guess-who%E2%80%99s-drone-power-now-turkey-177801

[103] Fukuyama, "Droning On in the Middle East", *op. cit.*

[104] Jalel Harchaoui, "The Pendulum: How Russia Sways Its Way to More Influence in Libya", *War on the Rocks*, January 7, 2021. https://warontherocks.com/2021/01/the-pendulum-how-russia-sways-its-way-to-more-influence-in-libya/

[105] Sinem Adar, Hürcan Aslı Aksoy, Salim Çevik, Daria Isachenko, and Moritz Rau, "Visualizing Turkey's Foreign Policy Activism", *SWP-CATS*, 17 December 2020. https://www.cats-network.eu/topics/visualizing-turkeys-foreign-policy-activism/

[106] Michaël Tanchum, "How Did the Eastern Mediterranean Become the Eye of a Geopolitical Storm?", *Foreign Policy*, August 18, 2020. https://foreignpolicy.com/2020/08/18/eastern-mediterranean-greece-turkey-warship-geopolitical-showdown/

[107] Steven A. Cook, "Erdogan Is Libya's Man Without a Plan", *Foreign Policy*, July 9, 2020. https://foreignpolicy.com/2020/07/09/erdogan-is-libyas-man-without-a-plan/

[108] Federica Saini Fasanotti, "Order from Chaos: The New Great Dangerous Game in the Eastern Mediterranean", *Brookings Institute*, August 28, 2020. https://www.brookings.edu/blog/order-from-chaos/2020/08/28/the-new-great-dangerous-game-in-the-eastern-mediterranean

[109] Nael Shama, "The Geopolitics of a Latent International Conflict in Eastern Mediterranean", *Aljazeera Centre for Studies*, December 23, 2019. https://studies.aljazeera.net/en/reports/2019/12/geopolitics-latent-international-conflict-eastern-mediterranean-191223074025635.html

[110] Luca Franza, "EU-Turkey 5 Years Later: The Relaunch of Cooperation Passes through Energy", *Istituto Affari Internazionale*, March 18, 2021. https://www.affarinternazionali.it/2021/03/ue-turchia-5-anni-dopo-dallenergia-passa-il-rilancio-della-cooperazione/

[111] Yunus Emre Açıkgönül, "Turkey's East Med Policy: Victory at Home, Isolation Abroad", *Heinrich Böll Stiftung*, September 12, 2020. https://tr.boell.org/en/2020/09/12/turkeys-east-med-policy-victory-home-isolation-abroad

[112] Tanchum, "How Did the Eastern Mediterranean Become the Eye of a Geopolitical Storm", *op. cit.*

[113] Emmanuel Karagiannis, "The Silent Rise of Greece as a Mediterranean Power", *RUSI*, November 16, 2020. https://rusi.org/commentary/silent-rise-greece-mediterranean-power

[114] Tanchum, *op. cit.*

[115] Yannis Palaiologos, "Europe Fails to Contain Turkey", *Wall Street Journal*, September 30, 2020. https://www.wsj.com/articles/europe-fails-to-contain-turkey-11601507708

[116] Alexis Papachelas, "From Bismarck to Merkel", *Kathimerini*, February 7, 2021. https://www.ekathimerini.com/opinion/262093/from-bismarck-to-merkel/

[117] Nektaria Stamouli, "Greece Blasts Berlin for Shunning Plea for Turkey Arms Embargo", *Politico*, November 28, 2020. https://www.politico.eu/article/greece-blasts-berlin-for-shunning-plea-for-turkey-arms-embargo/

[118] Exploratory talks have been an exercise that brought together Greek and Turkish officials to decide how negotiations about the bilateral disputes on the Aegean, ranging from maritime delimitation to the continental shelf, can be conducted. They started in 2002 and after 60 rounds which did not yield any results, were interrupted in 2016. Encouraged by the EU to defuse the tensions in the Eastern Mediterranean, the 61st round began in January 2021. The Turkish side was interested in the undertaking to impress the European Commission and to prevent the possible sanctions against Turkey that could be brought into force at the EU summit in March 2021.

[119] https://www.yenisafak.com/gundem/cumhurbaskani-erdogandan-micotakise-tepki-cilgin-turkleri-iyi-tani yacaksin-3598463; https://tr.sputniknews.com/turkiye/202102101043775932-erdogandan-micotakise-cilgin

-turkleri-iyi-taniyacaksin/

120 Tom Ellis, "Erdogan Threatens Mitsotakis", op-ed, *Kathimerini*, February 11, 2021. https://www.ekathimerini.com/opinion/262241/erdogan-threatens-mitsotakis/

121 Açıkgönül, "Turkey's East Med Policy", *op. cit.*

122 Yunus Emre Açıkgönül, "Untold Legal Principles Favoring Turkey in Aegean Maritime Disputes", *FeniksPolitik*, February 26, 2021. https://fenikspolitik.org/2021/02/26/untold-legal-principles-favouring-turkey-in-aegean-maritime-disputes/

123 Ryan Gingeras, "What Can a Retired Sailor Teach Us About Turkey", *War on the Rocks*, October 21, 2020.

124 *Al Marsad*, "Turkey Makes Maritime EEZ to Israel as Extension of the Border Drawn with Sarraj for Libya", December 7, 2020.

125 Gingeras, "What Can a Retired Sailor Teach Us About Turkey", *op. cit.*

126 Ryan Gingeras, "Blue Homeland: The Heated Politics Behind Turkey's New Maritime Strategy", *War on the Rocks*, June 2, 2020.

127 Matthieu Cailleaud interview with Cem Gürdeniz, "Qu'est-ce que la 'Patrie Bleue'? Une Conversation avec l'idéologue de la doctrine géopolitique Turc [What Is the "Blue Homeland?" A Conversation with the Ideologue of the Turkish Geopolitical Doctrine], *Le Grand Continent*, Geopolitical Study Group, Paris, October 26, 2020.

128 Ibid.

129 Ibid.

130 Ibid.

131 Ibid.

132 Cailleaud interview with Cem Gürdeniz , *op. cit.*

133 Ibid.

134 David Gauthier-Villars, "An Assertive Turkey Muscles into Russia's Backyard", *The Wall Street Journal*, December 11, 2020. https://www.wsj.com/articles/an-assertive-turkey-muscles-into-russias-backyard-11607696623

135 Vladimir Socor, "The South Caucasus: New Realities After the Armenia-Azerbaijan War", *Eurasia Daily Monitor*, Vol. 17, No. 179 (December 16, 2020). https://jamestown.org/program/the-south-caucasus-new-realities-after-the-armenia-azerbaijan-war-part-one/

136 Thomas de Waal, "Unfinished Business in the Armenia-Azerbaijan Conflict", *Carnegie Europe,* February 11, 2021. https://carnegieeurope.eu/2021/02/11/unfinished-business-in-armenia-azerbaijan-conflict-pub-8384

137 http://en.kremlin.ru/events/president/news/64384; https://en.president.az/articles/45923; https://www.primeminister.am/en/press-release/item/2020/11/10/Announcement/

138 https://reliefweb.int/report/armenia/how-goble-plan-was-born-and-how-it-remains-political-factor

139 Thomas de Waal, *Black Garden, Armenia and Azerbaijan Through Peace and War,* New York University Press, 2013, 274-278.

140 http://en.kremlin.ru/events/president/news/64384; https://en.president.az/articles/45923; https://www.primeminister.am/en/press-release/item/2020/11/10/Announcement/

141 *The Economist*, "Peace for Now: A Peace Deal Ends a Bloody War over Nagorno-Karabagh", November 12, 2020. https://www.economist.com/europe/2020/11/12/a-peace-deal-ends-a-bloody-war-over-nagorno-karabakh

142 Paul Antonopoulos, "Is Azerbaijan Preparing a New War against Armenia?", *Greek City Times*, March 11, 2021. https://greekcitytimes.com/2021/03/11/azerbaijan-new-war-armenia/?amp

143 Ibid.

144 https://menafn.com/1101703022/President-Aliyev-gives-speech-at-virtual-Summit-of-Economic-Cooperation-Organization-

145 Ibid.

146 *Azertac* (Azerbaijan State News Agency), "Informal Summit of Cooperation Council of Turkic-Speaking States Was Held in Video Conference Format, Azerbaijani President Ilham Aliyev Made a Speech at the Summit", March 31, 2021. https://azertag.az/en/xeber/Informal_Summit_of_Cooperation_Council_of_Turkic_Speaking_States_was_held_in_video_conference_format_Azerbaijani_President_Ilham_Aliyev_made_a_speech_at_the_Summit

147 Vasif Huseynov, "Azerbaijan Embarks on Construction of Nakhchivan Railway (Part Two)", *Eurasian Daily Monitor*, Vol. 18, No. 59 (April 13, 2021). https://jamestown.org/program/azerbaijan-embarks-on-construction-of-nakhchivan-railway-part-two/

148 Ayca Alemdaroglu, "Sultan Tepe, Erdogan Is Turning Turkey into a Chinese Client State", *Foreign Policy*, September 16, 2020. https://foreignpolicy.com/2020/09/16/erdogan-is-turning-turkey-into-a-chinese-client-state/; Didier Chaudet, "Analyse, Vers un Rapprochement entre la Chine et la Turquie?", *Asialyst*, November 28, 2020. https://asialyst.com/fr/2020/11/28/chine-turquie-rapprochement/

149 Alemdaroglu, "Sultan Tepe", *op. cit.*

150 Michaël Tanchum, "Has Turkey Outfoxed China to Become a Rising Eurasian Power", *The Turkey Analyst*,

January 19, 2021. https://www.turkeyanalyst.org/publications/turkey-analyst-articles/item/659-turkey-outfoxed-china-in-azerbaijan-to-become-a-rising-eurasian-power?.html

[151] Connor Dilleen, "Turkey Forges a Strategic Future Independent of Russia and the West", *The Strategist*, Australian Strategic Policy Institute, December 21, 2020. https://www.aspistrategist.org.au/turkey-forges-a-strategic-future-independent-of-russia-and-the-west/

[152] Dimitar Bechev, "What Does the Nagorno-Karabagh Deal Mean for Turkey and Russia?", *Aljazeera*, November 18, 2020. https://www.aljazeera.com/opinions/2020/11/18/the-nagorno-karabakh-settlement-and-turkish-russian-relations

[153] Kuzzat Altay, "Why Erdogan Has Abandoned the Uyghurs", *Foreign Policy*, March 2, 2021. https://foreignpolicy.com/2021/03/02/why-erdogan-has-abandoned-the uyghurs/?utm_source=PostUp&utm_medium=email&utm_campaign=30788&utm_term=Editors%20Picks%20OC&?tpcc=30788

[154] Dilleen, "Turkey Forges a Strategic Future", op cit.

[155] Igor Delanoë, "Bras de fer dans russo-turc dans le Caucause", *Le Monde diplomatique*, December 8, 2020. https://www.monde-diplomatique.fr/2020/12/DELANOE/62586; Igor Delanoë, "Russia and Turkey, Friends or Enemies?", *Le Monde diplomatique English Edition*, December 8, 2020. https://mondediplo.com/7 search?s=Igor+Delanoë

[156] Anton Mardasov and Kirill Semyonov, "Best Frenemies: Russia and Turkey", *Riddle*, November 26, 2020. https://www.ridl.io/en/best-frenemies-russia-and-turkey/

[157] Nicholas Danforth, "What did Turkey gain from the Armenia-Azerbaijan War?", *Eurasianet*, December 11, 2020. https://eurasianet.org/perspectives-what-did-turkey-gain-from-the-armenia-azerbaijan-war; Güney Yıldız, "Turkish-Russian Adverserial Collaboration in Syria, Libya, and Nagorno-Karabakh", *SWP Comment*, March 2021.

[158] Natalie Nougayrède, "The Two Angry Men on Europe's Borders: Loud, Proud, and Impossible to Ignore", *The Guardian*, October 29, 2014. https://www.theguardian.com/commentisfree/2014/29/europe-two-angry-men-west-vladimir-putin-recep-tayyip-erdogan-russias-turkey.

[159] *The Economist*, "The Odd Couple", *op. cit.*

[160] Institut Montaigne, "Shaky Bridges between Russia, Turkey and the EU: Three Questions to Andrey Kortunov", November 2, 2020. https://www.institutmontaigne.org/en/blog/shaky-bridges-between-russia-turkey-and-eu

[161] Kremlin, "Interview with Vladimir Putin: Replies to Media Questions on Developments in Nagorno-Karabakh", November 17, 2020. http://en.kremlin.ru/events/president/news/64431

[162] Ibid.

[163] *The Economist*, "The Odd Couple", *op. cit.*

[164] Ibid.

[165] Fiona Hill and Omer Taspinar, "Turkey and Russia: Axis of the Excluded?", *Survival*, Vol. 48, No. 1 (March 2006), 81-92

[166] *The Moscow Times*, "Russia, Turkey Open Joint Military Center in Azerbaijan", February 3, 2021. https://www.themoscowtimes.com/2021/02/03/russia-turkey-open-joint-military-center-in-azerbaijan-a72818

[167] Ibid.

[168] David Rosenberg, "Turkey Doesn't Have the Economic Bite to Back Up Erdogan's Bark", *Haaretz*, October 28, 2020. https://www.haaretz.com/middle-east-news/turkey-erdogan-doesn-t-have-the-economic-bite-to-back-up-erdogan-s-bark-1.9263259

[169] Ibid.

[170] Ferhat Gurini, "Turkey's Unpromising Defense Industry", Carnegie Endowment for Peace, October 09, 2020.

[171] Ibid.

[172] Ibid.

[173] Rosenberg, "Turkey Doesn't Have the Economic Bite to Back Up Erdogan's Bark", op. cit.

[174] Ibid.

[175] Allison Meakem, "The Year in Review: Turkey's Year of Living Dangerously", *Foreign Policy*, December 25, 2020. https://foreignpolicy.com/2020/12/25/turkeys-year-of-living-dangerously/

[176] Krzysztof Strachota, "Dwie Turcje" [Two Turkeys], *Tygodnik Powszechny* [Weekly Standard], October 5, 2020. https://www.tygodnikpowszechny.pl/dwie-turcje-165079

[177] Ibid.

[178] Ibid.

[179] Caroline Finkel, Osman's Dream: The Story of the Ottoman Empire 1300-1923, Great Britain: John Murray Publishers, 2005.

[180] Christopher de Bellaigue, "Turkey's Hidden Past", *The New York Review of Books*, March 8, 2001.

[181] M. Şükrü Hanioğlu, "Dünya 'Biz'i Parçalamak için mi Savaştı?", *Sabah*, November 25, 2018; *Sabah Daily*, "Has the World Fought to Partition 'Us'?", November 25, 2018. https://www.sabah.com.tr/yazarlar/

hanioglu/2018/11/25/dunya-bizi-parcalamak-icin-mi-savasti

182 Özel, "2021: Year of Decisions", *op. cit.*

183 Cengiz Çandar, "Turkey's 'Soft Power' Strategy: A New Vision for a Multipolar World", *Seta Policy Brief*, No. 38, December 2009.

184 Ibid.

185 Dilleen, "Turkey Forges a Strategic Future Independent of Russia", *op. cit.*

186 Emil Avdaliani, "Turkey's Foreign Policy Balancing Act", *Besa Center Perspective Paper*, No. 1972, March 21, 2021. https://besacenter.org/perspectives-papers/turkey-foreign-policy-balancing/

187 Rouleau, "The Challenges to Turkey", op. cit.

188 Dilleen, "Turkey Forges a Strategic Future Independent of Russia", *op. cit.*

189 https://www.state.gov/secretary-antony-j-blinken-and-nato-secretary-general-jens-stoltenberg-at-a-moderated-conversation-with-rosa-balfour/

190 Josep Borrell, European Union External Action Service (EEAS), "EU-Turkey Relations: The Need to Build Bridges", *From the Blog*, March 30, 2021. https://eeas.europa.eu/headquarters/headquarters-homepage/9593
0/eu-turkey-relations-need-build-bridges_en

191 Marc Pierini, "Turkey Needs the EU", *Euronews*, September 3, 2018. https://www.euronews.com/2018/09/03/turkey-needs-the-eu-the-question-is-how-much-its-relationship-will-cost-

192 Nicholas Danforth, "It Is Time to Let Turkey Go", *Foreign Policy*, December 15, 2020. https://foreignpolicy.com/2020/12/15/it-is-time-to-let-turkey-go/

193 Nicholas Danforth, "Turkey and the West: A Hostile Dance", *Eliamep,* March 19, 2021. https://www.eliamep.gr/wp-content/uploads/2021/03/Policy-paper-60-Nick-Danforth-final.pdf

194 Gideon Rose, "Foreign Policy for Pragmatists", *Foreign Affairs*, March/April 2021. https://www.foreignaffairs.com/articles/united-states/2021-02-16/foreign-policy-pragmatists

195 Walter Russell Mead, "The End of the Wilsonian Era, Why Liberal Internationalism Failed", *Foreign Affairs*, January/February 2021. https://www.foreignaffairs.com/articles/united-states/2020-12-08/end-wilsonian-era

196 Richard N. Haass, "How a World Order Ends", *Foreign Affairs*, January/February 2019. https://www.foreignaffairs.com/articles/2018-12-11/how-world-order-ends

197 G. John Ikenberry, "The Illusion of Geopolitics", *Foreign Affairs*, May/June 2014. https://www.foreignaffairs.com/articles/china/2014-04-17/illusion-geopolitics

198 Vali Nasr, "The Middle East's Next Conflicts Won't Be Between Arab States and Iran", *Foreign Policy*, March 2, 2021. https://foreignpolicy.com/2021/03/02/the-middle-easts-next-conflicts-wont-be-between-arab-states-and-iran/

199 Richard N. Haass, "The New Middle East", *Foreign Affairs*, November/December 2006. https://www.foreignaffairs.com/articles/middle-east/2006-11-01/new-middle-east

200 Henry Kissinger, World Order: Reflections on the Character of Nations and the Course of History, New York: Penguin Group, 2014, 96-97.

201 Shlomo Roiter Jesner, "Erdogan's Economic Hail Mary Won't Work", *Foreign Policy*, November 30, 2020. https://foreignpolicy.com/2020/11/30/turkey-economic-problem-erdogan-mismanagement/

202 Danforth, "Turkey and the West: A Hostile Dance", *op. cit.*

203 Andreas Krieg and Jean-Marc Rickli, Surrogate Warfare, The Transformation of War in the Twenty-First Century, Georgetown, 2019.

204 Aris Roussinos, "Anarchy Is Coming", *UnHerd*, March 22, 2021. https://unherd.com/2021/03/anarchy-is-coming/

205 David E. Sagner, "That Was Fast: Blowups with China and Russia in Biden's First 60 Days", *New York Times*, (updated) March 25, 2021. https://www.nytimes.com/2021/03/20/us/politics/china-russia-biden.html

206 Gideon Rachman, "A Second Cold War Is Tracking the First, US-Led Western Alliance Is Once Again Squaring Up to Russia and China", *Financial Times*, Opinion Geopolitics, March 29, 2021. https://www.ft.com/content/b724fbb0-6c62-4175-85c9-b17ac98dde7d

207 Ibid.

208 President of Ukraine Volodymyr Zelenskyy Official Website, "Ukraine and Turkey Share a Common Vision of Security Threats in the Black Sea Region and Ways to Respond to Them", April 10, 2021. https://www.president.gov.ua/en/news/ukrayina-j-turechchina-mayut-spilne-bachennya-bezpekovih-zag-67917

209 President of Ukraine Volodymyr Zelenskyy Official Website, President Of Ukraine Had a Phone Conversation with the Secretary General of NATO, April 6, 2021. https://www.president.gov.ua/en/news/prezident-ukrayini-proviv-telefonnu-rozmovu-z-generalnim-sek-67813

210 Dimitar Bechev, "Ukraine-Turkey Cooperation Has Its Limits", *AlJazeera*, April 18, 2021. https://www.aljazeera.com/opinions/2021/4/18/ukraine-turkey-cooperation-has-its-benefits-but-also-limits

211 Sagner, "That Was Fast", *op. cit.*

212 Rachman, "Second Cold War Is Tracking the First", *op. cit.*

213 Sagner, "That Was Fast", *op. cit.*

214 *Foreign Policy*, "Blinken Accuses China of Uyghur Genocide in Xinjiang", March 31, 2021. https://foreignpolicy.com/2021/03/31/blinken-uyghur-china-human-rights-report/; U.S. Department of State, "2020 Country Reports on Human Right Practices", Bureau of Democracy, Human Rights and Labor, March 30, 2021. https://www.state.gov/reports/2020-country-reports-on-human-rights-practices/

215 Andrew Doran, "Stop Giving Erdogan a Veto Over U.S. Recognition of the Armenian Genocide", *Foreign Policy*, April 23, 2021. https://foreignpolicy.com/2021/04/23/armenian-genocide-turkey-erdogan-biden-recognition-allies-nato-syria-russia/

INDEX

145, 150,151, 153, 154, 158, 159, 160,
163, 164, 165, 166, 167, 168, 169, 170,
172, 177, 179, 181, 182, 183, 184, 185

S

S-400, 14, 17, 125, 154, 172
Saudi Arabia, 14, 17, 31, 53, 57, 58, 84, 85, 91
Sea, v, 21, 78, 86, 88, 95, 96, 98, 101, 103, 111, 113, 115, 119, 120, 124, 125, 130, 133, 135, 166, 167, 168, 185
Second Karabagh War, 109, 110, 112, 116, 123
Seville Map, 96
Shaposhnikov, 108, 109
Shargh, 28, 176
Shusha, 108, 110, 112
Sisi, 87
Somalia, 18, 21, 22
Strategic Depth, 44, 46, 177
Surrogate Warfare, 164, 165, 185
Sweden, v, 3, 97, 108, 140
Syria, v, 3, 4, 6, 14, 17, 18, 19, 22, 28, 32, 45, 46, 49, 50, 51, 52, 53, 56, 57, 58, 59, 60, 61, 65, 68, 72, 73, 74, 75, 76, 77, 78, 79, 86, 99, 103, 124, 127, 132, 145, 151, 155, 164, 165, 166, 168, 172, 179, 182
Syunik, 114, 115, 117

T

Tajikistan, 111, 115
Tayyip, vii, 2, 13, 14, 18, 19, 20, 21, 28, 29, 31, 34, 39, 43, 49, 50, 51, 54, 56, 57, 60, 66, 67, 68, 70, 77, 93, 103, 115, 120, 127, 128, 130, 132, 135, 141, 149, 163,

167, 169
Tel Abyad, 74
The Economist, 68, 113, 128, 132, 178, 181, 182, 183
Total, 85, 86, 87
Trilateral Agreement, 112, 117
Tripoli, 13, 17, 45, 78, 83, 84, 89, 107
Tripolitania, 45
Tsar Nicholas I, 143
Turkmenistan, 111, 115
Tygodnik Powszechny, 143

U

UAE, 14, 31, 73, 78, 84, 85, 87, 88, 98, 179
Ukraine, 9, 11, 17, 124, 128, 140, 165, 166, 167, 168, 169, 185
United Arab Emirates, 4, 83, 85, 91, 107
Uyghur, 123, 171, 185
Uyghurs, 123, 171, 182
Uzbekistan, 111, 115, 122

W

Wall Street Journal, 19, 92, 108, 175, 180, 181

X

Xinjiang, 123, 169, 171, 185

Y

Yerevan, 107, 109

Z

Zangezur, 111, 113, 114, 115, 116, 117